P.S. I Think of You Often

YOU OFTEN

A JOURNEY INTO UNDERSTANDING

BRENDA LAFACE

THE
SELF
PUBLISHING
AGENCY

Brenda Laface
P.S. I Think of You Often: A Journey Into Understanding

TSPA The Self Publishing Agency Inc.
Copyright © 2025 by Brenda Laface
First Edition

Softcover ISBN 978-1-998537-01-3
eBook ISBN 978-1-998537-02-0

Book Design | Ashley Russell Designs
Editor | Alisen Santa Ana
Publishing Management | TSPA The Self Publishing Agency, Inc.

This book is dedicated to all who seek meaning and purpose.

"Who looks outside dreams; who looks inside, awakes."
(C.G. Jung's *Letters, Vol. 1: 1906-1950*)

CONTENTS

Memories—Messages to Be Mined for Meaning

INTRODUCTION

I was born on February 24, 1955, at the Royal Columbian Hospital in New Westminster, British Columbia (B.C.) in Canada. After spending the first ten months of my life in a foster home in Port Moody, B.C., I was then adopted by a couple who lived in Trail, B.C. As such, I was raised in Trail.

In having spent most of my childhood feeling lost, alone, and terribly confused, I entered adolescence and young adulthood troubled and emotionally unstable. Anxious to find a normal life, I married and had children, but I was not happy. In fact, I was extremely unhappy, and as a result, became increasingly unwell as time went by. Unable to contain my pain any longer, I eventually blew myself up, and in blowing myself up, I blew up my family's life.

I have been writing my story in the stars for over thirty years, and during these years, my story has undergone much change. The memories have always remained the same, crisp, and clear, but in so far as every new day came with the benefit of yesterday's thoughts and experiences, ever-more light continued to be shed. Deeper meanings emerged from the magical method inherent in the gestalt of my life. And so it is that my book has now, finally, come together in a way that feels right, true, and complete.

Although this book contains my story, it is not intended to merely tell a story. By including reflections on my past and expanded perspectives about those with whom I shared my past, my intent is to portray a process. By elucidating colliding contextualized considerations and conclusions gleaned from within the tainted, tangled madness that was my life, I hope to convey the introspective process that led me out of intergenerational trauma into freedom—the freedom to live and learn into a spiritual understanding of my life. In sharing the sanctity secreted away in a story as sordid as my own, I hope to encourage others to search for the sanctity in their own.

I could not have made this journey alone. In knowing I needed help in understanding what ailed me, I engaged a local psychotherapist, George Reilly, whom I saw bi-weekly for almost ten years. 'Twas not till years later, while attending university, that I learned my guiding light must have drawn heavily from the works of Carl Gustav Jung because he taught me to walk back through time, examine my memories, thoughts, feelings, dreams, and intuitions. He taught me to ask myself hard questions and listen to the answers that would well up inside of me. He also instructed me to pay attention to symbols, situations, and synchronicities that resonated with me.

In examining my life in this way, I was, in time, able to depressurize, defuse, and depersonalize my experiences enough to detach from them and view them from within the context of my family of origin, my family of adoption placement, and then finally from within the context of a cosmic whole seeking its end. It has been since awakening to this latter—far larger—perspective that everything in me, and for me, has changed. I am no longer a rose seeking to be loved and admired via encultured commodification. I am more akin to a daisy, happy to be alive in a reality where we are all, individual by individual, seeking an understanding of the larger *Self*, to which we all belong.

In feeling as detached from my former self as I now do, the narrative I share is communicated in the third person. I—Brenda—write of a past life, the life of Rose who through extrapolated interpretations of her experiences, was able to transcend her former self. My use of a third person narrative is intended as a metaphorical device only. It is in no way intended to conceal my identity or alter the reality of my self-perceived experiences. The names of those with whom I shared my life, however, have all been changed except for in the case of my best friend, Chris, who in having been privy to my many hijinks, requested I use her real name. I was happy to oblige.

Although I took no pleasure in the first bit of my life, I have surely come to appreciate it for the road it has taken me down. I am happier now than I could ever have imagined myself being, and in looking back on it all, I believe/know my life and my journey have been nothing short of a miracle—a bloody miracle—exquisite in both purpose and design.

I hope you enjoy my book.

"Life can only be understood backwards,
but it must be lived forwards."

—Søren Kierkegaard, nineteenth century Danish existentialist

PROLOGUE
What Was Lost Must Be Found

Telling my truth was something I always wanted to do. I always knew how I felt, what I thought and wanted, but I would not—could not—under any circumstance let myself out. Fear, frustration, anger, and self-hatred would have my mind raging as a chorus of internal voices rocked, reeled, and rammed against the walls of the cautiously circumscribed psychic cocoon I kept myself captive within. I fantasized about telling my truth, longed to do so since my childhood, but for reasons I did not yet understand, I would never—could never—allow myself into my world. I was, had always been, a shut-in, a prisoner of an existence-denied life.

I *was*, that is, until with a bang, I *was not*. After an entire lifetime of being totally unwilling or unable to speak my truth—the truth, the whole truth, and nothing but the truth—came ripping and tearing out of me with a vengeance I had never before, and would never again, experience.

THE BEGINNING OF THE END

1

THE DAY THE SHIT HIT THE FAN
Call to Battle

T he shit hit the fan on Thursday, October 1, 1992.

This particular Thursday started out as any normal weekday for Rose. Hubby was up and gone, having caught the co-op bus that took him to work at the smelter in Trail by 6:00 am. She was up by 7:00 am to rouse the kids. After dressing, the girls—aged ten and eight years old—went out to do their chores—feed the chickens, cats, and dogs before they all sat down for breakfast. There was no fooling around because the girls had to be down at the bottom of the driveway of their Beaver Falls home by 8:20 am to catch the bus that took them to their elementary school in Fruitvale, a small neighbouring town. And by 8:30 am, Rose needed to have her four-year-old son down the driveway, and then across the highway, to the half-day playschool he attended. Once all that was done, Rose tidied up the kitchen, readied herself, and set off to complete the day's errands. There were bills to pay, and it was already almost 9:30 am.

Whilst at the bank, as she hoped, Rose ran into the bank manager, a friend—an acquaintance really—who two years earlier had captured the imaginings of her heart, soul, and every hope, wish, and desire she'd ever had. She played with the image of them being together constantly. She was sure she loved him. Did he love her? He was living with a woman he'd been with for many years ... so ... Rose did not know for sure, but she believed he must because whenever their eyes locked, she felt their souls enmesh until they could take no more, and they both had to look away. This time, however, as if being captured and possessed by some alternate version of herself, Rose did not take her gaze away; she asked her irresistible muse if he wanted to go for lunch sometime.

"Yes, that sounds great," he replied. "I'll give you a call next week."

Rose was delighted—ecstatic—exceptionally excited. She couldn't believe she had done what she had done, but, nevertheless, she began wondering when he would call. Where would they go? What should she wear? What should she say? She created beautiful sets and scandalous scenes. She escaped into ecstasy until pulling back into the family driveway, when she was struck by what she had done. With that, the voices in Rose's head flew into overdrive.

Oh my GOD! I am a married woman, and I asked a man to go for lunch. What does this mean? Am I a slut? Everyone is going to think I'm a slut. How could ... why would I do such a thing? Randy and I have been working so hard on our marriage.

Horror—absolute horror—had Rose pacing the house till noon when she had to walk down the driveway and then across the highway to pick her son up from playschool.

"What's wrong, Mommy?"

"Nothing sweetheart." Rose couldn't tell her son what she had done. How could she? Once back in the house, she fixed her son some lunch, and sent him off to play with whatever might entertain him. She needed a drink, perhaps a few.

Under stress—mild to extreme—Rose did one of two things. She would go for a nap, shut her eyes so as to shut out the world, and let sleep dissipate whatever emotional crisis was crippling her at the time. Forcing herself to sleep was a strategy Rose had been employing since childhood, and it worked quite well when the world was pressing in on her. When she was the culprit, how ever manic due to her own miserably myopic mismanagement, she used alcohol to calm herself down. Mellowed by alcohol, she could usually get her battalion of internal critics to release her into the recognizance of a singular sorry self so she could grapple with whatever correction or edification might make right the horrific wrong she had committed.

Although Rose's strategy usually worked, not this time. This time, she had really done it. This time, Pandora's box had burst wide open, and Rose had broadcasted her most unacceptable self into the world. Even in her hysteria, Rose knew she was doomed. As such, her wine had no option but to continue serving itself. By 3:00 pm, Rose was drowning in her cups but still no closer to personal consolation. Realizing she needed to get her son out of the house and that the girls would be home from school in less than an hour, Rose needed to make a plan.

There was a group of six or seven married couples that partied together and sometimes went houseboating on the

Shuswap Lake. Carol, one of these friends, lived close by, and Rose knew she would be home. Since having her children, Rose had never, ever, gotten herself into this sort of shape before, but now, here she was. What was she going to do? She decided to call her houseboat friend.

"Can you please come and get my little boy and maybe collect the girls from school for me? I'm having a really bad day (life)."

Before Rose knew it, Carol arrived, collected her son, and demanded her car keys.

"But I need my keys. I have to pick Randy up from the dentist at 5:00 pm."

"No, Rose! You are too drunk to drive. Randy is going to have to find his own way home."

Carol left with Rose's son and her car keys. It was too late for Rose to call the dentist's office to tell her husband she would not be able to pick him up ... so ... what was she going to do? She could not stand him up, let him stand there waiting to no avail. How was he going to get home?

Rose decided to call her youngest brother, Jerry, to see what they could figure out. They were not close or anything. The only time Rose ever saw him was at their mom's, during one of her tedious Sunday night dinners, but for some reason, Rose felt like he might understand, he might be the least judgmental, so she called him.

Due to her hysterical overconsumption, Rose had no recollection of what she said to her brother, or why her brother decided to come and pick her up so she could meet her husband in town. But, in knowing, after her phone call that her kids were safe, the situation handled, Rose poured herself more wine. What transpired between her last glass of wine and being slumped in the passenger seat of her brother's pick-up truck, watching as Randy came out of the dentist's office, also remained a mystery, as did the logic of she and Randy ending up at a bar—as if she was not already drunk enough. All Rose remembered was that it was then and there, as her husband of twelve years sat and listened, that she finally burst out of herself.

"So, Rose ... what is it you have ... need to tell me?"

"RANDY ... I DO NOT LOVE YOU! I HAVE NEVER LOVED YOU. YOU MAKE MY SKIN CRAWL EVERY TIME YOU TOUCH ME. THE ONLY REASON I HAVEN'T COMMITTED SUICIDE A MILLION TIMES OVER IS BECAUSE I DO NOT WANT TO DO TO MY KIDS, WHAT WAS DONE TO ME. I DO NOT WANT TO ABANDON THEM."

Randy just sat and listened as Rose pugnaciously power-puked the reality of their onerously one-sided partnership. Rose knew she was being heartless, but she could not stop. She could not, it would seem, contain her malfeasance for even one moment longer. She was like an exploding pincushion, and her husband, sole beneficiary of her brutally blunt barbs, was bleeding from every pore of his body.

Once the tirade was done, Rose was spent.

Rose never recalled the details of how she and Randy got home, or the morning after the horrific night before. All Rose remembered, vividly, was the tormented relief she'd experienced after the hermetically sealed chamber containing her self-administered homeopathic horror burst, and the rivers of anger, rage, fear, resentment, and self-loathing that flowed and continued to flow for days—perhaps weeks—after the abscess of emotional poisons she had been stockpiling for years, was unceremoniously lanced. During those days—perhaps weeks—Rose felt like she was experiencing the pain of the entire world, all of existence throughout time. She felt like she understood the anguish—agony—carried by every individual who had ever lived.

By means of a punch thrown by the powerful potential pressing the outpouring of a prohibited passion, I was finally forced out of myself. My loathsomely dishonest self was finally carried across its event horizon to where a battle would ensue, a battle that only the universe—the powers that be—knew a bottle ... box ... of wine could ensure, a battle that would not just be with myself, but would also be with the life I had so callously and calculatingly created for myself.

2

THE STAGE IS SET
Oh, What a Tangled Web We Weave

R ose and Randy were friends long before they got together romantically. And their getting together was far from a Cinderella story, about as far from a Cinderella story as one can get.

Rose met her husband-to-be through her friend Chris, her bestie since Grade Eleven. Belonging to the same gaggle of girls, Rose and Chris had been comrades since the end of Grade Eight, but it was only toward the end of high school that the girls became bosom buddies, singing to the same tune.

Chris's mom had grown up right across the street from Rose's dad. They'd known each other's families but did not *know* each other, as they moved in different circles. Chris's mom was a widow with seven children of whom Chris was the youngest by seven years. Chris's dad had died of a heart attack when Chris was only five years old. With five older brothers and an older sister, Chris felt like she was on her own. Rose too, felt she was alone in the world. Perhaps it was this commonality that brought the two of them together, or, perhaps it was because both girls lacked having an adult male influence in their life. Yes, Rose had a dad. He was there—in the background—never interacting, so Rose did not feel his presence in her life. Whatever the case may be, two days after their graduation year, 1973, Rose, Chris, and eventually Rose's high school boyfriend, all moved to Red Deer, Alberta (A.B.). Less than two months after their arrival, Chris, due to missing her boyfriend too much, moved back home.

Eight months later Rose followed.

Once home, Rose reconnected with Chris, who by this time, had befriended a young couple from the prairies, Lois, and her fiancé Randy, who lived in the apartment below her and her mom's. Chris had also become acquainted with the couples' cohort of friends and relatives. And so, Chris's friends quickly became Rose's friends. They would all meet up after work to discuss the evening's entertainment—weekends, of course, always being a cause for a party of some kind. One summer, Chris and Rose even accompanied Lois, Randy, and their transplanted friends and relatives on one of their semi-annual cavalcades back to the prairies. It was a great adventure, such tremendous fun.

Through the years, group affiliates came and went, but Rose, betwixt and between romantic interests, two more failed attempts at leaving her hometown, a near marriage, and a subsequent string of tawdry debasing one-night stands, was steadfast. When things went badly, Rose had pals who would help her party her pain into the past.

'Twasn't till the group travelled to a Supertramp concert in Spokane, Washington, sometime in 1979, that Rose finally took note of the malfunction in Randy's fun meter. Once again, he got so trashed he could not possibly be having fun—he missed the concert.

"Why … why does he do that?"

Finally, reluctantly, someone told her. "Randy is in love with you and has been for ages!"

"What? Yikes!" Rose was horrified! "Are you kidding me?"

But what could she do? From then on, Rose tried to stay as far away from Randy as possible … but … she needed her friends. They were all she had.

Shortly after the concert, it came to Rose's attention that one of the girls in their group, Petra, was going through a rough patch and needed a place to live. All the apartments she'd looked at were dumps. Rose mulled it over. She did have a spare bedroom that she'd fixed up, but she hadn't lived with anyone for a while. Rose wasn't sure it would work or not but …

What the heck … she needs a place to live, and the company will be nice for a change.

The girls did fine together. Both had day jobs. They were both party girls and Rose was really enjoying the company. They had fun, a lot of fun. All was well, very well until, six or seven months later, on the night of January 25, 1980, when a bunch of them ended up at Rose's house after leaving the bar. Lois had gone home tired, but the rest of them were not yet ready to call it quits. 'Twas that night, that infamous night, that Rose allowed herself to fall into the arms of a friend she barely liked anymore; she fell into the arms of Lois's fiancé … Randy.

Waking the next morning, Rose was aghast.

Oh my God! What have I done?

There were still people asleep on her living room floor, so she knew everyone was privy to her loathsome betrayal.

Now what?

As consumed with guilt and shame as she was, Rose could not just go crazy and throw everyone—including Randy—out of the house, as was her first impulse. No, after doing something so hollowly heartless and horrendously heinous the humiliation would have killed her. There had to be another solution.

Wait ... Randy and I are friends, sort of, and I have heard that it is always best to be friends first ... the rest will come. A lot of people in arranged marriages are very happy together. Maybe this is what is supposed to happen.

Rose had long been miserable, and at least Randy loved her. As far as Rose was concerned, no one else ever had, or would, so ... maybe this was fate, a blessing in disguise. Maybe, if she really went for it, Rose would finally be able to get a life, get married and have kids, build a family that loved her.

And so, it was with stifled compassion for her friend Lois, stealth mortification for herself, and a seductively summoned exuberance toward a future, that Rose proceeded under the auspices of a giant ruse she promised herself she would never, ever, tell anyone about. As such, Rose owned the whole sordid affair as if it were her own, as if it were something she herself had longed for, and her feigning of affection must have been very effective, because ... everyone bought it.

Rose began seeing Randy almost daily.

Shortly after Rose and Randy started seeing each other, Rose developed a habit she could not understand. In private, Rose would overeat. After coming home from the bar, Rose would cook herself up a box of Kraft dinner, eat the whole works, then stick her finger down her throat to throw it all back up. She didn't want to gain weight.

One day she baked bran muffins, ate all twelve of them, and then spent the next two hours trying to "un-eat" what she had just eaten. Sometimes in desperation, Rose would do the same thing with raw macaroni and sometimes even coffee grounds. Rose would get so mad at herself, but it was like a compulsion. She just couldn't seem to stop.

Why am I doing this? It is sooooo stupid.

After a couple of months of hearing sorrowful tales from Lois about how she thought Randy was cheating on her, and sorrowful excuses from Randy about how the time had not yet been right to tell his fiancée, the truth, it was Rose—Rose—who finally told her friend Lois what was going on.

Yes, it was hard, but it was something Rose felt she had to do. She felt she had to do it for her friend. She owed her friend the truth and it needed to be done so she could prosper from the proposition proffered her by fate.

A day or two later, with nothing but his car and a suitcase, Randy moved into the rickety old house Rose had bought herself a few years earlier. And Lois—Rose's friend—well

… she was destroyed, a broken woman who left town soon thereafter. Rose was sorry for that but …

Rose's new roommate Petra moved out shortly after Randy moved in. The house was a little cramped with three people and … needless to say, the dynamic had changed. As such, Petra took the opportunity to move in with her boyfriend, another member of their extended group.

In May 1980, four months into the future Rose had sketched out for herself, Mount St. Helens flipped its lid. After the unexpected explosion, smoke and ash hung in the air for months, blocking Rose's, and everyone else's, view of their surroundings. With the winds of time and nature's tears, however, things cleared up and life went on.

The following Christmas, it was Rose, instead of Lois, who accompanied Randy back home for Christmas. Yes, it was a time of mortifying humiliation, but Rose got through it. The only blip occurred during gift giving. A couple of girls in the family received engagement rings for Christmas. Rose received a full-length burgundy leather coat. She was heartbroken.

After all I have put myself through …

The voices in her head were harried with bitterness and despair, so much so that despite her best efforts at maintaining a stiff upper lip, Rose's resentful heart demanded tears breech her reserve. With this, Rose excused herself under the guise of missing her family during the Christmas season. Anyone who knew the least little bit about Rose would know how ridiculously false that statement was. Not only did Rose not miss her family, but she also absolutely hated Christmas, and she hated burgundy.

On the trip home, it was decided that the couple—Randy and Rose—would marry that coming spring of 1981.

"Hell no ... of course I was not expecting an engagement ring. I don't even like engagement rings." *Liar, liar, pants on fire!* Rose had so wanted an engagement ring.

With impending nuptials, Rose was gifted her inheritance—her grandmother's house—the house her mom was born and raised in, Rose's favourite house in the whole world even though it was just up the hill, nearly right next door, to her mom and dad's. Rose had long loved her gran's house, and her mom knew it, so her mom said she thought it only right that someday her daughter would live in it and raise her family there.

As a child, Granny's house and garden had been Rose's sanctuary. It was her special place, the only place she ever felt whole and at peace. Now, she was being gifted the opportunity to go back there, so it was with great excitement that Rose sold the rickety old house she'd bought a few years earlier, and she and her soon to be betrothed, moved into the house, of her former refuge, but future (perceived) contentment.

Mesmerized by the rationalized fate Rose had foisted upon herself, visions of white picket fences and children, lots, and lots of children, began dancing in Rose's head. The main floor only had a master bedroom, but the upstairs—the attic—had one large bedroom and a dormitory type of room that could easily fit four. Rose was sure she was headed for the future of her dreams.

I can now identify that cohabitating with Petra may have marked the beginning of my eventual end. I had always been better on my own. Yes, I worked by day and partied by night and weekends, but I always came home, most often alone, to my own space. I had downtime, time to water my many house plants, play with my pets, work on, or clean my little house and yard. Once Petra moved in, however, in both being party gals anxious to get on with life, we were always cooking something up we hoped would lead us to where we wanted to go.

Could the strange habit I developed of filling myself up, only to then be driven to empty myself out, have had anything to do with the pseudo-sustenance I was force-feeding my starving soul? The behaviour only lasted till I became pregnant. I was worried it might hurt my baby, so I stopped. Just like that, I stopped.

Without warning, Mount St. Helens erupted. It erupted because internal pressures had exceeded the mountain's ability to contain its molten hot lava. Is that how it always works? No one ever knows when something—someone—is about to blow, until it or he or she does. My warning had been issued but ... I did not yet know how to interpret my reality.

And so, the universe had set the stage for a disaster, a disaster just waiting to happen, and as in all great tragedies, it did. I made a deal with the devil, my deepest need/desire—

presumably—fulfilled in exchange for my soul. It was done. Signed, sealed, and in the mail.

3

THE HAPPY HOMEMAKER
More Than Enough to Do

T he couple was married May 1981 in their garden—Rose's granny's garden—just as Rose's mother before her had been. The entire day was intended to be spent outside, but it rained, so everything was quickly moved mid-celebration, into a run-down little hall Rose's mom had secured just in case. Rose got so drunk she barely recalled the reception.

Rose had no idea what she had signed herself up for, but she did get a little taste during her Mexican honeymoon ... in *hell.* In so far as newly-weds are, or should be, madly in love, the whole connubial bliss thing was ... shall we say ... extremely hard to endure.

Although Randy said he never wanted children, Rose had other plans, so she was in seventh heaven when she learned she had conceived during their honeymoon. Both Rose and Randy's parents were thrilled. In believing her strategy worked like a charm, Rose couldn't help but congratulate herself on the adage she embraced.

See Rose ... you gotta do what you gotta to do if you wanna get what you wanna get.

Toward the end of her pregnancy, Rose had a very troubling nightmare. In her dream, she gave birth to a baby with two heads, two heads and only one body, so surgical separation was not an option. Upon waking, Rose was unnerved. She didn't understand what it meant.

'Twas in front of a multitude of curious professionals that Rose's first baby was born, March 23, 1982, a girl delivered breech after twenty-four hours of labouring in love. And deeply in love was exactly how Rose felt when she first laid eyes on her perfect, single-headed, angel of mercy.

For the very first time in Rose's life, she was happy to be female, a woman. *Men can't do this*, Rose thought to herself, self-satisfied, sometimes, even mumbling this statement to herself aloud.

Although Rose could not help but feel guilty about her daughter's deeply bruised bottom, which was caused by her body giving birth ass-backward, bashing little buttocks, hour after hour, against and finally through the barrier of her beginning, Rose would make up for it. She would see to it!

This little girl was the light of Rose's life, but in so filling her life, Randy, the dad, was reduced to a sine qua non securities sponsor, and it was Rose's job to still keep him satisfied. Not a fun job, but Rose knew it was mandatory, part of the deal, so she complied without complaint.

Was Randy aware of his wife's ever-present discomfort with marital relations? Well, maybe, sort of. Rose was never an enthusiastic participant and Randy often gave voice to his wife's lack of initiative in this department. That withstanding, Randy must have been content enough because he forged on.

"What?"

"No ... I am never in the mood for sex."

"Never?"

"No ... never."

Randy was aghast and totally unsympathetic.

"That's not normal Rose. You are not normal. You need to get some help."

While Rose did offer Randy a smidgen of the truth, in that she had never been a big fan of sex, her inability to express the fact that she had never—never—been even remotely attracted to Randy was a huge lie of omission, a lie she truly believed she *should* be able to circumnavigate. Given there were many things, in life, that needed to be done whether you liked it or not, Rose believed that if she could just come to terms with the fact that she was a wife and coitus was part of her job ... everything would be fine.

"Okay ... I will try and get some help."

After delivering an abridged version of her situation, Rose's doctor recommended she see a psychologist who specialized in hypnosis. The doctor indicated that perhaps Rose was burying something that needed to come out.

Shortly thereafter, the couple travelled to Kelowna for an appointment with a psychologist who specialized in hypnosis. During her session—while hypnotized—Rose saw herself as a little girl being coaxed into a barn or a similar outbuilding to be sexually assaulted by a young man she trusted.

"That's weird," remarked Rose, "I do not remember anything like that ever happening to me." Although Rose could not, at all, identify with what she'd seen in her mind's eye while hypnotized, she could not help but feel that the trusted young man she'd seen had something to do with her husband. As incendiary as that inclination was, Rose decided to keep that little tidbit—thought—to herself.

Needless to say, Rose's hypnotic revelation did nothing to appease her situation. She could not, for the life of her, recall ever having been sexually abused by someone she trusted.

Rose's first little darlin' was not yet one years old, when she realized she was once again with child. Again, she could not have been happier. A couple of months before her second child was due, however, her oldest brother, Tom, called to say that unless Randy began doing a little more work around the yard, their dad was going to drop dead of a heart attack. Knowing full well it was her mother who had put her brother up to his call, the next morning, Rose's little family stormed down to her parents' place.

Rose knew from the start that there were always strings attached when it came to her mom. She just hadn't realized that she and Randy were not living up to the conditions of her inheritance.

"You want us out … we're out!" Rose barked.

"Why don't you wait till after the new baby comes?"

"No, as soon as we find a place, we will be gone."

Without haste a search for new hearth and home commenced.

Ever since Rose was young, she wanted to live on a large piece of property that sported a house and a myriad of outbuildings. Was this a residual desire left over from childhood, memories of being with her gran in her granny's yard? Maybe … Rose didn't know exactly why she'd always wanted a house with property and outbuildings. But she knew—just knew—she always had. Never once did it occur to Rose that her desired homestead was similar to the scene of her hypnotic vision's crime.

Sure enough, 'twasn't long before she and Randy found the perfect place in Beaver Falls, a village halfway between Montrose and Fruitvale, bedroom communities of Trail. It was perfect. It was an older, fairly decrepit three-bedroom house that laid on an acreage spotted with fruit trees and a series of outbuildings: a barn, chicken house, and several different sheds. Both Rose and Randy knew that eventually the house would need work, but for the time being, it was perfect, and it could be, would be, theirs—no invisible strings attached.

On November 12, 1983, nary a month after Rose and Randy moved, nineteen months after the arrival of their first daughter, Rose and Randy became the proud parents of yet another beautiful, little baby girl. Although not breech, it was another gruelling labour. After thirty-two hours and an epidural, this little darlin' was still refusing her birth. It was only by hauling her out by the head, a high forceps delivery that left indelicate indents on the temples of her new little darlin's head, bruising the be-Jesus out of Rose's backside, that Rose had another little light to brighten up her otherwise darkly disturbed life.

One night, while sitting on the couch nursing her new daughter, Rose started to cry. She could not help but cry and cry as she pondered her plight.

Now, with two children, I will have to continue to have sex with Randy forever.

Rose knew exactly why she was crying. Rose believed Randy to be a kind, loving husband and father. He and Rose had the same values and sense of humour. They could talk about this, that, and the next thing for hours on end, but none of this made up for the disdain Rose felt in having to accommodate him all the time. Rose hated Randy for wanting her all the time and she hated herself for having to comply all the time. Rose was—felt—trapped.

Unable to confess to why, why she was crying, Rose offered up postpartum depression—a hormonal imbalance she had heard about that allegedly caused depression in women who had recently given birth. Rose thought it a perfectly plausible excuse, and she wondered if perhaps all women who suffered postpartum depression actually suffered due to the cementing of their circumstances.

Daughter number one had such a frail little cry, and waited, kept time with the kind of day Rose was having, whereas daughter number two was loud and beat to the sound of her own drum. She wanted what she wanted, and she wanted it right now! It was exhausting. Rose was exhausted all the time. Although Rose knew it was supposed to take some time after the birth of her second child to regain her energy, her spark for life, she was not bouncing back the way she thought she should, so she made an appointment with her doctor.

Her doctor suggested that perhaps she was depressed.

"Are you kidding me? Don't you think I'd know if I was depressed?" Rose was furious. She'd been chronically depressed for the better part of her life, so she knew what it felt like to be depressed and she wasn't that. She finally had everything she had ever wanted so …

"Idiot!" Rose half-mumbled as she stormed out of her doctor's office.

Maybe, it's just harder than I thought, having two kids.

'Twas their first spring on the homestead, spring 1984, when Rose and Randy got chickens to fill their chicken coop. They got layers and meat birds. The chicks were so damn cute. Rose's oldest loved to go out and visit with them. By late summer the chicks were birds and that was when all the trouble started.

Rose had a dog, Clifford, who had travelled through thick and thin with her, had been her closest companion and confidant for years. Anyway, Clifford had never spent any time around anything as neat looking and tasty as chickens before, and he couldn't resist. Rose tried scolding him but that didn't work. Randy tried locking the chickens up better, but that didn't work. Randy also tried corporal punishment. Last but not least, Randy tied a dead chicken around Clifford's neck for two or three days. Needless to say, Clifford did not come in the house during that time. Apparently, that's what they used to do on the farm to cure dogs of their taste for chicken, but that didn't work either.

Eventually, Randy said, "If we intend to have chickens, Clifford has got to go!"

It was a huge dilemma solved only when a friend of theirs—a friend Rose had known since her church camp days—offered to take Clifford and give him a good home.

"I promise Rose," said the friend, "I will take really good care of him. He will be fine. You can come and visit him whenever you want."

"Okay then. I suppose …" Rose didn't cry as Clifford drove off. She was numb wondering just how she had consented to giving away her very best friend, a friend who had seen her through so much horrendous pain.

Less than a month later, Rose mentioned to Randy that she would like to visit Clifford. Randy said he would talk to their friend about it and make a plan.

The next night, Randy suggested he and Rose go out for a nice dinner.

"That sounds nice," Rose said.

Halfway through her lobster Newburg, Randy told Rose that Clifford had proven to be a far larger problem than their friend— THEIR FRIEND—had anticipated, so he had Clifford put down.

" ....
....
....

....

....

...."

In the aftermath of such devastating news, many things came to Rose's mind, but she could not say a word. Everything inside of her was gone. She could neither speak nor look at Randy for the rest of their meal. Once home, Rose went for a long—a very long—drive by herself. She needed to be— to feel—totally alone as she attempted to internalize/accept what had happened.

HOW COULD I HAVE ALLOWED THIS TO HAPPEN? Why didn't our FRIEND mention that things weren't working out? If he had, I would have taken Clifford back and personally KILLED EVERY ONE OF THOSE GOD DAMNED CHICKENS WITH MY BARE HANDS!

Rose hated the chickens from then on. If Randy did not feed and water the chickens then the chickens did not get their food bin filled or their poultry fountain topped-up. She'd help butcher and eat the suckers, but that was it. Once the girls were old enough, tending the chickens became one of their chores, but until that happened, Randy was in charge of the chickens. Rose hated the chickens, and she couldn't imagine how she would ever trust anyone—a friend—again.

As time went by, Rose found a daily rhythm robust enough to keep busily *beside* herself instead of *staidly* inside herself. She had a house to keep clean, a family to take care of, and a hobby farm with cats, dogs, chickens, sometimes ducks and a huge vegetable garden, fruit trees, and berry bushes to take care of.

She threw herself into the role of Mom, Olivia Walton, of *The Waltons,* by canning and preserving as many staples as she could. She made most gifts and busied herself making most of the girls' and her own clothes.

Sometimes, for no particular reason, Rose would look at Randy across the dinner table and think to herself: ... *why can't you just fall in love with someone else and leave me the fuck alone? Or ... why can't you just have a heart attack and die or something.*

Instead, as duplicitous as Rose was, she would dish out her disgust disguised as conversational delights.

"How was your day dear? Would you like dessert? How about a cup of tea?"

Rose knew it was sick but ... she could not, for the life of her, figure out why she felt the way she did. She thought—honestly believed—that because her husband was a good provider, and a seemingly good father, one far more involved with the kids than her own dad had ever been, there was something terribly wrong with her. As such ... she decided she best just suck it up. Denied anger, however, does not evaporate. As the saying goes, "Shit runs downhill."

One Saturday night, the man of the house was off playing hockey with the guys and Rose was left home alone with the kids (again). For whatever reason, trivial at best, Rose started on a huge rant wherein she eventually threw her little girls— who were roughly four and two years old—crying hysterically, into their shared bed.

Shortly after slamming the door behind her, Rose realized what she had done. Overcome with grief and sadness, guilty, shameful remorse begged Rose to go back into her daughters' bedroom to make whatever reparation she could. Her heart nearly broke after re-opening the door and seeing her two precious little angels, each in the other's arms, crying. One by one, Rose carried her little darlings to her bed, snuggled between them, all three of them hugging their way into heaven, until they soon fell asleep.

Had Randy moved the girls back to their own bed once he'd returned home? Rose had no idea, that little morsel never made it into her memory.

Time passed but relief was not forthcoming.

Rose noticed she had begun smoking and drinking way more than she had in quite some time. With this realization, she was worried she'd slip back into the despondently self-destructive desolation that had characterized her earlier pre-wedded life. She couldn't allow that. She had a family to consider. She was getting nowhere on her own, with the sex thing, and the more tormented she became, it seemed, the more Randy asked of her. And the whole incident with the girls … well … that had scared the absolute living shit out of Rose.

How could I have done that to my precious little girls?

W hat I did to myself is almost inconceivable, but the unconscious energy animating me was on a quest. I was on a journey I would not understand until I had taken it.

No longer on a frantic search, thinking I'd finally snafued what I'd been looking for, I was able to calm myself down enough to assume the "happy homemaker" role I was sure would make me happy, but was I happy? Instead of happy, how about I say I kept myself busy, as busily entertained with external things as I possibly could. This I did to limit time spent lollygagging around inside my own head.

4

CRY FOR HELP
Enter George

With the unprovoked hissy she'd thrown at her little girls, Rose knew she needed to get help, so once again, counselling came to mind. This time she needed to find a good one! One that could help her.

Rose ended up calling a local psychotherapist recommended by the therapist her old buddy Chris, and Chris's partner, had begun seeing down the coast. It was by this means that Rose found George, George Reilly, and Rose loved him. No, she did not literally love him. She did not develop a crush on him. She just loved talking to him. George actively encouraged Rose to talk, and while she talked, he listened, he listened intently. He never got a sad, judgy, surprised, or disapproving look on his face. All he ever did was nod as if he understood what Rose was rattling on about. If he didn't understand or thought Rose might be stretching the truth, he'd stop her, ask for clarification. Rose thought George was the greatest thing since sliced bread, maybe even greater than sliced bread.

Rose loved her visits so much she suggested that both she and Randy, her non-consensual consort, should begin attending sessions together. George thought that was a great idea, but once the couple was there, Randy never said a word. For three or four appointments running, all he did was sit and listen.

When George quizzed him on it, Randy said, "Oh no, I am fine. It's Rose who has the problem."

Given that, Randy stopped attending. If he had nothing to contribute, George did not think there was much point in him attending. It was with enormous enthusiasm, however, that Rose continued to attend, and if necessary, would move heaven and earth to get there, get to her one hour bi-weekly appointments.

Although Rose thoroughly enjoyed her appointments with George, they didn't seem to be helping her much at home. She still found herself bitching and whining about her husband and his carnal desires to whatever compassionate companion she could find. She even tried speaking to her mother-in-law about it. They got along well, better than Rose had ever gotten along with her own mom so …

The advice Rose got back was as expected. "If we, as women, do not keep our husbands happy and satisfied, they will surely find another woman who will and then … then where would we be?"

Rose's oldest daughter had just turned four years old, and her youngest daughter was two years old when Rose became pregnant again. Even though she had recently busied herself even more by starting a bookkeeping and accounting business, Rose was, once again, delighted. This pregnancy did not, however, pan out.

She was five months along, at her mom's having Thanksgiving dinner, October 1986, when she began having cramps and started to bleed. She and Randy left the kids with their grandparents and zoomed to the hospital. The baby was dead, had been dead for a while, and Rose's body had begun trying to rid itself of the raunchy remains. All were amazed that Rose was not a lot sicker given the rot with which she was aggrieved. Once her labour began, Rose was wheeled into surgery for a D&C. She knew what that procedure was because she'd had two of them prior that were not quite as apropos.

The next morning, Rose was beside herself both physically and mentally. The nurses tried their best by explaining that miscarriages are just nature's way but ... Rose was heartbroken. She already had her brand-new little baby girl or boy's name picked out. The doctor explained that it was going to take a couple of days for her body to clear itself of the poisons produced by the corpse, contrary to nature, she continued to carry inside her, and until it did, she would feel as she felt—feverish and achy—like she was on death's doorstep. Were it not for her kids, not wanting to abandon her kids as she had been, she could have gladly lost the will to live.

During Rose's first night in the hospital, she had a very upsetting waking dream or hallucination of sorts. In this hallucination, Rose saw herself tempestuously running after Randy as he threatened to leave her forever. With this, she became paralyzed, unable to move or scream. Luckily a nurse happened to pass by, saw the fear in Rose's eyes, and by whatever means, snapped her back into the present. Rose was grateful to the nurse who saved her from herself, and then stayed with her, drank tea with her until she could regain some measure of composure. Although neither doctor nor nurse would agree, to Rose's mind, it was the pain meds—codeine—that caused her episode.

Not too long after Rose had returned home from the hospital, she learned that the heat exchanger in their furnace was broken, and they were all being exposed to carbon monoxide. Rose felt she should have guessed that something like that was going on given they'd had to replace the canary her oldest daughter received for her birthday, three times. The first time, Rose thought it was the bamboo cage, that somehow the bird had choked on a shard of bamboo. The next time Rose thought it was probably the ink on the newspaper she used to line the cage, perhaps the lead content of the ink. The third time, Rose had absolutely no idea why the bird died. Had carbon monoxide poisoning been the cause of Rose's miscarriage?

Rose was advised to avoid conception for at least six months after her miscarriage so her body could right itself. And it could not have been much more than six months later that Rose conceived yet again. By that time, her oldest had just turned six years old and her youngest was four years old.

This pregnancy was, by far, Rose's most difficult. Right from the beginning she felt lousy, nauseous, tired, crabby, and uncomfortable. And despite continuing to see George, the ante on her unhappiness had upped itself to where she was forever fantasizing about driving through the guardrail and over the edge of the treacherously steep, windy road etched into the mountainside that separated their house from town.

Unable to relax or sleep as she used to, Rose would get up at two or three in the morning to cry and cry, cry herself dry before the next day began, but this she did quietly, silently, because no one was to ever know how truly tortured she found her life. Consequently, Rose was always so screaming tired that she could barely draw breath. Sometimes the girls would have to get up and do their chores, get their own breakfast unattended because Rose was too tired to get out of bed.

As her pregnancy progressed, Rose began to feel like something was wrong, terribly wrong. She could no longer feel her baby move like it used to. This withstanding, her doctor assured her that all was well.

"The baby is fine."

Rose was skeptical but … what did she know?

Finally, the day arrived, April 20, 1988. After sixteen hours of labour, Rose was rushed off for an emergency C-section. The umbilical cord was wrapped around the baby's neck. Then, and only then, as her unborn child was being lifted from the womb of his creation, was it discovered that her brand-new baby boy had, indeed, been in a death spiral. Rose's placenta was almost completely detached from the uterine wall, so her as yet unborn child was slowly being starved to death. Given his length and weight, it was estimated that he had lost over a pound, a whole lot for a newborn. The poor little guy, he looked like a skeleton wearing the skin of a snake mid-shed. He was so thin—skin and bone—and his whole body was so dry, peeling off.

For medical reasons or otherwise, Rose's new little son was an exceptionally unhappy little boy. He had trouble eating, cried all the time and refused to sleep more than two or three hours at a time for the first two or three years of his life. The only way Rose could ever get her little man to sleep was if she lay down and hugged him to her breast as hard as she possibly could. With that, he would scream, continue to scream at the top of his lungs, as Rose cried softly, until the tortured torment of his terror turned into the serene silence of a slumbering child. Only after her babe was asleep would Rose slip out from under him to attend to the chores of the day.

Little did Rose know her little baby son's very survival was in question. Everyone else, doctor, husband, and parents all knew, but for whatever reason, had deemed Rose too fragile to be told the truth. It was not until his three-month check-up with the paediatrician that Rose was told.

"You no longer need to worry, Mom. Your son will be fine. He is gaining weight as he should, and his vitals are perfect."

Rose was aghast! Of course, she was delighted that her son was going to survive, but she was furious that she had been denied the truth. What if he had died without her having had an opportunity to give him the daily pep-talk he needed, that he should have received? What if she was forever unable to infuse his little soul with the workings of her heart? What if she'd had to let him go, give him back, like she'd had to give back the last child who inhabited her womb? Rose was furious and deeply hurt, yet, also, so relieved, that she cried for days.

Rose was thankful she told her doctor prior to the arrival of her third child that she wanted a tubal ligation. The doctor was skeptical saying she was far too young, at thirty-three, to be limiting her options in that way, but Rose knew—*just knew*—after this last pregnancy, that she was done. She had two beautiful daughters and a son, animals, and a yard to care for, a Mom-Walton image to maintain, a couple of part-time bookkeeping jobs to stay on top of, and a part-time, morning and weekend job as office manager at the local Royal Canadian Legion that she had taken on prior to getting pregnant the last time. Finally, Rose had found her fill. She had enough. She had way more than enough, but was she happy?

Through my years of struggle, I had tried many different counsellors. Most often I went once or twice. I neither needed nor wanted sympathy. I needed and wanted help, help I could intuit the counsellors I'd previously seen were unable to offer. Right from the get-go, however, George was different. He seemed to know when I was blowing smoke up his ass and he didn't—wouldn't—buy it, any of it.

He would stop me and stare steadily into my eyes, as if to say, "Really, Rose?" Finally, someone who, by expectantly awaiting the truth, fostered my ability to find it.

Such a coincidence, me having a miscarriage at exactly the same time the heat exchanger in our furnace was belching out carbon monoxide. Was the canary in the coal mine—bird cage—trying to tell me something about the toxic emotional and environmental atmosphere my child was attempting to grow within?

As I became increasingly efficient at managing my chores, I began marshalling myself a myriad more. More and more till the irrationality of my self-imposed expectation—the expectation that I could eventually make myself want to do something that I did not want to do—had me, once again, unable to hold my centre. My long-denied discontent began leaking out and onto the very family I had for so long coveted having. Repressed rage toward my husband was one thing, but after having caught myself splashing frustrated anger onto my little darlings, I knew I was at the end of my rope.

And so, 'twas only after having been tightly enough wound in the web of my own terribly misguided making that the world around me began to drum up sufficient unfortunate events to crack me wide open. It was from within that gaping hole that my light finally found a way to start shining through. It was from within that gaping hole that purpose and meaning would eventually shine light on my life.

A SERIES OF MOST
UNFORTUNATE EVENTS

5

HOUSE FIASCO
Flooded by Foreboding

B efore they knew it, Rose and Randy's son was approaching two years old, and would need out of his crib. While their house had three bedrooms, the third was very small and had been doing double duty as Rose's office and her son's bedroom. Because there was barely enough room for a desk, filing cabinet, a crib, and a small combination dresser/change table, the time was now.

A contractor was signed on. Randy's brother, also a contractor, came out from the prairies to help. All of Rose and Randy's friends offered their expertise whenever they were able, and Rose's dad was on stand-by. And ... whatever Rose was thinking—if she was, indeed, thinking at all—the family decided to move in with Rose's parents, for the duration of the renos.

Everything was set.

Work began February 1990. Unsurprisingly, things did not go well at Rose's parents. They were only there a couple of weeks prior to wanting—needing—to leave. By either coincidence, or secretly betrothed design, an older man Rose had befriended from the Legion—Grandpa Dave—so called by the kids, offered the family his tiny little house. Because Rose was reduced to tears after a single stern look from her mom, there was great relief in being able to temporarily move into a tiny one-bedroom, six-hundred square foot house of their own. Rose suspected Grandpa Dave had vacated his house so she and her family could move in but … it felt like a gift Rose thought unkind to call out.

The whole exercise—remodelling—was unbelievably stressful and unbelievably aggravating. Randy worked full-time through the process, so it was Rose's responsibility to do this, do that, go here, go there, all while having to stay on top of five or six small bookkeeping jobs as well as trying to keep the kids' lives as normal as possible.

During one of her appointments, Rose mentioned to George, "Those bloody drywall guys are making me crazy. They hardly ever show up for work, and when they do, they are usually piss-drunk but … you know George … it's almost like I need to get mad; I need to feel furious about something."

George nodded approvingly. "So … you are angry, Rose … what are you angry about?"

During the course of things, Rose and Randy ran out of money several times, each time having to sweet-talk their bank manager, the delightfully handsome man with whom Rose was becoming ever-more enamoured.

The nightmare lasted five long months, but finally—finally—the house was done. It was done and it was beautiful with its dark oak hardwood floors, white-spindled staircase, and brand-new top-of-the-line appliances. Euphoria accompanied Randy and Rose as they moved their family into their brand-new digs a day or two before the August long weekend, 1990.

Once all the harried hassles were over, Rose and Randy were convinced it had all been worth it, so to celebrate, they decided to take the kids to the lake for the weekend. They all needed to get away, blow off a little steam, and one of their friends—the friend that had put Clifford down—had a huge cabin at the lake that always welcomed friends. The Clifford issue was never discussed. To bring something such as that up would have been far too traumatic and ... to what end. Clifford was dead.

The family packed up and left late Friday afternoon. After having a wonderful time laughing and playing in the sun all day Saturday and Sunday morning, Rose, Randy, and their children headed home.

Upon opening their fancy new front door, however, they were greeted by water pouring out of every light fixture on the main floor. There were no words to express the anguished horror that overtook the pair. After rushing across their newly installed but ruinously puddled and warped hardwood floor to turn off the main water valve, Rose put the kids to bed so she and her husband could sit and cry, cry quietly together until they polished off the better part of a bottle of rum.

No matter how hard I try ... things just aren't going to work out, are they?

A top floor water line had ruptured. No one could say when, but the result ... with a bathroom and the bedrooms on the top floor, all could still sleep in their own beds, but with the main floor off limits, all family time—cooking, eating, clean-up and recreating—was moved to their half-basement, moved into their tiny two-hundred square foot rumpus room. It was damp, dark, and dreary, but it would have to do.

Through everything, I attended my counselling sessions religiously. I so loved having someone to whom I could spill my guts. With George, I was allowing myself the first real "friend" I'd had ever had. Given the safety of his office, I was learning how to be myself. I was learning how to say what I really thought—meant—rather than couch my words in vague drivel or say what I thought others wanted to hear. Not only did this help quiet all the voices in my head, in speaking my truth so honestly and forthrightly, I was beginning to feel emotions I had long learned to deny, emotions I had long deemed far too unacceptable or far too painful to feel, never mind, air. With thoughts and emotions being spun together, I began to see how my inner life was being reflected in my outer life. Previously locked doors were beginning to open.

'Twas the end of September 1990 before we could move back upstairs to fully fill and feel the fruits of our disheartening ad hoc do-over. Luckily, insurance covered most of it, but nothing was the same, and I knew nothing could—ever would—be the same. I could not put a finger on exactly what was different—things just felt different—somehow ruined. A crack in the disastrously deceitful delusion I had used to fortify the factiously, fabricated foundation upon which I'd built my life was beginning to form. The shattering of my precariously partitioned psyche had begun.

6

SEXUAL ABUSE?
Reckoning Reality

In contrast to the delight Rose experienced visiting her maternal grandmother, Rose despaired, and seriously despised the bi-monthly trips up to visit her paternal grandmother, an aunt and uncle, and an additional single uncle who all shared the same house. This was the home her dad grew-up in. Before every visit, Rose would spend the day agonizing over what was to come. Inevitably, she would be so stressed out that she vomited en route. Rose's mom thought it was car sickness, but Rose knew otherwise.

The problem: every visit, Rose had to sit on her creepy old uncle's knee. He gave Rose the creeps from across the room, never mind while balancing herself on one of his bony knees. Sometimes he would stick his face out for a kiss on the lips. His breath was absolutely putrid. Rose's mom said it was because he had liver disease.

Y u c k! Rose would be screaming silently at the top of her lungs as she dutifully complied. Rose's mom realized the situation made her daughter extremely uncomfortable but ...

"Poor Aunty and Uncle, they couldn't have children of their own … all he asks is that you sit on his knee. He is so terribly fond of you."

Rose had no idea when this particular horror began. All she knew was that despite having always been very tall for her age, it continued till she was nine or ten. Why she was allowed to quit visiting, Rose couldn't ever say, but at some point she did, and for that she was eternally grateful.

As unfortunate as the previous situation had been for Rose, when it was discovered that she was struggling in her Grade Ten French class, it was this uncle that Rose's mom engaged as a tutor. In his day, he had apparently been a fabulous French teacher. However long it was that Rose went to him for help, Rose knew it was never going to help. She did not have a problem with French, she just couldn't—wouldn't—speak it. If publicly pressed for a word or two, Rose would don a dismissively detached, almost arrogant air, and purposely blow it worse than she might have had she actually tried her best. By then, Rose was so screaming insecure and self-conscious that she would far rather not try—fail French—than sound like an idiot.

After relaying this story to George, Rose asked, "So … what the hell was up with Mom wanting—expecting—me to continue sitting on that disgusting old man's knee? And then … sending me to exactly the same creepy old uncle for tutoring? Why did she do that?"

"I have no idea, Rose. Why don't you ask her?"

"Are you kidding me? There is no way I would ask Mom about that ... she refuses to talk about things she does not want to talk about."

In addition to the aforementioned story, Rose also told George about being hypnotized, told him what she had seen— but failed to feel—during her session. While Rose wanted to know where her vision had come from and why she might have had it, George didn't have much to say.

"I don't know what it was Rose? Do you have any ideas?"

"Not a clue," Rose had said, so the topic was left to float as she continued to wander aimlessly in and out of her life experiences.

Whatever topic brought the question up, during one particularly noteworthy appointment George asked, "Rose, why do you do things—keep doing things—you do not want to do?"

"Huh ... you are right George. I am forever ... have forever been doing things, forcing myself to do things I do not want to do ... I think it's because I don't want to hurt people's feelings."

George's next question had Rose stumped. "Well ... why do other people's feelings matter so much more than your own?"

"Huh! I've never really thought about it like that before." *Why do other people's feelings matter so much more than my own? They really shouldn't ... should they?*

As Rose continued to consider the question, George mentioned that very often this sort of behaviour emerges due to early childhood sexual abuse.

"You know George … it is really funny you bring this up, because, as you know, this is the second time sexual abuse has been brought up—out—and I racked my brain for years, after being hypnotized, trying to think of when I might have been sexually assaulted."

The only thing that ever came to mind for Rose was *that* uncle of hers … whose knee she was expected—forced—to sit on.

"But that wasn't—isn't—sexual abuse … is it George?"

Rose and George then explored Rose's remembrances around her uncle, but no breakthroughs were forthcoming.

"Well Rose … sometimes people repress those memories because they are too painful."

After having sexual abuse brought up for a second time, Rose became obsessed with uncovering some sort of sinister truth she could not, no matter how hard she tried, gain access to.

Could some sort of sexual abuse have occurred prior to my being adopted? Had it happened during my ten-month stint in a foster home?

Rose's little brother and sister were all adopted. She wondered if maybe sexual abuse was common within foster homes because she did remember one of her little brothers getting into trouble for drawing breasts and penises on all the Yogi Bear and Boo Boos in his colouring book. She'd heard that sort of thing was indicative of sexual abuse.

But maybe … could it have been my dad? It had to have come from somewhere … wouldn't it have?

In a desperate attempt to quench her curiosity Rose called up her dad one morning and asked him if he would come over for lunch. He was retired so Rose knew it wouldn't be a problem. She really needed to tell him her situation and ask him if he knew anything. Rose knew there was no point in asking her mom. Her mom wouldn't talk about hard stuff. She would just remain silent until the topic was changed.

Rose's dad said he would come over, but he would have to make up some dumb excuse as to why, or her mom would be all over him. He told Rose's mom that she and Randy needed some sort of plumbing advice.

Whatever ... thought Rose.

It was a delicate subject to be sure, but Rose was in a state so ... after lunch and a little small talk, Rose launched right into it. To begin, Rose explained the theory her therapist had come up with. Immediately Rose's dad started to cry. Rose had never before seen her dad cry. She hadn't even asked him the *big* question yet, so she was terribly surprised when he starting to cry.

He continued to cry as he said, "No, never ... neither your mother nor I have ever done anything like that."

Now, what struck Rose was why ... why had he mentioned Mom? Rose hadn't even mentioned her mom.

Once Rose got her bearings back, she and her dad went on to have a fabulous chat, the best talk they'd ever had and about really hard things. Rose and her dad had never talked like they talked that afternoon. He told her about his childhood, being one of ten children, how he was always so afraid of his mom and so maybe that was why he always submitted to his wife, Rose's mom. Rose asked him about his relationship with her little sister and her brothers. He told Rose all kinds of things about himself that he said he had never told anyone else. The brick-and-mortar wall that had always existed between them vanished that afternoon. Before he left, Rose and her dad hugged. Rose had no recollection of ever hugging her dad before that.

Rose ended up having absolutely no idea if her dad told the truth or not, but all that seemed to matter, was that they talked.

A week or so after their private conversation, Rose's parents came over for dinner. After dinner, Rose's dad signalled her to meet him outside. Once outside, Rose found her dad standing around the corner crying. Again, she was astonished. In querying him, Rose's dad said he was worried she hated him now.

"What?" Rose asked wondering … had her dad lied to her and been unable to fess up? Did he know something about mom that he could not get out? Rose wondered, and continued to wonder ad nauseam, but what was done—or not—was done. Rose hugged her dad again, tightly but tenderly. He was in pain. She had caused that and for that Rose was sorry.

"No, dad … I love you."

Rose was anxious for her next appointment with George.

"So, George … don't you think it's weird that my dad brought up my mom without me even mentioning her?"

"Yes, it's a bit odd."

"Given my dad's reaction, do you think he sexually abused me?"

"Well, Rose … the discussion had clearly upset him, but I don't know. The topic can upset people for many different reasons. As much as you want answers … you may never get them."

Did my dad sexually abuse me? I don't know and will never know but it no longer seems to matter. In having no better way to explain it, I'll say … I am over it. And my mom?

When I first I got pregnant, mom had said, "Well … let's hope it is a girl. Girls should always be the oldest."

I was taken aback and wondered, but then, after hearing about a young girl who had been gang-raped, my mom said, "They should have just killed the poor girl."

Had my mom been sexually abused? Why else would she think that poor girl would have been better off dead? Mom having been sexually abused would certainly go a long way in accounting for her attitudinal anomalies.

With George always actively encouraging me to babble on and on about whatever came to mind, I began listening to myself—hearing myself talk. In being stopped and asked questions, I began to take note of the many inconsistencies in my thinking and the total lack of congruence between my feelings and my actions. Without knowing what he was doing or why, George was leading me deeper and deeper into myself, and with this, my cognitive dissonance began to reveal itself.

Funny my being unable to connect the reason I first started seeing George to sexual abuse of some kind. Prior to being married, I would have to steel myself—preferably have a drink or two—prior to being able to perform as the modern day, swinging single I pretended—wanted, assumed, or expected—myself to be. After the incessant grinding of marriage, however, I eventually discovered that if I held my breath, as if underwater, and only came up for air, when necessary, things would be a lot easier. Most often that worked. Only on the odd occasion would I be unable to hold back my sobs as I forced myself into compliance. If perhaps my body betrayed the anguish in my mind, I would lament the cruelty of my world. Unrestricted sexual consent had always been a self-imposed expectation, so I had been consenting to my own sexual abuse for years, both pre and post wedded bliss. Did I believe what I was doing was normal? Yes, I think I did.

The topic of sexual abuse never again came up. My supposition is that George thought it best to let me stew in my own juices. Given our conversations there could have been no doubt in George's mind that I was—and had long been—sexually abusing myself but ... I wasn't there yet so ...

Although I continued to cherish the comfort I found in my bi-weekly visits with George, were they helping me with things at home? No, not yet. That would take more doing, more time, and a lot more self-reflection ... self-realization.

7

LOSS OF A PARENT
Homeopathy of the Heart

The following spring of 1991, Rose's dad went in for back surgery. Although his back had bothered him since he was in his twenties—his lacrosse days—until then, he had refused the surgery doctors recommended he have. Rose had no idea why he finally decided to go for it then, but he did.

During the operation, a blood clot became lodged in his pelvis, and he was rendered paralyzed from the waist down. His doctor said he would never walk again. The family was mortified given Rose's dad's propensity for being constantly on the move. All were convinced immobility would kill him, but all were wrong.

After anguishing through months of physiotherapy, with the help of a walker, Rose's dad was back on his feet. He was back on his feet in time for his fiftieth wedding anniversary on September 12, 1991. All celebrated, all marvelled at their grand achievement. Rose and her siblings believed their parents should have gotten divorced years, if not decades, earlier but ...

A month and six days after Rose's parents' fiftieth wedding anniversary, Rose received an ever-to-remain notable telephone call during her favourite soap opera, *Days of Our Lives*. It was her oldest brother, Tom, calling to tell her that she needed to get to the hospital tout de suite because their dad had a heart attack, or something, and he would probably not survive.

"You're kidding?"

"Of course, I am not kidding. Why would I kid about something like that?"

After the moment it took for Rose to have what her brother said sink in, Rose flew into panic mode.

Desperately trying to figure out what to do first, she called her husband at work to tell him what had happened. Immediately after she'd hung up, Rose was furious at herself for having called him ... even offering to pick him up prior to going to the hospital. The drive in to pick him up would take thirty minutes, then commuting to the hospital, another twenty ...

All Rose could think was, *What if Dad dies before I get there?*

Despite how irrational she knew it was, Rose hated her husband for needing to be picked up from work. However Rose had arranged to have her children taken care of, she remembered not ... by the time she and Randy arrived at the hospital, everyone was already there—her mom, her siblings, and her dad's surviving siblings.

Apparently, a massive brain aneurysm exploded while Rose's dad was washing his car. Her little nephew had found him. By its size, the doctor believed that her dad would have been brain dead by the time he hit the floor. There was no hope, so rather than prolong the inevitable, Rose's mom decided they should let him go.

The family room Rose's dad was in was stacked with mournful attendants, backed as far as possible against the walls. The room felt stifled in cautiously calculated self-conscious fear. Rose surmised that everyone was scared to death of death, so no one wanted to be anywhere near her dad for longer than it took to give him a quick peck on the cheek and utter a private phrase or two.

What is wrong with you people? He is dying for Christ's sake, and he might be scared shitless!

Rose couldn't stand it, her dad being so alone and perhaps afraid. She did not want her dad to be afraid any longer, so she sat next to him and held his hand as she continued to remind him that she knew he'd done his best and that she loved him.

"All you need to do now, Daddy, is let go. Just let it all go. It will be okay. I promise!" Rose didn't know how she knew. She just did.

Although Rose's dad was already brain dead, it was another four hours before his heart stopped beating. Seconds after his heart stopped, his lungs released their final breath. With his final breath, Rose's dad gently squeezed his daughter's hand. The nurse said it was a normal, pre-death spasm, muscles tensing before relaxing forever, but Rose did not believe her.

You know I am here don't you, Dad? You know that you are loved right? Rose knew that little squeeze was her dad's goodbye to her, and she cherished it. She also knew that her dad's rest—his reward for living—was finally upon him.

After her dad died, Rose spent a lot of time thinking about him and his life. First off, in feeling like she could have crawled into bed with her dad so as to hug him, comfort him from this world into the next, Rose was convinced her dad had never abused her. If he had, that would have been the last thing she wanted to do.

After Rose's initial—aforementioned—conclusion, she pondered broader aspects of her dad's life. Everyone outside the house loved her dad to bits, thought he was a friendly, jolly fellow, but at home he was such a miserable, mean, cranky old sot. He was perceived one way in the world and another way at home. Rose wondered how her parents were perceived outside the home because when they were together at home, they treated each other terribly. You would have sworn that they hated each other, but no … it was only after seeing—feeling—her dad's pain, seeing him trembling and awash in tears by the time her mom finally arrived for her weekend visit to the distant rehabilitation centre that housed him, it was only after seeing—feeling—her mom's pain, in losing the love of her life, that Rose finally realized her parents must have *truly* loved each other. Despite appearances, and the havoc their dysfunctional turmoil caused within the family, Rose's parents had truly loved and needed each other. *How? And for God's sake, why?*

What struck Rose the most, however, was the irony of how her dad died. He died of a massive brain aneurysm. *All that cognitive dissonance. I guess his brain just couldn't take it anymore. It finally blew-up.*

With this, Rose could not help but wonder how her cognitive dissonance was affecting her health, and by extension, the health and happiness of her own little family.

I had never been afraid of death. In fact, I had been pretending I was dead since childhood. Whenever I woke up in the dark—without light—in the middle of the night, I would stiffen up and pretend I was dead. That was the only way I could clear my fear sufficiently to allow myself to fall—f a l l—asleep. I used to believe that death was the reward for having faced, in the best bravest way one knew how, the torturous trials of life, always having to try one's best to figure things out, to be okay. Many, many, were times when I implored the universe to reveal why I was *here* ... why I was alive, believing I had never—and never would have—asked to be born.

Was it extreme cognitive dissonance that had killed my dad? Maybe, maybe not, but in pondering my dad's life, after his death, I woke up to yet another glimpse of myself. Yet more conscious awareness was breathing itself into my unnecessarily miserable life.

8

CANCER AND CURIOSITY
Twin Tolls of Truth

A couple of months after Rose's dad died, winter of 1991, she was invited back into the workforce. An insurance agency in town remembered her from her former pre-motherhood life and wondered if she was interested in coming back to work. She would have to rewrite the licensing exam, but they were willing to sponsor her. No, Randy was not pleased, but Rose really felt like she needed to get out of the house, get a life, so she promised hubby she would make it work, and she went for it.

In addition to thoroughly enjoying being out and about, going for lunch every day with the girls, Rose was being thrown into constant contact with the bank manager who had set her life and loins on fire during the re-modelling escapade. Rose knew it was not a good situation, but it was a delightful diversion and it drove the determination behind the doubling down of diligence required to meet the demands of working outside the home.

It was while wistfully wandering around in a world of wishful thinking, as a re-licensed insurance agent, that Rose learned that British Columbia's Adoption Reunion Registry was going from passive to active. Previously, in order to reunite a family, both parent *and* child (over the age of nineteen) had to have voluntarily placed their name on the passive registry. When that happened, the powers-that-be would work to unite mother with child. As of January 1, 1992, however, either a parent *or* child (over the age of nineteen) could register an active search to be conducted on their behalf.

To Rose's mind, this was kismet, so she couldn't quit blabbing about it. She had always believed that someday, if and when the time was right, she would find out where she came from, and with she and George trekking so deeply into the tumultuous terrain of her past, it was a miracle—the timing could not have been more perfect. Finally, at the age of thirty-six—soon to be thirty-seven—the *time* was upon her. It was here. Finally, there was a chance—a good chance—Rose would find her story, her *real* story. All would be dealt with on a first come first serve basis, and because her name was already on the passive registry, Rose knew she would be one of the first.

Rose wasn't worried about her mom. She figured her mom would be genuinely excited for her because her mom had always professed to understanding how being adopted—the missing piece of her daughter's life—might elicit colossal curiosity.

"It is only natural for you to be curious …" It was her mom, after all, who had written to Victoria, B.C., for information on her daughter's history prior to her foiled marriage plans. "You have a right to know your medical history before you start a family."

It was also her mom who had put her daughter's name on the passive registry when it opened years earlier.

As such, it was without delay, with great outrageously gushing gusto that Rose made the necessary calls, filled out the necessary forms and sent in her $250 administration fee. All she needed to do was wait.

A month or so into her waiting, Rose's mom appeared at her office minutes before Rose's afternoon coffee break. Apparently, Rose's mom wanted, needed, to have a quick word with her daughter. Rather than going somewhere for a coffee and a chat, as Rose suggested, her mom insisted they just meet out front, on the sidewalk.

The whole thing seemed a little cloak-and-dagger to Rose, but ... she said, "Just a sec . . . I will get my coat."

Upon Rose's arrival outside, her mom blurted out, in no uncertain terms, that she had uterine cancer. She had a fast-growing malignant tumor the size of a grapefruit that required immediate surgery, radiation, and chemotherapy.

"What ...?" Rose was in shock. She could barely breathe but before she could get herself together enough to say anything, her mom turned around and began walking away.

With great effort Rose managed to call out, "But, Mom ... aren't you scared? Do you need a hug?"

But her mom did not turn around. She just continued to walk away.

Rose's next memory was of her and her mom sitting in the oncologist's office listening to a doctor explaining her mom's upcoming surgery, and what to expect post-surgery.

Rose had wanted to accompany her mom to the coast for her surgery and treatment. She knew her mom would be going through some pretty tough stuff, had heard about cancer treatments, and she didn't believe her mom should go through *it* alone, but time, and time again, her mom refused. Rose was not happy about it but … she had long learned it was best not to argue with her mom. And so it was that Rose taxied her mom to the airport, waited with her till it was time, and then waved to her as she watched her mom board the plane. Rose continued to watch as the plane took off … going up, up and away, into the wild blue yonder.

During the course of her mom's multi-stage treatment, Rose and her mom spoke on the phone several times, and Rose's mom always said things were going fine. She sounded a little hoarse, but she said was fine, just eager to get home.

How long was her mom gone? A week, ten days … or was it two weeks? Rose remembered not. All she remembered was the horror she'd felt as she watched the stewardess wheel her mom out of the plane in a wheelchair that had a neck brace attached to it.

Oh my God! I LET HER GO BY HERSELF! Stricken, Rose's eyes filled with tears of incalculable incredulity, but in knowing how her mom felt about tears, she did her best to roll them back.

Barely recognizable, the vital, able-bodied woman Rose had watched board the plane days earlier, had vanished. In her stead, was a sad, lifeless looking skeletal being who resembled an Auschwitz survivor more than she resembled her mom. It was all Rose could do not to crumple up and die on the spot.

Rose quit her job the next day. Someone needed to look after her mom. Since Rose's dad died, her mom had lived alone, and in her current condition, she certainly could not look after herself. She couldn't walk. She could barely talk. She couldn't eat. And although extremely dehydrated, she could barely keep water down.

Rose's mom was supposed to return for her second treatment in a couple of weeks, but by then she was barely eating and the ringing in her ears had still not stopped. The fight was on. Rose's mom did not want further treatment and Rose did not blame her. Rose's brothers and sister were furious with Rose for standing in solidarity with a mother who would prefer to die.

"Well, so would I," screamed Rose before the rant in her head continued … *wouldn't you? … you selfish freaking assholes?*

As you recall, death had never been Rose's enemy.

The oncologist was a jackass when Rose's mom, with Rose at her side, told him she was refusing further treatment. In response to her refusal of further treatment, the doctor told her, point-blank without emotion, that without treatment she would be dead in three months. Rose's mom said she did not care, and Rose could not help but despise the insensitive tactless prick sitting in front them.

They left.

It took Rose's mom a while, but eventually she was back working in her garden.

'Twas mid-April, Rose's mom was on the mend, well enough to be back in her greenhouse preparing for the coming gardening season, when Rose heard back from the adoption people. Back at the beginning of the whole process, Rose was told that reunions could only be arranged if both parties consented. Not only did her birth mom consent, she wanted Rose to call her that very night. Rose dang near exploded with excitement.

Immediately, she took to the phone. She had to tell everyone she knew her news. All were put on red alert.

YES! I am finally going to find out where I came from.

Rose was manic with excitement, but she was also a little afraid. What was she afraid of? Perhaps a lifetime of not knowing … What was the truth? Did she really want to hear the truth? With her mind working a mile a minute, Rose somehow got through the rest of her day, dinner, and doing dishes. At 7:00 pm that evening—with ciggies and a glass of wine at the ready—sitting alone at the kitchen table, Rose made her call.

I n compassionately witnessing – validating – my many recollections, commentaries, complaints, and contemplations, George was helping me to realize that I'd always had a life, a life that was my own, filled with my own perceptions, thoughts, emotions, realities, hopes, dreams, and desires. I was not, and had never been, a mere accoutrement in the lives of others. I was my own person. Hence my unwavering confidence in pushing full steam ahead into meeting my birth mother.

Because Mom would never talk about hard things, I quit asking her hard questions. I would have loved to have been privy to the mind of my mom, but she simply wouldn't ... perhaps couldn't ... share.

At one point during the whole cancer thing, I had asked, "Don't you feel like crying, Mom?"

Her response was, "No ... if I ever started to cry, I don't think I'd ever be able to stop."

Just how plugged up with emotion had my poor mom been? Perhaps she and I were far more alike than I'd ever dreamt.

9

THE CALL
Mirror, Mirror of My Soul

See ... I do have an older brother. I knew it! I have always known it! I knew I was not supposed to be the oldest.

Rose hated being the oldest; it always felt wrong, just plain wrong. Rose learned she was the youngest of four biological siblings. The first of four was a boy, nine years Rose's senior.

It turned out Rose's biological father died of Hodgkin's lymphoma many years earlier, when Rose was just seventeen years old, the year she attempted suicide. Her biological mother had moved to a neighbouring community, Salmo, of all places, shortly after Rose was born. Rose couldn't believe it. She had spent her entire life living a mere forty kilometres away from her biological mother. They could have, unwittingly, stood in the same line at a grocery store.

Rose's husband, it turned out, had been taking the co-op bus and working alongside Rose's older brother for the past five years. Rose's youngest daughter and her biological brother's youngest son knew each other too, because they were in the same grade at the same elementary school. Her oldest sister, four years her senior, was married with kids and living on Vancouver Island.

The oddest thing ... Rose's oldest sister's name was Ewin, a name Rose had not heard since she worked with two women of the same name a lifetime earlier. The other sister, two years her senior, who lived in Vancouver, also made reminiscent bells go off in Rose's head. This sister, at one point in her life, had had rheumatic fever, an illness Rose once thought she had pulled out of thin air. Rose was amazed.

So ... maybe I hadn't just plucked "rheumatic fever" out of thin air. Maybe it was hanging in the very air to which I have always been attached. Rose was amazed. Had it been a coincidence or was it something else?

Rose also learned that she had a half-brother—nineteen months her junior—and a half-sister—four years her junior—who lived in Salmo, the same small town as her mother. This half-sister was married with sons close to her own son's age. She had even dated a young man Rose had attended school with, a young man who had lived down the street from where she grew up. It was all so much to take in, so amazing. Rose felt like they should all be on *The Oprah Winfrey Show*.

Rose and her biological mother were on the phone for over an hour that night, so long Rose had waited, so much to learn and understand. She learned that her birth mother had been born in 1922, the same year her adoptive mom had been born. Before contact was cut off for the night, it was agreed that the two would meet for lunch that coming weekend. They agreed to meet in the restaurant of a local hotel at noon. Rose was so excited.

Rose met her birth mother for the first time on April 28, 1992, two days before her birth mother's sixty-ninth birthday. That morning, Rose went to the florist to buy two single, long-stem, red roses, one for each mom. En route to the restaurant, Rose made a pit-stop at her mom's.

"Here, Mom, I am going to meet my birth mother for lunch today and I thought ... well ... I thought I would bring you each a rose, a rose for each mom."

Rose did not have to be a mind-reader to know her mom was not thrilled by her daughter's gesture. Rose made a mistake. She hadn't meant to ... but ... she did.

When Rose arrived at the restaurant, her birth mother and husband were already seated.

They both stood, as Rose nervously, approached. After handing her birth mother her gift of a rose, hugs were given all around. As they sat down, Rose's birth mother handed her daughter a little gift-wrapped box. Inside was a tiny set of diamond studs.

"I hope you have pierced ears ..." her birth mother offered with trepidation.

"Yes ... I do ... and the earrings are beautiful." By this time, Rose was crying almost uncontrollably. A long pause preceded, until Rose said, "Thank you ... these are the first diamonds I have ever received."

Seeing her mother's face for the very first time was a moment Rose would never forget. Without effort, it engraved itself deeply into Rose's memory. Immediately upon looking into her mother's face, Rose noticed that they had the same nose. It was a long hook-type nose that permitted, what Rose thought, an unsightly view inside one's nostrils. Her birth mother's hair was a lot thicker than Rose's, and it was a dark blond, lighter than Rose's brown hair. Would Rose have recognized her mother if she had not known who she was? No, she did not think so, but then, Rose did not think she would recognize herself if she passed herself on the street.

After talking to her birth mother for a while, however, after hearing the pitch and cadence of her voice and seeing the wild emotional flailing in her birth mother's mannerisms, Rose knew it. She could feel it. Her mother was every bit as nutty and neurotic as she had ever been. Maybe she had indeed come from this planet. Rose felt more at home than she ever had. Every cell in her body relaxed, and for the very first time, Rose was at peace.

Apparently, Rose's birth mother was abandoned as a baby. She'd spent the first while in an orphanage but was eventually sent to live with an aunt and uncle who lived on a farm somewhere out in the middle of nowhere Manitoba. She stayed with her aunt and uncle until she was rescued by social services at thirteen years old, due to physical and sexual abuse. At nineteen years old, Rose's birth mom married Rose's dad, but it had been an unhappy marriage. She had married out of loneliness. It was only after having three children, and then meeting someone new—her current husband—that she felt she could leave Rose's dad.

Unfortunately, by then, she was pregnant with Rose. She had tried on several occasions to abort Rose, and told her, "I am afraid dear you were hell-bent on being born."

All things considered, both she and her new beau felt it best to give the baby—Rose—up for adoption. All parties in the know were told that the baby—Rose—was born dead.

When Rose's biological mother was first contacted by the Adoption Reunion Registry people to see if she would be willing to reunite with the daughter she had given up for adoption, so many years earlier, she said she'd replied, "Yes ... of course. A day hasn't gone by that I haven't thought of the little girl I gave away."

Even though it was going to be hard because neither Rose's full biological siblings, nor her half siblings, knew of her existence, Rose's birth mom was all in, right from the beginning. For this, Rose was eternally grateful because if her birth mother had not consented ... well then ... that would have been it ... end of story.

"Thank you, Mom—thank you—this means so very much to me. I have wondered about you—been lost without you—my entire life. But why did you abandon me if being abandoned had hurt you so much?"

"I didn't abandon you Rose ... I put you up for adoption. I helped pick the family that would raise you as their own."

"Oh." Rose did not want to argue the point, but to her mind, she had indeed been abandoned.

Funnily enough, as Rose was to later learn, she was the only one of her siblings who looked almost identical to their mother.

Upon visiting her biological brother's house one day, a mutual acquaintance of Rose and her older brother's asked, "Why do you have a picture of Rose on your wall?"

Rose's biological brother laughed and said, "That's not Rose … it's a picture of my mom when she was younger. It turns out, Rose is my sister."

This little story made Rose feel so proud, so self-assured, because it proved to Rose, and the world, that, *Yes, I was born on this planet! I do belong here … I have never really been alone.*

Now … the fact that Rose's birth mother's life pattern was so astonishingly similar to her own, given their total lack of environmental interaction, gave Rose pause—huge pause—but the fact that her birth mother had been sexually abused in one of the outbuildings on the farm in which she lived—under the same circumstances as Rose had experienced while hypnotized—was, to Rose's mind, freaking incredible. It was so mind-blowing that Rose was certain no one—absolutely no one—was ever going to believe her.

"How is this even possible George? It's like I've lived my mother's life, lived inside my mother's existence without ever having known a thing about her."

Rose knew—could tell—George believed her, but he had no explanation at the ready. He just smiled and nodded approvingly at Rose's most recent realization.

There was and would be much more to learn and a tremendous amount to consider, but for the time being, Rose's main focus was on getting to know her blood relatives. She felt more at home with her kin than she ever had in the home she grew up in. As such, Rose ate, drank, and made merry with them as often as she could.

Rose knew it would probably take a while for everyone to meet everyone else, but Mother's Day was coming up and so Rose suggested, "Maybe we should have a giant barbecue and invite both families so everyone gets a chance to meet everyone else?"

Rose, Randy, and the kids thought it was a great idea. Plans were made. Invites were extended. Everyone who could, said they would attend. Rose believed it was going to be great. She was sure of it.

The weather co-operated. It was a beautiful, sunny Sunday, but after everyone arrived and Rose cheerily introduced her mom to her biological mother, and her biological mother thanked her adoptive mom for raising her daughter, Rose's mom took Rose aside to say she was awfully glad her dad was dead because this would have broken his heart.

"At least your brothers aren't doing this!"

Rose was spontaneously splayed and eviscerated by the scourge intended to sabotage her effervescent exuberance. The energy animating Rose effused, and she thought she was going to disappear. Rose used alcohol to hold herself together as she catatonically saw the day through promising herself, over and over, over, and over and over again, that ties between adoptive mom and birth mother would, henceforth, remain severed.

But why didn't she just tell me the truth? Why did she let me believe she was supportive when really, she wasn't? Rose was sick inside. If only she had known. If she had known, she would never have proceeded as she had.

Why ... why do people lie to each other? Despite being a prevaricator extraordinaire herself, Rose was confounded. *I wonder what else Mom has been lying to me about.*

Given the horror of it all, Rose began to wonder if maybe it was the mutiny enacted against her, by her eldest daughter, that had caused her mom to get uterine cancer. Cancer of the womb. Rose was heartbroken.

W hy was I so afraid of the dark that I needed to pretend I was dead to fall asleep? Could it have had anything to do with the emotional reality within which I was immersed prior to birth? Could it have been the fact that my mom had tried to abort me? How about the fact that everyone was told that I had been born dead? How much of our pre-birth experience is locked inside of us?

Evolutionary biology suggests that humanity's wide diversity of behaviours is the result of an evolutionarily engineered capacity for behavioural plasticity. Given the pre-programing of our own special little set of needs, desires, and circumstances, we are unaware of why we do what we do and fall into behavioural options most likely to ensure the continued survival of our "selfish genes."[1] If evolutionary forces can carve out our physical means of survival, why not our mental and emotional as well? After all, who would cognitively reason oneself into a drug addiction, prostitution, or some other sort of shame inducing self-loathing and/or social condemnation? Who would abandon a child if they thought there was any other way? Had my birth mother simply found herself in the same situation as her mother before her? I represented the second consecutive generation of abandonment. I wonder if my maternal grandmother had been abandoned at birth. That would make me the third consecutive generation of abandonment.

I was so confounded by the countess similarities between myself and my biological mother's life, the sexual abuse thing, marrying someone out of lonely desperation, and then having three children prior to leaving the situation. It seemed almost too absurd to be real but ...

The emerging biological discipline of epigenetics,[2] is demonstrating how the environmental and lifestyle choices of an individual can influence both the physical and mental health of the next generation. Not only does a biological parent's diet affect their future child's risk of cardiovascular disease and diabetes, but severe stress—trauma—caused by physical, mental, emotional, or sexual abuse, as well as issues of abandonment, poverty, and food insecurity, can predispose future offspring to theme-specific inter-generation anxieties without them even having to suffer the same circumstances.

So, why did I choose to terminate two pregnancies, not so apropos D&Cs, rather than carry my first two pregnancies to term? I could have given those two children life and then given them up for adoption. It's not like I didn't—don't—think with remorse about the two sweet souls I denied life. Whenever I muse on the love I have for my children, they are always there, in the background, being loved dearly. Did I abort them because I feared abandoning them?

Could a fear of abandoning my children have been something I carried in my genes? Had I genetically inherited my lack of voice, my propensity for self-betrayal, and sexual abuse *victimology* epigenetically from my biological mother as well? It makes sense, more sense than anything else I have been able to come up with.

With all of this, it seems that every little thing matters, matters a lot to the health and well-being of not only our *self* but also the future we bring into being. The Hopi believe it takes seven generations for wrongs to fully unwind. How did they understand this without the benefit of our modern-day science? After hundreds — perhaps thousands — of years of careful observation, recognizable patterns emerged and were passed down, generation after generation, as the wisdom of ancestors. The Hopi are from Arizona, USA. I am sure our many Canadian indigenous peoples also carry knowledge that would be of great benefit to us all.

So much of the wisdom of our forefathers, both indigenous and not, has been lost ... from nature's signs and cycles to plant medicines, and pre-industrial farming techniques. Why did we allow these losses? I do not — simply cannot — understand.

For the longest time, I believed that people who could not have children of their own were probably not supposed to have children. I have since come to realize, however, that my earlier views were the result of externalized anger and resentment, anger and resentment that I carried toward myself, and my unwillingness or inability to speak. I have met countless individuals who in having been adopted themselves, feel no animosity whatsoever toward their situation. They feel nothing but gratitude.

Adoption is a magnificent gift. It is a social mechanism designed to permanently bring together childless couples and parentless children. I wonder who I would have been, what I would have been like, if I had not been adopted, had remained orphaned — genuinely alone — my entire life?

With these considerations though ... I also wonder if adoptive parents know ... I wonder if my parents knew what they were getting themselves into when they adopted four different children from four different lineages unknown, who had been removed from the ground of their being, from all they innately were, all they had already experienced. Every child does come from somewhere. There is no tabula rasa starting point.

Eventually, my brothers did the same thing I did. They searched for and found their birth mothers and extended family. They just did it after our mom was gone. Should I have waited? I probably would have if I'd known how my mom really felt but ... if I had waited, if I had not experienced the excruciating pain wrought by my mom's lack of emotional congruence, would the foundational awareness necessary for me to start inquiring into my own emotional duplicity have been sufficiently laid?

10

THE GIFT IN DESTINY'S DESIGN
The Journey Begins

Although Rose had not given herself permission to tell her husband of twelve long years that she did not love him and never had, she was glad the tremor of her long-denied truth had torn its way through her soul. Yes, it was painful—extremely painful—but it was also a relief, a giant relief to have her pipes finally flushed.

After her giant exhale, after the emotional eruption that smashed Rose's self-concept to smithereens and punctured the reservoir of pain and suffering that had given her previous life form, Rose was empty, amorphous, and so unstably grounded, that she had no idea who she was. Clearly, she was not who—or what—she thought she was because what had come out of her mouth had not only shocked Randy, but it caused Rose, herself, to feel apoplectic.

Oh my GOD! What did I do to myself ... to my life ... to Randy? How could I have married someone I did not love, barely even liked? And for God's sake why ... why did I do it?

Randy said he wanted to stay married no matter what, but Rose didn't know what she wanted. Did she want to stay married, or did she want to get divorced? Neither option felt immediately doable. They had children to consider, children to love and support, so before Rose could allow herself to move forward in any tangible way, she needed time. She needed time to figure stuff out. She needed to figure out what the hell had happened to make her do such an incredibly stupid thing.

G eorge and I had been exploring my life, jumping back and forth, and that had helped me to start unwinding things, but with what had just happened, I knew I was going to have to go back, all the way back. I was going to have to dig deep and retrace my steps so I could understand exactly whose fault it was that I had made such a horrendous mess of my life. Was it Randy's fault for tricking me into something I didn't want? Was it the fact that I was adopted? Was it my parents' fault for screwing me up so badly? What the hell was it?

Till I could figure stuff out, I decided to bide my time. I would live day to day, uncommitted to an outcome, until it became clear, in my mind, what I wanted, what I needed to do.

At some level, I knew I was stuck, had been stuck my entire life. I had always known how I felt, what I thought, and what I wanted, but I didn't think any of that mattered to living the life I wanted. I kept it all inside of me—to myself—never allowing myself to be heard, hence seen. And so, for the next few years, with help from my time-travel companion, George, I explored every factual remnant I could dig up and every personal reminiscence I had. I wanted to pick up and examine every shard of stained glass that had drawn blood. 'Twas my hope that by fitting it all back together, into some sort of frame, I would better understand the ground that created a figure such as myself.

And so, I became obsessed with my life. Did the egocentricity of the endeavour I was about to embark on occur to me? No, it did not. All I cared about was insight because I knew—just knew—insight was going to be my only salvation. Insight, and insight alone, would be—could be—my only *saving grace*.[3]

With that, my journey was on, and it was *on* with an intensity of spirit I had never before known. I had finally found a *purpose*; I finally understood my *reason for being*.[4] I needed to understand a completely non-sensical life—my own.

MEMORIES—MESSAGES TO BE MINED FOR MEANING

11

THE CATTLE GUARD
Behind Bars

Rose's earliest memory was of herself, alone, in a park somewhere. She must have been very young because she was barely able to walk, not very steady on her feet. She was staring down at a prison door looking thing, something she was later able to identify as a cattle guard, the horizontal piping laid at the entrance of a road or fenced field intended to prevent one's herd from entering or escaping. Rose remembered being totally captured by it, until she looked up and saw her mom, dad, and another couple within sight but quite far away. Had they called to her? Is that why she looked up? Were they worried she might hurt herself? Funny thing though … the way Rose remembered it, the cattle guard was between her and the grouping of adults.

How is that even possible? How had I gotten to the other side?

Rose thought George might have more insight into the conundrum contained in her memory than she did, so she asked, "What do you think it means, George?"

"I have no idea. What do you think it means?"

Rose did not know. She would have to think on it.

I have no tangible proof of this memory, and it contains no emotional tone, but I do still, for whatever reason, carry the scenario. I wonder why my budding young awareness decided to snap a pic of such an inane event? Could it have been intended as foreshadowing, foreshadowing of the prison cell I would eventually be called to free myself from?

12

EARLIEST PHOTOS
No Bells Ringing

While Rose had a few pictures of herself taken during her first few years of life, she could not identify with herself in any of them. In looking back through old photos with her family, after her dad passed, Rose recognized her mom, but for some reason, she could never recognize her dad, even when she was in the picture with him.

"Why do think that is George? Why am I never able to recognize my dad in pictures taken when I was young?"

"I don't know, Rose. Why do you think that is?"

"I don't know ... I will have to think on it."

Years ago, after my perspective had expanded, I had a dream that pulled sharply on my not being able to recognize myself or my dad in early photos. In this dream, I was dancing with the bank manager muse of my past, but when I looked up, into his face, who I saw was my dad—my adoptive dad as an older man—then, I saw my oldest biological brother's face, and finally, the face of the man I knew to be my biological father. In beholding the man who had sired me, a man I recognized from old photos that my birth mother had shown me, I knew—just knew—I had spent my entire life feeling a void where this man should have stood. When I awoke from this dream, I was awash in tears. Through my entire workday, the emotional turmoil and release this dream evoked had me fighting back tears. Could the reason I failed to recognize my dad in early photos have been because the man in the photo was not the dad *my earliest knowing* knew I *should* have had?

This dream also caused me to rethink my relationship with my mom. It is often said that the loss of one's mother in childhood is one of the most traumatic losses a child can face. By the time babies are born, they can hear quite well. They can recognize the voices of various family members, especially that of their mother's. This fact was established when studies showed that a newborn will turn their little head toward a voice they have come to know, while still in utero.

In recognizing a voice, the voice being recognized must cause a feeling of familiarity. But what would cause that? To recognize a voice, the energetic pattern of that auditory stimulus must be stored in the brain. With repeated exposure to a voice, each specific voice, a highly unique pattern of energy must travel along an identical neural pathway every time it is heard. Eventually, in etching and re-etching itself—time and time again—that voice must trigger an electrical firing that forces the owner of said etching to come to attention, an attention that spontaneously causes a sense of familiarity ... a sense of familiarity that reflectively triggers a newborn to turn their little head to determine from whence said voice emerged.

But what is this sense of familiarity? Is it a memory? No, it has no content. Is it an emotion? No, although it may anchor us to a previous time, be it ever so subliminal, it is without feeling tone. It is just a moment of conscious awareness that feels familiar. It must be somewhat akin to the feeling of déjà vu, a moment that suggests you've experienced this something—whatever it is—before. When we recognize something or feel something is familiar, we feel a sense of re-acquaintance, an attachment, or a sense of belonging to some prior time and place. In newborns, this sense of familiarity elicits a reflexive response that directs the acquisition of associational information, info that informs a child's understanding of the world. Thus, the child reflexively seeks out their mother, the place from where it came.

Given my hypothesizing, children must be born with an innate need to attach, a need to orient themselves, a need to know where in this world they are meant to be or belong. Is this why I felt as I did about my mom? No matter what she did, it was wrong. She was wrong. She had the wrong voice, smell, and energy. Despite having been there for me, she was not the mother *my earliest knowing* knew I *should* have had, so ... I rejected her.

My birth mother hated her birth mother. Why ... because she'd abandoned her?

13

THE PORTRAIT
A Compilation of Period Specific Truths

Rose had clear memories attached to a professional photograph taken of her when she was eighteen months old. She remembered the blanket-covered box she sat on and the big lights on either side of the room. What she remembered looking at, however, was the big blank screen upon which the picture was going to be taken. Rose knew that couldn't be right. The screen would have had to be behind her, right?

Rose also remembered the brown checkered dress she wore to have her photograph taken. It was terribly uncomfortable, shiny on the outside but very stiff and itchy on the inside. Rose always believed she still had her ponytail at that time, and she was always convinced that she had been hanging on to her beloved stuffed rabbit, Bugsy, for dear life.

When looking at this photo, later in life, Rose was amazed by the incompleteness and incorrectness of her memory. She did not remember the light blue trim on the dress, and she did not remember her matching light blue ankle-socks. In addition to this, Rose clearly did not still sport a ponytail. By this time, she already had her hideous, short, curly do. And instead of hanging on to Bugsy for dear life, she was holding some strange short-eared bear. What astonished Rose the most, however, was the fact that she was smiling. As Rose recalled, she had been scared shitless during her photo-shoot, during her entire childhood.

In pondering the discrepancies between her memory of the event and the actual photo, Rose was called back to how much it hurt when her mom washed her hair. Her mom scratched and scraped so hard that Rose figured she must have had her claws out.

At some point, Rose started to wash her own hair, and when she did, in catching herself ripping and tearing at her scalp like her mom used to, she asked herself why she was doing what she was doing. In being unable to come up with an answer she stopped. Just like that, Rose was able to stop. It was so simple. Rose never scraped or tore at her scalp again.

Rose was also called back to how much it hurt when, every night before bed, her mom would brush and brush her hair until she tied it up in rags. The rags would be tied so tightly. It hurt so much, but apparently, after being tied up in rags, Rose's hair would fall into the loveliest ringlets. That only lasted until Rose's ponytail was abruptly and unceremoniously cut off at the elastic.

Rose had a picture in her mind of her mom sitting in one of the big green upholstered chairs in the corner of the living room, when she called her daughter over, saying, "Come here and turn around."

Rose had no idea what was about to happen, but she was sure she was wearing that brown checkered dress when it did. Rose's mom said she cut off her daughter's hair so it would grow in thicker.

Then, there was Bugsy, the stuffed rabbit Rose was sure she had been holding in the aforementioned photo. Bugsy was a pink and white stuffed rabbit Rose took everywhere with her for years. She so loved—so needed—that rabbit. He was the only toy Rose ever recalled being attached to. If inadvertently left behind somewhere, Rose would be beside herself until Bugsy made it safely back into her arms. Rose had no idea when or from whom she first received her crazy wabbit. What she most remembered about him, however, was the reoccurring nightmare Bugsy took centre stage in. It was her worst dream ever and it was always the same.

Rose would set Bugsy down on a little sill that formed the entrance into a big brick fireplace, this so as to put her hands to some other use. The next thing Rose would know, evil looking flames that were laughing uproariously would leap out of the fireplace and snatch Bugsy. They would snatch him and commence burning him up right in front of Rose's eyes. Holy! Rose would wake up in controlled hysteria—unable to move or scream—every single time she had the dream, and the last time was when she was about sixteen years old.

Other early childhood memories would get triggered from time to time, and Rose would reflect on them with anger, sadness, confusion, and sometimes horror, but then she would just let them go, let them go as random scenarios that for whatever reason, haunted her, from time to time.

With my memory of this photograph and its accompanying morsels, it is as if my mind's eye created a mosaic, a compilation of period specific truths coalesced around a moment, a single moment deemed representative enough to be saved.

I wonder why I do not remember the photographer standing in front of me taking my picture. All I have is the remembrance of whiteness in front of me. In being afraid at such a tender age, had my awareness gone within, retreated into the light I still carried within?

More often than not, the memories I carry do not have a beginning, middle and end. They are situational snapshots that stopped dead when my emotional reality became too intense to feel. At those times, 'twas as if my thinking/feeling mind would suddenly withdraw, retreat to somewhere safe, leaving me on automatic pilot—automatic pilot until my limbic system, once again, became overwhelmed and I formed a new flash memory.

I have spent a lot of time wondering why I remember what I do, the way I do, and I have come to the conclusion that my memories were formed as tools that could come in handy later, should I choose to use them. By mining my memories for meaning, I was able to see where I'd *been* so as to understand where I *was*. By that means, I was able to change the trajectory of my future.

I wish I had paid attention to my memories earlier. They certainly laid enough breadcrumbs to lead me back into the frightfully fraught folly of my past, but never, not once, did I consider that they may have been trying to help guide me into a different, less painful, way of being. Nope! Never once did I look inside myself for answers. My gaze had been trained outward, and unfortunately, that is where it stayed until inward was the only place I had left to go.

When my youngest daughter was little, she had long, very thick, blond hair that she absolutely hated to have brushed, so she would whine and cry every time. My solution, apparently, was to abruptly and unceremoniously, cut her ponytail off at the elastic, and it was apparently, just as devasting for her as it had been for me, a generation earlier. Had I allowed my memory of that event to inform me ... I probably would not have done what I did.

Had I scraped and torn at my children's scalps when I washed their hair? No, I did not. And why was that? Because ... well ... I decided—made a conscious effort—to stop scraping and tearing when I first began washing my own hair, long before my children were even a twinkle in my eye.

As a very crispy critter, fur long since worn off, Bugsy now sits in a box frame mounted on a wall in my spare bedroom where he can forever be remembered as the benignly comforting companion, he once was.

Last thing about the aforementioned photo ... again, after I had begun to view my life from a far wider perspective, I had a dream wherein I was an old woman crouched down beside that little girl sitting on the blanket-covered box waiting to have her picture taken, and whispered softy, "It's okay darlin', you are going to be fine. We made it."

When I woke up, I had tears in my eyes. I so remembered being that little girl.

14

JOYFUL INNOCENCE
Granny's Enduring Endowment

Most of Rose's best memories were ones she carried from her earliest childhood years, and they were centred around time spent with her granny. Granny was Rose's mom's mom who lived right up the hill from Rose's family. They all lived on the same mountainside. Granny was a slender, nimble, hardworking, old woman who mostly always wore exactly the same thing—a pair of blue jeans, or dungarees as they were called back then, one of her many tartan-flannel-collared shirts, a sweater over top when it was coolish, and a red bandana over her short, artificially curly, thinning, grey hair. Rose used to watch when her mom gave her granny a Toni—a permanent— from time to time.

Rose spent a lot of time at her granny's house. She never understood why she spent as much time there as she did. She just remembered being there … a lot. And it was great. Rose loved it.

Rose's gran's house was a normal size, not too big, but not too small. It was old but tidy and clean. Her furniture was nice enough. It looked comfortable where it was placed, and it provided comfort when you used it. There was no plastic on the couch or protective runners on the floor, and you were allowed to bring food into the living room. All of Granny's rugs were homemade. Rose's granny would buy old wool coats from rummage sales, cut them into strips and then make the most beautiful, braided rugs. Her house was full of them. If you spilled something while at Granny's house, it was no big deal. You would help Granny clean it up and carry on without feeling like you had done something unforgivable.

Rose's favourite spot in her gran's house was the cozy, bright kitchen. She and her gran would chat and chat as they sat at her gran's little fold-down, yellow Arborite and stainless-steel kitchen table. The matching chairs were even padded so they did not hurt your bum. And Granny's kitchen always smelled so good. Whether just boiling water to make tea, cooking a pot of soup, or baking some delicious delight, Granny's wood burner was always on the go.

What Rose loved most, however, was spending time with her gran in her granny's garden. Granny's garden was huge, and it was a natural paradise, so beautiful the way the lawns gave room to trees and gently erupted into rockeries, multi-coloured flowerbeds, and fishponds. There were pansies, poppies, primroses, daffodils, delphiniums, and dahlias. And then, of course, there were the daisies. Rose loved the daisies. They were so innocent looking: so happy, free, and glad to be alive.

Every spring, sometime after watching her patch her fishponds with cement carefully mixed with a shovel in her wheelbarrow, Rose and her gran would inspect the newly hatched fish. They would have to bend over, get really close, before they could see the little darlings swimming around in the shallow troughs carefully crafted around each pond for that very purpose.

"The babies like to be warm dear. And you have to keep the little ones away from the big ones because the big ones will eat the little ones if they can."

When it was warm enough, Rose and her gran would have lunch, homemade oatcakes, and cottage cheese, on a red and white-checkered tablecloth Rose's gran laid under her favourite tree, the big maple in front of her kitchen window. Rose would even be allowed to drink tea with her gran. Granted it was half milk with a generous portion of sugar, but it was tea with Granny nevertheless.

Rose and her granny were forever wandering aimlessly around the yard chatting, laughing, and looking at this, chatting, laughing, and looking at that. There were bugs, butterflies, birds and very often a bat hanging upside down in the rafters of the garden shed. Sometimes they would see a garter snake slither by or spy a frog watching them watch him.

"Snakes and frogs are a garden's best friends, dear. They eat all the bugs."

When hundreds of squawking birds flocked into the giant side by each Lombardi poplar in the back garden, Granny would say, "Oh … the birds must be having a party." Or if the weather was changing, she'd say: "The birds must know it is going to rain so they are looking for a place to stay dry."

Rose thought her granny was so wise. To her, at the age she was, Rose believed her gran knew everything, every single thing about her wildly natural hodgepodge of colours blooming and life buzzing. When Rose was with her gran, the world felt like a miracle. It was a wonder where everything was happy and fit together perfectly.

On Sundays, Rose's mom and she would go to church with granny. Granny was a member of the Presbyterian Church, and so was Rose's mom. They both belonged to the Lady's Circle, so having Rose start down the same path was more than logical.

One Sunday when Rose's dad must have needed the car, the three of them took a taxi to and from church. Rose remembered that as being quite the adventure. She had never been in a taxi before. Rose also remembered that for a treat, every now and again, they would all go to the Tastee-Freeze for an ice-cream sundae, or a banana split, after church. Once Rose was old enough for Sunday School, she went there while her mom and gran were at church.

One Sunday morning, Rose read the 23rd Psalm from the pulpit. How, or why that came about, Rose had no idea.

Rose loved Sunday School, all the singing, colouring, and stories. The only story Rose ever remembered was the one about little Samuel, God calling on him in the middle of the night. The reason Rose remembered that story was because she too had heard someone calling her in the middle of the night. There she was, lying in her bed, hallway light streaming through her bedroom door not quite shut because she was petrified of the pitch black, when all of a sudden someone called out her name.

What? Is that Mom and Dad calling me? Then she heard it again.

Yes! They are calling me. But they know I am in bed! Again, Rose heard her name being called. After this third time, Rose got out of bed and went—stormed as Rose recalled—into the kitchen.

"Yes, what do you want? I was in bed."

Rose carried a mental snapshot of her mom and dad sitting there that night, sitting across from each other at the kitchen table staring at her with looks of befuddlement on their faces. They had absolutely no idea what Rose was talking about. After looking at each other and then partaking in a fairly substantial silence, they replied.

"We did not call you." Question marks flashed in their eyes.

"Oh," Rose responded, as she turned around more than just a little befuddled herself.

Once back in bed, Rose lay there forever trying to figure out what had just happened. Had she really heard someone call her name? She was sure she had. In fact, she was positive she had, yet, who could it have been if not for her mom and dad?

I know, maybe it was God who was calling me, like he had called little Samuel? Sorry God. I didn't mean to ignore you. I didn't realize it was you. Please call me again, okay? Next time I will know it is you.

Rose heard her name called out from undisclosed locations many times in her life, but she never again wondered if it was God calling to her.

Once Rose was in kindergarten, Granny would come down to their house for lunch. Rose and her brothers loved that because their gran always had a little bag of candies: liquorice babies, jube-jubes, jellybeans and the like, in one of the front pockets of her blue jeans. Then, when their mom wasn't looking, Granny would sneak them a candy or two or three.

D id I love my granny? I know I loved being with my gran. Her essence carried me on the clouds. Whilst with my gran, I felt good, relaxed, like everything was as it should be. It was during my early years with my gran that I developed my deep love and respect for the natural world. It was my gran who first showed me that everything fits, belongs together, because we are all part of the same thing.

15

CHILDHOOD WONDER
Starry, Starry Night

Once old enough to go, Rose started going to church camp. It was a week a year, during summer vacation, and Rose loved it. It was the highlight of her life for five or six years running. The camp was located on Wasa Lake, north of Cranbrook, in the East Kootenays.

As you drove into the camp, there was a corral with three, maybe four, horses on the right side. Ruby was Rose's favourite horse. She was the most spirited of the horses, and yes … she did kick Rose in the shins once leaving a huge black and blue horseshoe-shaped welt. It hurt like crazy, but Rose knew it wasn't Ruby's fault. Rose just hadn't realized that you weren't supposed to stand directly behind a horse. And in having failed to cinch Ruby's saddle properly one day, Rose and her saddle—feet stuck in the stirrups—slid dang near under Ruby's belly before she stopped dead on the side of the road. But, as time went on—or the years passed—Ruby and Rose grew to love each other. On the days it was Rose's turn to ride, she would ask the cooks for a carrot or an apple for her beloved Ruby.

The camp itself was comprised of a bunch of cabins. There were four girls' cabins, each with four sets of bunkbeds and a cot by the door for the cabin leader. There was only one boys' cabin, and it was huge. It had eight or more sets of bunkbeds and two or more cots for cabin leaders. Rose wasn't sure about the inside of the boys' cabin because girls were never allowed in it. There was a separate wash house with sinks and toilets: girls on one side, boys on the other. The kitchen, dining hall, and rec room or lounge area were all in the same building. It was a huge rectangular building with a veranda out front and a large porch out back. The dining hall had a series of long tables that provided great fun when food fights broke out. The lounge area had a big fireplace, lots of comfy couches and a pool table.

On the last night of every camp, a kangaroo court was held to celebrate, condone, or absolve, if necessary, any noteworthy events of the preceding week. 'Twas like a family of friends reviewing and revelling in a time of their life.

Off the kitchen was an outdoor chapel with little wooden tables for crafts and little wooden benches to sit on for talks and storytime. One year, one of the boys attempted to skin a dead squirrel on one of the craft tables. Needless to say, no one was pleased about that but …

To this place in or under heaven, every summer, fifty or so similarly aged girls and boys from all over the Presbytery, would meet up. They would all have to get up at dawn's crack for either calisthenics or a quick dip in the lake. Rose always chose the calisthenics. Cold water, first thing in the morning, did not work for Rose. After brekky and chores, cleaning up their beds and cabins, helping the cooks peel potatoes or something, they would all sit through a mini-church service and a related craft. Then, everyone would get to do whatever was planned for the day—swimming, canoeing, sailing, horseback riding, hiking, or games of sport.

One year, sufficiently convinced that she had learned to sail well enough to go out by herself, Rose sank one of the tiny two-seater sailboats. Luckily, someone had been watching and came out to rescue her.

Every night, after it got dark, they would all take their flashlights and go down to a campfire on the beach where they would drink hot chocolate and have a sing-along.

Rose relished her memories of church camp. Such joy, such carefree abandon. It was so similar to being with her gran, it allowed Rose's mind to open up to things she did not understand, brief glimpses of things she would forget … forget until the next time … forget until she forgot for a long time.

At home, after abruptly snapping awake in the middle of a dark empty night, Rose would just stiffen up, be very still— pretend she was dead—till she fell asleep. But this one night, in knowing she was at camp—camp being akin to her gran's garden—Rose decided to get up and go outside.

Once outside on the stoop, surrounded by overwhelming calm and blackness, Rose's gaze went up to the sky. There sprinkled in the vastness before her were stars, thousands, if not millions—billions—of brightly lit little suns, all twinkling down at her. In the face of such awe-inspiring magic, Rose's heart nearly burst. She understood the meaning of *glory on high.* She was, after all, at church camp. In looking up at the wonder above her, Rose could see the stars looking at her. She could feel them sending their love out into the vastness of space. With this, Rose understood that she was not but a miniscule spec in the grand scheme of things, and it didn't matter a whit what she did or didn't do, everything was and would always be fine … just fine. The pressure was off. After thanking the stars for what she experienced, Rose went back to bed, closed her eyes, and allowed herself to fall fretless, back into the void. She fell asleep.

You know, I have thought about this memory a million different times, and on pretty much every occasion, I cannot help but wonder … how on earth I managed to crawl out of my sleeping bag, get down from the upper bunk in the corner of the room—the bunk I had every year—and get out the door in the pitch black, without anyone hearing me. The cabin leader's bed was always right next to the door, and on many other occasions, kids had been caught trying to sneak out. So … is this memory really a memory or was it a dream? Either way, it was a wonderful experience I never told anyone about because it felt far too personal, far too special to share.

16

NATURE'S NURTURANCE
Creekside Reverie

One day, when Rose was nine or ten years old, she, her two brothers, and her dad, arrived at her dad's favourite fishing hole. Rose's dad loved to creek fish. It soon became more than apparent that the group was short one fishing rod: three rods, four fisher-people. In being the sweet, self-martyring child that Rose was, she cheerfully told the guys to go on ahead, secretly believing she would—could—fashion a rod the *Tom Sawyer way,* and fish the heck out of the whole dang works of them.

Needless to say, Rose's initial reaction to her total lack of suitable supplies was to feel overwhelming despair. As such, she climbed onto a big rock and began doing what she did best, that *being,* wandering around inside her head.

With the sun shining ever so brightly on her face, it suddenly occurred to Rose that the creek running so swiftly beside her was completely made up of tiny raindrops or drops of water that had fallen from the sky, came from springs within the earth, or were the result of melting snow. All of these raindrops would have had to join hands and decide to go in exactly the same direction for this marvel of a creek to be possible. In doing this, these raindrops gave life and home to fish, plants, bugs, and even herself, since she too, was dependent upon the very essence of what raindrops were. With this revelation Rose felt at one with the creek, everything in it and everything around it. Complete joy filled Rose's heart.

I have no idea how long I sat staring at that creek, but it must have been an hour or more, because as I remember it, at the very time my revelation was complete, the fishermen of the day were coming back with a great deal more than their fair share of nature's bounty. Again ... childhood wonder, and again, a story I never shared because it too felt far too personal, far too special. It felt like a secret between me and the universe that wasn't intended to be shared.[5]

17

DESCENT INTO DARKNESS
Innocence Lost

Rose's granny died when Rose was twelve years old. But before her death, Granny took a fall down one of her rockeries and was not found till she failed to come down for lunch the next day. After that, it was like Rose's granny was already gone. She was still there in body, bedridden, but it was like she and Rose had somehow already said their goodbyes.

Rose was neither sad nor resentful in having to make and help her gran drink the home-made eggnog: raw egg, banana, vanilla extract, and milk combo blended by a hand mixer—her gran needed to keep her strength up. She didn't mind sitting vigil at her bedside or staying overnight on her couch. And even though her house had begun to smell something terrible, like something was terribly wrong, Rose did not mind being at her gran's. In fact, she loved it, because while there, she could be herself and could read for as long as she wanted from whichever book she wanted as long she found it at her gran's. You see, Rose was not permitted to do much reading at home as her mom did not believe reading was a good use of one's time.

Rose remembered reading *The Adventures of Tom Sawyer,* *The Adventures of Huckleberry Finn, The Jungle Book, Tarzan,* a large collection of *National Geographic* magazines and a whole raft of Perry Mason paperbacks. Rose realized there were probably a lot more books she had read while at her gran's, but those were the ones she remembered reading.

While trying to reimagine—feel—herself back on her gran's long, comfy couch reading *Tom Sawyer*, Rose was stopped in her tracks. *This can't be right.*

Had Rose read *Tom Sawyer* before her granny got sick, before the aforementioned ill-fated fishing trip, or after? It made no sense to Rose that she would try and fashion a fishing rod the *Tom Sawyer way*, prior to reading about Tom Sawyer and … it made no sense that she would be out fishing after her gran got sick, because after her gran got sick, she was forever at her gran's house. Rose was confused as hell but …

There you go … she thought. *That's memories for you.*

Quite often, Rose would read aloud at her gran's bedside. She wasn't sure her gran was paying attention, but Rose didn't care. Even if her gran was just sleeping, Rose believed she would somehow know Rose was there with her.

Rose didn't remember how long her granny was sick before she died, but she remembered, clearly, the day it happened. Upon arriving home, Rose's uncle—her mom's youngest brother—was preparing lunch. With that, Rose knew something was up. How long was it before her gran's funeral? Rose had no idea. However long it was, Rose remembered that there was a lineup of people waiting to greet her and her family as they entered the church for her gran's service. After being instructed by her mom to plant a kiss on the cold, waxy cheek of a carefully costumed corpse, Rose thought ... *that is not my granny.*

Once back at her parents' house for the post-funeral gathering, all Rose was concerned about was how she looked. Rose's mom had borrowed from her cousin a flashy two-piece, navy blue wool suit for her daughter to wear for the occasion, and Rose was allowed to wear nylons and clip-on earrings for the very first time. Although there was a myriad of people standing around chatting and crying, Rose spent most of her time checking her reflection in the mirror. She hated her hair, thought her hairdo made her look stupid, and she agonized over the many pimples that had begun poking their little heads out.

Did she even cry that day? Rose remembered not. Rose believed that by then, she and her gran had long since parted ways. By the time Rose's gran died, Rose was lost, lost, alone, and terribly confused. And unfortunately, she remained that way for a very, very, long time.

I can now, once again, touch who I was—how I felt—as a little girl in my gran's cozy, little house or in her big, beautiful yard. I can also now, once again, touch who I was—how I felt—while feeling the love that emanated from the night sky and the marvel I experienced beside the wonder of that living creek, so very long ago. In feeling a kinship with the world around me, I was happy and at peace. While in those locations, I had a deep wordless understanding of how everything—including myself—naturally fit, flowed, and functioned together. Unfortunately, I lost my connection, my ability to commune with that feeling. But did I lose it because I was supposed to? Did I lose it because my life, all along, had been dedicated to re-discovering it—finding home—once again?

18

DISORIENTATION
A World I Did Not Understand

Rose had no early childhood memories of being in her parents' backyard, even though it was, had always been, every bit as expansive as her gran's lovingly tended habitat. Part of the reason for this may have been that the landscaping of Rose's parents' yard only found its beginning as Rose was finding hers.

In early pictures, Rose's parents' acre and a half appeared as nothing but barren mountainside, much as the rest of the surrounding countryside, mostly just sandy dirt, rocks, and scraggly old shrubs. This was apparently owing to the toxic chemicals that forever belched out of the smokestacks of the giant lead and zinc smelter that gave birth to the city where Rose grew up, that gave the city its birth and kept it, its local residents and the local hockey team alive and prosperous through good times and bad. Although environmental concerns around the smelter's operation began in the 1920s, 'twas not till the 1950s that Cominco's harmful waste began to be converted into pellets, sold all over the world, as Elephant Brand fertilizer.

Without all the noxious fumes to fight, nature started to come back. So started the *greening* of Rose's community (and the eventual *greening* of the world).

Upon learning the story of her city, Rose was curious, and said, "But Dad … if it is poisonous enough to kill plants when it comes out of the smokestacks, how can it be safe when you throw it on the ground?"

Rose's dad did not have an answer. No one seemed to have an answer. Rose did not understand so she remained skeptical …

Rose was older but not that much older when she began to take notice of the way her parents were fashioning their yard. It was different; it looked and felt very different than her gran's.

Rose had a clear memory of her dad cutting down the last tree—a Silver Birch—on their property. She had so loved that tree for its thin sheets of silvery bark that she could peel off and use as paper.

"Why are you cutting it down, Dad?"

"Because it makes a horrible mess when it drops its leaves."

"Oh …" Rose didn't get it. Her granny didn't seem to mind all the leaves and she had a ton of trees.

Rose's mom and dad put in many, many lawns but apart from the times when a photographer would strategically place Rose and her brothers, like plastic pink flamingos in positions consistent with various and assorted games of frivolity, no one was allowed on them. All walking, sitting, and lying down had to be done on one of the little cement sidewalks or patios. The lawns were for viewing purposes only. Any sort of trespassing would apparently cause unsightly yellow spots.

Really? Do Granny's lawns have ugly yellow spots on them? Rose had never noticed any yellow spots and she could not understand why anyone would want lawns if you couldn't use them for anything.

There was no carefully crafted trough around the edge of Rose's mom and dad's fishpond. No green sludge or slime for the bugs and babies to hide in. Snakes and frogs were, at best, discouraged, and at worst, immediately put to death.

All the flower beds and borders were meticulously organized. The plants were organized according to a pre-planned colour scheme and were located in varietal specific locations, equally spaced in straight lines, cordoned off by little cement walls. The rockeries were also very well groomed, only one or two plants per pocket. Mom was forever plucking plants, sometimes flowers, out of her rockeries.

At some point in her childhood, Rose asked her mom why she pulled so many of her pretty flowers out. Her mom said it was because they were weeds. Again, Rose didn't understand. Eventually she decided to look the word "weed" up in the dictionary. According to the Webster Dictionary, a weed was any undesired, uncultivated plant, growing so as to crowd out a desired crop or disfigure a lawn. With that, Rose couldn't help but wonder if the plants knew they were undesired, uncultivated and perhaps disfiguring an otherwise picture-perfect scene. The plants hadn't decided to grow in the wrong place. One day they just up and found themselves there, found themselves there only to be plucked up and tossed. Rose did not understand. Something or someone must have wanted that plant where it was, or it wouldn't have popped up there in the first place. Would it have? Could it have? With this, Rose wondered ...

Am I a weed? Is that why I was adopted?

Rose made a point of remembering the names of her favourite weeds. There were pansies of all different sizes and colours, so cute with their little faces. Most often they reminded Rose of little old men. There were poppies. They too came in a multitude of colours. Rose liked the Oriental poppies the best. Their gossamer appearance made them seem so delicate and trusting. Then there were the daisies, and as you know, Rose loved daisies. Their air of innocence, a myriad of white petals around a giant yellow sun. Oh, how Rose used to mourn the poor little weeds.

Rose's mom had a whole bed of roses. They too came in a variety of colours, but Rose never really cared for any of them. Her granny had a climbing rose that covered an arbour. Rose liked that but her mom's roses were all so prim and proper looking. They were perfectly groomed. Rose guessed that was because they weren't weeds. They never showed up where they weren't supposed to. Rose used to watch as her mom fussed over her roses. She'd prune them, cut off growths she didn't like. She'd tie them onto sticks so they would stand up straight. And once a bud had bloomed and then withered, she'd deadhead it so it would grow a new bud or what ... a new head? Rose hated the word deadhead. It sounded so mean.

Their tortures and training aside, those roses could be mean little suckers as well. You had to be very careful while working with them because they had thorns. They would bite. Every once in a while, Rose's mom would catch a thorn, but she would never worry too much about it.

"Yes, it hurts," Rose's mom would confess, "but it will come out once it gets infected."

"Why don't you take it out before it gets infected?"

"Trying to dig it out hurts a lot, Rose, and it may break off or you could push it in deeper. Once it festers, it will pop out on its own."

Yes, eventually it would pop out on its own, as Rose witnessed many, many times. Once all puffy and red, the sore would explode, and then the thorn would pop out with the puss. Yikes! Rose could not figure out how that could be less painful. Again, she did not understand.

Even though Rose's mom and dad's garden had won numerous garden contests, appeared several times in *Beautiful British Columbia* and a magazine put out by Cominco, the company who owned the smelter in town, Rose did not like it. It was not nature; it was not natural. It looked far too controlled, far too contrived. It did not look happy or relaxed. It looked nervous, worried it might do something wrong. Yes, Rose's parents' garden was very different than her gran's, and Rose could feel the difference deep down inside of her. It broke her heart. It made her feel lost and alone, not part of the world she found herself in.

Rose's parents' house was also very different from her granny's house. It was huge and it only had really fancy, very expensive stuff in it. It had hardwood floors that got cold in the winter.

Rose couldn't even relax in her bedroom. It too was too fancy. The wallpaper, sheets and bedspread always matched. You weren't allowed to sit or lay on top of the bedspread, that would ruin it apparently. Everything had a place and Rose had to make sure everything was always in its place. Everything had to be just so, and you always had to be very careful not to damage anything. No food or drinks were allowed anywhere but on the kitchen table, and maybe, on special occasions, in the rumpus room downstairs. Rose didn't care for it. She couldn't understand why anyone would want to live in a place where you were always on pins and needles worrying about what could happen.

It's just a house ... where we live, that's all. Who cares?

Rose so wished she lived in a normal house, a house like her granny's or any one of her classmates. Just a house ... a place to hang your hat, as they say. Rose hated the fact that all the kids at school knew she lived in the big fancy house, in one of the poorer parts of town. They were all so impressed, but Rose knew if they had to live there ... they wouldn't be happy about it either. It wasn't warm, cozy, or relaxing. Much as she felt in her parents' garden, she felt lost, alone, and terribly uncomfortable in the house she grew up in.

Because Rose's parents' house was the talk of town, as people arrived to tour her parents' version of Victoria's Butchart Gardens, they also arrived to tour her parents' house. The tours were not an economic enterprise. No money ever changed hands. Rose surmised her mom and dad were just very proud to present their picturesque setting to snoopy spectators.

Rose could see and feel in her mind's little eye the last tour of hearth and home she participated in. As remembered, Rose was accompanying her parents as they escorted a fairly large group of tourists from room to room.

Upon leaving the bathtub room, re-entering the main toilet area, Rose must have thought to herself: *since we are here ...* and had then whipped down her pants—or had she whipped up her dress? Either way, her panties came down and she commenced doing what needed to be done.

In response to gasps, Rose looked up and into a morass of unfamiliar faces, all of whom had eyes of incredulity, trained to her gaze. Exactly how this episode ended—how Rose exited the bathroom—forever escaped Rose, but she was convinced that she had spent the rest of the day in bed crying. The shame she had felt was almost overwhelming.

Despite the fact that Rose had absolutely no interest in dolls, thought dolls were stupid, she kept getting dolls, Christmas after Christmas, birthday after birthday, dolls, dolls, dolls, nothing but dolls. Rose had a zillion dolls, a doll buggy, and a miniature playpen to store all said dolls. In addition to this, Rose had an entire dresser drawer full of clothes and accessories for her dolls. She couldn't understand why she kept getting dolls when she never, ever, played with them. Rose's mom thought her daughter should be a lot more grateful for all the dolls she had because she, herself, had only ever been given one doll and her brothers broke it in very short order.

By the time Rose was four, maybe five years old, she had the whole works of her dolls and doll equipment packed up and stored in the attic.

Turning into the cynical young adult Rose eventually became, she thought that maybe the reason she got so many dolls was because girls were supposed to like dolls, and/or, dolls suited the fussy, frilly, decor of her *girly* bedroom.

A s I became older, my perceptual understanding was forced to narrow. I had to begin seeing myself—feeling myself—as isolated and alone in a world of atomized objects to be managed and controlled. Through the years, I experienced brief moments of sublime unity, but they always came out of the blue and they never lasted long. They were like tastes that did not linger in the fractured reality I had entered.

I used to hate—resent—my mom and dad's house and garden, but I no longer do. I can now appreciate that what they managed to build with their own hands was truly remarkable, but, at what cost? They worked themselves to the bone—non-stop for decades—not to feed their family, but for praise from peers.

Were my parents attempting to build a legacy they hoped their children would someday embrace and carry forward?

Maybe, but after living the expectations that come of such efforts ...

The last thing Mom said to my little sister, Annie, before she died was:

"Burn the house down ..."

With the beginning having become far clearer in light of the end ... had Mom understood life—all manner of things— differently? Eventually my parents' legacy fell into ruins. The community grieved but ... rightly or wrongly, us kids ... we wanted a different life for ourselves and our families.

19

ADOPTED
No Tree to Refer to

Rose's mom, of German and Scottish descent, was born in 1922, and was the youngest of three. She had two older brothers, all born in their parents' bed in Trail, B.C.

Rose's dad, of Italian descent, was born in 1919, and came somewhere in a line of ten. He too was born in his parents' bed, but that bed was in the neighbouring city of Rossland, B.C.

"Six miles up where the prices are down," so said a radio commercial from Rose's childhood.

According to Rose's mom, she and Rose's dad got together young—she was thirteen, and he was sixteen years old. They met through their mutual love of sports. Rose's mom was into track and field and won many trophies in the hurdles and the hundred-yard-dash, and Rose's dad belonged to the local hockey and lacrosse teams, which in their day, won many championships.

When WWII broke out in Europe, in 1939, everyone in the area was very concerned because Trail was home to one of the three smelters in the world that produced the heavy water necessary to make nuclear weapons. Because of this, there was a good chance Trail could be bombed, so all were on constant alert for an air-raid siren. It was apparently a combination of this fear and fear of the coming draft—authorizing conscription if deemed necessary—that Rose's parents decided to marry a lot earlier than they might otherwise have. Due to the times, conflicting ethnicities, and religious backgrounds, neither set of parents were very happy when the couple decided to marry in September of 1941, but they did it anyway, at the age of nineteen and twenty-two respectively.

Rose's dad signed up for the Royal Canadian Air Force. If he was going to have to go to war, his preference was the Air Force, so that is what he did. Rose's mom travelled around with her husband during his training, but once deployed, she returned to her hometown of Trail, where she got an apartment and waited for her husband's return.

'Twas not till the end of the war, September 1945, and Rose's dad was home that the couple bought the property just down from where Rose's mom had grown up, just down from Rose's gran's, and began preparing for the family—the large family—they intended to have.

Rose's dad was a blue-collar worker, a tradesman—lead-burner—at the smelter in town, and her mom was a self-employed bookkeeper and accountant. While living in the property's old, run-down existing house, Rose's mom and dad commenced building a humongous, state-of-the-art brick house, all the bricks having come from an old Japanese internment camp somewhere in the Slocan Valley. In order to achieve their aims, Rose's dad worked as much overtime as he could get his hands on. As a couple, they were shooting for the moon.

After almost thirteen heartbreaking years of being unable to have children of their own, Rose's parents decided to adopt. They adopted four children in all. Rose's mom was thirty-three and her dad was thirty-six when Rose arrived in Trail, B.C. with her new parents. Roughly two years later, Rose received a little brother who was nine months old.

Upon first setting eyes on her new little brother, Rose could not help but think, *Look at his ears ... he looks like Dumbo the Elephant.*

And roughly two years after that, she received another little brother who was eleven months old. *Holy moly ... is he ever fat!*

Eventually, a little—not so little—sister arrived. She was already eight years old, and by then, Rose was sixteen years old.

Rose had known she was adopted for as long as she could remember. In having absolutely no memory of ever being told for the very first time, it was something Rose figured she'd been told, or somehow just knew, right from the beginning. The recommended storyline of the day, however, went something like this:

"We adopted you because you are a very *special* little girl. Most parents do not get to choose their children, but we chose you because you were such a good little girl."

This tall, little tale must have made Rose feel exceptionally proud of herself because her opening line during every new introduction was:

"I am adopted you know." For the longest time this was Rose's story. It was her story, and for a while, it was enough.

It was enough until one snowy morning, bundled up like the Michelin Man, Rose was sleigh-riding down the sidewalk in front of neighbouring houses, when all of a sudden, a cranky old neighbour lady opened her front door and started screaming at Rose in a thick Italian accent. Something about the sidewalk and being such a brat, her own mother didn't even want her.

What? Rose remembered thinking forlornly. *What is she talking about?* Dragging her sleigh behind her, Rose ran home crying.

Her mom's comforting response came in the form of a reminder: "But Rose, you already know you are adopted."

Yes, Rose knew she was adopted but prior to this incident, Rose did not believe she knew what being adopted really meant. Rose had no recall of anyone ever explaining to her exactly what it meant to be adopted, so, after this event, Rose figured she must have figured it out for herself.

In Grade Five, Rose befriended a little boy who swore he was from Mars. Most people, teachers included, stayed as far away from this little guy as they could, but Rose kind of liked him. Rose wondered if maybe she too was from Mars and that's why she felt as she did, so conspicuous and out of place all the time. Rose was shocked but delighted when this little guy kissed her underwater at the local swimming pool. Unfortunately, Rose's little Martian friend was not around for long. One day he just disappeared. Rose thought maybe he went home.

I wonder what it is like on Mars ...?

The next time the fact that she was adopted twigged Rose's curiosity, was after not being permitted to go to one of her classmate's homes.

"But why ... why can't I go, Mom?"

"Because ... I knew that little girl's mom when she was young."

"What does that have to do with anything?" Rose was curious.

"Well ... 'apples do not fall far from their tree.'"

"What does that mean?" Rose was flummoxed. She did not understand.

Eventually, under duress, Rose's mom confided in her daughter. Apparently, this classmate's mom had become pregnant prior to being married to her classmate's father.

"Oh ... does that matter?" Rose wanted to know why it mattered but her mom had no comment.

"But why ... why does that matter?" No response was forthcoming. Rose's mom had clearly said all she was going to say on the topic.

Given the hidden gravity of such information, given that this information was sufficient to forbid Rose from visiting her classmate's home, the next day at school, Rose felt compelled to share what she had learned.

By late that afternoon, word was out. There was crying, commotion, and calls of contrition, but permeating it all was Rose's steadfast curiosity.

I wonder what tree I fell out of?

Back in those days, kids would get a little sex education in the Grade Six. 'Twasn't till then that Rose began to wonder if she was adopted because there was absolutely no way her parents would do what was necessary to conceive their own child. Both Rose and her friends thought the whole thing was gross.

Rose was somewhere between ten and twelve years old when she first started to become interested in astrology. Having been born under a Piscean moon, it made sense to Rose that she would be considered one of the dreamers of the zodiac: highly emotional, spiritual, imaginative, idealistic, and often able to sense and feel things others cannot. Rose was always so anxious and self-conscious, always so confused about who she was and how she was supposed to act/be. It bugged her to no end that she would never be able to have a proper ephemeris, or a numerological accounting done. For that, she needed the exact time of day she was born, and no one seemed to have that information.

It was easy, however, for Rose to find out what day of the week she was born on. She had been born on a Thursday.

Monday's child is fair of face
Tuesday's child is full of grace
Wednesday's child is full of woe
Thursday's child has far to go
Friday's child is loving and giving
Saturday's child works hard for a living
And the child that is born on the Sabbath day
is Bonny and blithe, good and gay.[6]

Thursday's child has far to go! What the heck does that mean? Even learning that was problematic for Rose. There seemed to be no end to Rose's frustration.

As Rose got older, she became increasingly more dissatisfied with herself, her parents, and her life. She would often wonder if her mom had wanted her so she could have a slave, someone to do all the work—housework—she did not want to do. On Saturdays, she had to clean the house before she went anywhere or could do anything, and on Sundays it was laundry, lunch, and baking something for lunches for the coming week. But then again ... her brothers weren't slaves. They never seemed to have to do anything. Rose felt so downtrodden.

Considering her plight, Rose started fantasizing about getting a job in the hospital where she was born. She had been born in the Royal Columbian Hospital in New Westminster, B.C. She wanted to get a job there so she could look up who her real mother was, what time she was born, and just for fun, perhaps how much she weighed at birth, because judging from pictures of herself when she first arrived at her new home, she was humungous. Looking at her baby pictures, Rose was always struck by her dead-pan countenance, how unhappy she looked even as a baby ... dead eyes coming out of a blank stare.

Could I have been broken right from the beginning?

For the longest time Rose blamed a lot of her problems in life on the fact that she was adopted. She couldn't believe that anyone in their right mind—never mind a professional—would suggest telling a child that they are *special*—somehow more *special* than any other child, was a good idea. Talk about performance anxiety. Wouldn't nonsense such as that put a tremendous amount of pressure on a child? Heaven-forbid an adopted child stop being good. Would they be given back ... back to what ... to where? Rose couldn't help but wonder if it was this imprudent little lie that inspired her to become such an insecure, overly compliant child, a child whose will would stifle its own voice.

You know, it makes me laugh now: "Thursday's child has far to go." At the time I had no idea what that could have meant but now ... I understand completely. I had a hell of a long way to go.

20

LOST, ALONE, AND TERRIBLY CONFUSED
Culturing the Rose

Rose had no idea what she did—how she amused herself as a young child. The first thing she recalled was being signed up for Scottish dancing, even though she would have preferred ballet.

"Rose you are far too big and awkward for ballet. Ballet dancers are tiny little things. Besides, I took Scottish dancing lessons when I was young, and your Sunday school teacher teaches it," Rose's mother assured.

Rose's dance class was every Friday evening for an hour. Rose didn't mind them. Apart from the fact that they were black, Rose really liked the dance shoes her mom bought her. They were kind of like ballerina slippers. Rose's dad made her a set of wooden swords for the sword dance. He used the same wood he used to make the little sticks her mom tied her roses to.

Rose's mom thought her daughter was a pretty good dancer, so Rose performed in all the local recitals. The two aspects of her dance class that Rose was not fussy about were: number one, because she was so tall for her age, she always had to dance the boys' part. *But I am a girl ...* Secondly, Rose did not like performing for an audience. What if she screwed up? Her mom would be so disappointed.

When first attending school, Rose befriended a little girl named Susan who lived a couple of doors over. The youngest of three, Susan had an older sister who was already married, and a teenage brother whose bedroom was in the attic. Both being the same age and in the same class at school, Rose and Susan would walk to and from school together every day, and by so doing, became great friends.

Rose's mom approved of Susan's family even though they were Catholic, so on weekends, Rose would be allowed to go over to Susan's house to play, or the girls would go swimming, skating, or to a Saturday afternoon matinee together. Sometimes Rose would be allowed to accompany Susan's family to Saturday afternoon union picnics. Rose loved all the games, races, and playing bingo with Susan's mom. Every once in a while, Rose would even be allowed to stay overnight at Susan's house so long as she was home by 8:00 am the next morning.

"But why so early, Mom? Susan's family doesn't get up that early on weekends."

"Because I said so."

Rose loved staying over, chatting, and giggling with her friend before they went to sleep, but having to get up by herself, so as to dash home by 8:00 am, was so nerve-wracking. Sometimes she would be so worried about sleeping in that she'd barely sleep a wink. Plus ... it was kind of embarrassing.

Susan had long hair. All the girls had long hair and Rose couldn't understand why she wasn't allowed to grow her hair out, even a little. She always had to get short, hideous-looking pixie cuts that her mom used to put up in pin-curls. Every time Rose came home from the hairdresser, she would be beside herself, crying her eyes out.

I don't see how having short hair is going to increase the number of hair follicles on my head! It doesn't make sense.

'Twasn't till she was older that Rose noticed her mom used to style her short brown hair the same way she styled her own short strawberry blond hair.

Rose didn't understand why she always had to wear such hideous homemade clothes.

"The clothes I make you Rose are of far better quality than any clothes you can buy.

"But they are all the same ..."

Susan was allowed to bring her lunch to school and play with friends, but Rose was not.

"No Rose, I want you home for lunch."

"But why?"

"Because I said so."

Rose desperately wanted to learn how to skip Double-Dutch, but recess just didn't provide enough time.

Susan belonged to Brownies and took figure skating lessons, but Rose was not allowed to do either.

"But why?"

"Because I said so."

Rose did not find this to be a very satisfying answer, but more often than not, it was the one she got.

As the girls got older Susan started staying behind and playing with friends in the schoolyard after school or going to the park to play on the swings, teeter-totter, and monkey bars, but Rose wasn't allowed.

"But why not, Mom? Susan can."

"I don't care what Susan can do … good girls don't hang around schoolyards or go to the park."

What the heck does that mean? Rose's mom confounded the daylights out of Rose.

Rose never remembered exactly why she stopped her dance class, but whatever the reason, music lessons were next up.

"No education is ever complete without a musical education."

Rose was signed up for accordion lessons even though she would have preferred just about any other instrument. The family had a player piano downstairs in the rumpus room. Rose couldn't understand why she couldn't just take piano lessons.

To this, Rose's mom responded, "My mother insisted I take piano lessons when I was your age. The accordion is way better. It is far more versatile. You can bring it to the beach with you. Lots of people take accordion lessons and your dad knows someone who teaches accordion. You will love it. I am sure."

So, accordion lessons it was. Rose's mom and dad promptly bought their daughter a honking huge, top-of-the-line accordion.

What a nightmare. Rose could barely lift the dang thing off her bed once she had herself all strapped in.

"Don't worry, Rose, you will grow into it in no time."

Rose's lessons were once a week, exactly the same time as the television show *The Monkeys* was on. It was a television show about the band *The Monkeys* that all the kids at school watched. Rose was hugely disappointed about that, and she was also extremely disappointed that she had to practice an hour a day, every day. On school days she had to practice right after school, and on the weekend and during summer vacation, it was first thing in the morning. Rose's only reprieve was when she was at church camp for that one wonderful week every summer.

Rose would cry and cry, cry her little heart out as she sat practicing "Streets of Laredo," "Turkey in the Straw," or some other dippy tune.

"No, Rose, I didn't like practicing either, but it didn't kill me, so get going!"

One afternoon, thinking it was safe because her mom was out working in the garden, Rose laid her accordion on the bed and plopped herself down on the bed to read a book she had taken out of the school library. Low and behold, if her mom hadn't tippy toed into the house, flung open Rose's bedroom door and caught her daughter prone with a book in her hand. Yikes!

Rose hated that accordion. She hated it so much that a couple of years in, the shiny black top of Rose's top-of-the-line accordion was irrevocably marred by the salt laden tears that had cascaded down upon it. Not only had the salt from her tears eaten away the shiny finish, in eking its way under the edges of the eaten finish, it left faint white salt stains that refused to be polished out. Rose's mom was very annoyed with the permanent damage done to her daughter's accordion, but Rose couldn't help it. She cried endlessly while practicing.

Rose carried a remembrance of herself once playing her accordion in front of an audience at someone's wedding reception. How that came about, Rose never recalled.

One Sunday night, Rose's mom called her into the living room, so together, they could watch a local boy play his accordion on *Starlit Stairway*—a talent show broadcast from Spokane, Washington, a city just a few miles south of Rose's Trail.

"See Rose, maybe someday you can be on *Starlit Stairway*, like 'What's His Face.'"

Rose grimaced, horrified.

It wasn't till Rose was in Grade Six and made a complete fool of both her parents and herself at a school talent night that an abrupt end came to one of the very largest banes of Rose's existence.

Rose had not wanted to do it, but her mom said: "But you are so good Rose. You should feel proud of yourself and want to show off a little. I will sign you up."

So, once again, feeling under the gun of her mom's gleefully expectant glare, Rose complied.

As nervous and beside herself as she was, Rose inadvertently turned too many pages in her music book, and while giving it her all, jumped from one song right into the middle of a completely different song. Once cognizant of what she had done, paralyzed by fear and shame, Rose did the only thing she could. She finished the second piece up like a trooper. She finished up the piece that she had inadvertently zoomed into.

Rose had no recall of how she carried herself and her equipment off the stage, but her memory into the future contained the sound of the audience booing as she did so, looking so freaking stupid ... what with her tightly cropped pin-curled hair, her crisp, yellow blouse under the yellow and brown tartan rendition of her many identical jumpers.

"Really, dear, in different colours they all look so very different," her mother said.

A vision only made complete by her matching yellow ankle socks and brown oxfords, the oxfords she was teased mercilessly for at school: "Rose wears boys' shoes, Rose wears boys' shoes."

"Never mind dear, with those shoes you will have lovely shaped feet when you get older ... no, absolutely not ... saddle shoes are way too expensive and don't you dare ask for those stupid looking 'go-go boots' again."

On the way home that night, Rose was in the backseat sobbing uncontrollably when her mom suggested that perhaps she might like to hang up her gloves, hang up the gloves on her four or five years of accordion lessons.

Not another word was said about it. Rose's accordion and music stand were quickly and quietly packed up and placed in the attic next to Rose's long-surrendered collection of dolls and doll debris.

It was shortly after her accordion fiasco that Rose started having nightmares wherein she would find herself stark naked somewhere, either in the street, at someone's house, or in a classroom. She would try and hide but to no avail. Her shame would be celebrated by a crowd.

The accordion lessons were over, but Rose's angst over her life was far from over. Starting from back at the beginning of Grade Six, all the girls were supposed to shower after gym class, but Rose was not allowed to.

"But all the girls shower. Susan showers."

"I don't care what Susan does! You are not showering."

Rose's mom even had to write a letter to the school principal for that one. Rose was so embarrassed. She would have to wait around in the girls' locker room while all the other girls showered and dressed before they went back to class together.

Rose never understood the whole shower thing. Their family had a shower in the downstairs basement but …

Why do we have a shower if no one is ever allowed to use it? Is it because it makes a mess or is it because you must stand there naked?

Either way, Rose did not get it. At this juncture, not being allowed to go downtown by herself or with friends was also added to Rose's *no-go* list.

"Go downtown to do what … get into trouble?"

And except for birthday parties, Rose was never allowed to go over to any of her classmates' houses.

"Why are you gravitating toward *those* girls? What happened to Susan?"

Rose did not know how to answer that question, so she didn't. Rose and Susan had grown apart owing to the fact that Rose was not allowed to do *anything*.

After Rose's music career came to a screaming, or should one say, a sobbing stop, housework was on deck. It started out slow, but as Rose's skills increased, so too did her workload. While learning to become proficient at her chores, Rose would very often have to do things over and over again until she got it right.

"Did you dust the baseboards this time? Shall I check? Vacuuming …? Either the vacuum needs a new bag, or you are not doing a very good job."

Cleaning the bathroom, washing the floors, Rose's hands would get so sore from the Old Dutch and Spic and Span recommended for the job. Rose asked if she could use rubber gloves and a mop like they showed on television, but no such luck.

"Mops do not do nearly as good a job as getting down on your hands and knees. They do not get into the corners where all the crap is. Rubber gloves …" Rose's mom chortled amused. "Don't be so silly. There is nothing wrong with a working woman's hands."

And so, it continued … laundry, ironing, meal prep, baking … a whole lot more commissions to which Rose felt unfairly commanded.

"But why don't the boys have chores?"

"Oh … don't you worry, they most certainly will, once they are old enough."

Rose could never remember which came first, her bra or her complexion problems.

"No Rose … you do not yet need a brassiere. When you need one, I will get you one."

Most of the girls in Rose's classroom already had one. By the time Rose's mom handed her one, she was so embarrassed she pretended not to want it. Rose was sure her cover must have been blown because she wore it every single day, rinsing it out and hanging it to dry in her closet when need be.

When Rose sprouted her first couple of pimples, her mom told her it was normal at her age. As time went by, however, things got worse. Once Rose really broke out, her mom brought her to the doctor who recommended an antibacterial soap called Phisoderm. All the soap did was make Rose's face chapped, sore, and raw looking. Back to the doctor they went for more suggestions on washes, creams, and lotions. One of the products suggested was called Lemon something-or-other. Was it a wash, a lotion, or both? Whatever the case may be, the product smelled nice— like lemons—but neither it, nor anything else worked, so Rose began to pick and squeeze hoping that if she could just drain the little devils, she could make them go away faster. Yes, both the doctor and her mom told Rose many, many times to leave her face alone, but poor Rose, she couldn't seem to help herself. She just couldn't stop making her bad situation worse, and every time she looked in the mirror, she hated herself a little more.

With regard to Rose's monthlies ... sitting across from her dad reading the newspaper at the kitchen table one day, Rose was flipping through a magazine.

"Dad, what does m-e-n-s-t-r-u-a-t-i-o-n mean?"

Quickly and without lifting his head, Rose's dad said, "Go ask your mother."

Eek ... must be a bad question.

Rose didn't bother asking her mom. She didn't figure it was worth it if it was going to cause some sort of turmoil. Next thing Rose knew, a week, a month, or a year later, blood appeared in her panties.

What's going on? Why is there blood there, under where, under there?

Rose didn't know what to do. She was far too embarrassed to tell her mom, so for the time being, she decided to rinse her panties out and stash them under her bed. She needed time to think.

However, Rose's mom eventually found out. All Rose had of the incident was the memory of her mom standing at her bedroom door handing her a book from the library, *The Stork Didn't Bring You,* and a small, light blue box of Tampax tampons.

"Here's a book, read it. And here, bring these in the bathroom. The directions are in the box. I don't want you to have to use the same stinky old pads I used to have to use."

And that was it. Rose thought she must have been in that bathroom for hours. Her first discovery was that she had two, not one, but two holes down there.

Really? I am supposed to put it where? How am I supposed to do that?

Rose must have used half the box prior to meeting with any sort of success, but even once she had, she wasn't happy about it. She could feel it in there, half in and half out. Not only was it uncomfortable, but it also hurt. Most often she opted for massive wads of toilet paper. They were far more comfortable.

Thereafter, a day or two every month, Rose's boobs hurt, and it would feel like someone was trying to pull her spine out her belly button. You would think Rose was a budding young contortionist, the positions she would get herself into seeking relief. A hot water bottle and 222s were all Rose had available to her, and neither seemed to do a thing to relieve her suffering. One time Rose was in so much pain her mom took her to the doctor. The doctor thought maybe appendicitis or a kidney stone ... nope! After a brief exam ... just menstrual cramps.

"Yes, I am sorry, Rose. It is just the price of womanhood. All you can do is grin and bear it."

Great! On top of everything else ... now this ... I HATE MY LIFE!

As was previously mentioned, Rose was very big—tall—for her age and always had been. Since starting school, Rose had always been embarrassed about her height but never so much as after her mom bought her a bright green trench coat. After that, Rose's nickname at school became, "The Jolly (not so jolly) Green Giant," the brand name of a tinned vegetable company of the day. In Grade Seven, Rose was the tallest person—teachers included—in the school, but it was also in Grade Seven that Rose's height worked to her advantage. Because Rose was so tall, she was a shoo-in for both volleyball and basketball. With this, her mom allowed her to join the girls' intra-mural sports teams. Rose loved it, being with friends and riding the bus to other schools for games. And tournaments ... they were usually an all-day affair on Saturdays. Such great fun.

That summer, the summer between Grade Seven and Grade Eight, Rose was allowed to join a girls' softball team with her friends, but that was only because one of her mom's friends—acquaintances—was the coach. That little escapade, unfortunately, ended very badly for Rose.

Upon showing up for a scheduled game, it was discovered that the team they were supposed to play against had not shown up. Needless to say, the game was cancelled, and Rose's team won by default. But instead of going straight home, as Rose knew she should, she allowed some of the girls to convince her to go downtown. It was Fiesta Days.

"Your mom won't find out. How could she find out?"

Well, during the next meeting of Rose's mom's church group, one of the other ladies told Rose's mom that she had seen Rose downtown with a group of strays during Fiesta Days and was extremely surprised that Rose's mom would allow her daughter to do such a thing. Eek!

Again, as with reading a book instead of practicing her accordion, Rose had tried defying her mom's rules, and again, she was caught. Rose was beside herself. Did she feel guilty about it? No, she had wanted to go, and she went. Her remorse was solely attached to the fact she had been caught and her mom was mad at her. Rose hated it when her mom was mad or even the least little bit disappointed with her. Any sign or signal of this, and Rose would be in her bedroom agonizing and crying, convinced she was unworthy of love.

In addition to getting the wooden spoon for the very first—and last—time in her life, being as tall as she was—way taller than her mom—Rose had to voluntarily lay across her bed to receive her spanking. After that, she was grounded for the summer.

"The only thing you will be doing this summer, Little Missy, is chores."

Through her shame, bum still a burning, Rose wanted to know if she could still go to church camp. It was going to be her last year because she was aging out. She was twelve headed toward thirteen years old. She would be attending high school that coming September.

Thankfully, somehow, Rose was able to go to camp. Her mom said it was because she had already paid for it.

Yes! For once the universe is on my side.

Rose was so grateful. She had no idea how she would have coped without her yearly—one week—hiatus from hell. It's all she lived for, and it was as great that year as it was every year.

The rest of the summer passed. Rose accepted her situation, and in quietly doing so, her mom allowed her the odd reprieve from pseudo-Pleasantville. 'Twas the last summer Rose spent any time with her little friend, Susan, from down the street.

So ... not only did I traumatize my youngest daughter as I had been traumatized, by cutting her ponytail off at the elastic, I signed my oldest daughter up for Scottish dancing lessons, not because she was too big and awkward for ballet—not that I ever would have said that to her even if she had been—but because ... because why? Had I even asked her if she wanted Scottish dancing lessons? No, probably not.

The more I think about my life, think things through, the more I am visited by vignettes or pieces of verbiage I repeated with my own children. Why did I do that? I wonder how many things my mom unwittingly repeated from her childhood. So many things seem to get unwittingly passed down from one generation to the next.

Even though I can still hear the crowd booing after I made a complete bollocks of my accordion recital, I know the crowd could not possibly have been booing. 'Twas all in my head, me judging my poor little self because I did not live up to an expectation, my expectation, my mom's expectation, or had they merged by then? Thankfully, I never signed any of my kids up for accordion lessons.

Did my brothers ever have to take music lessons? No, they did not. Tom refused, so Jerry was off the hook.

Upon finding my old accordion in the attic of my parents' house some years later, Tom phoned me up and asked what I'd like done with it.

"You can take that bloody thing outside and axe the ever lovin' shit out of it for me, if you wouldn't mind."

There were two things Mom was right about: one is that I have rather lovely shaped feet, and two, I have taken the measure of every new miracle mop on the market, but none do as good a job as a rag, a bucket of sudsy water, and good old fashioned elbow grease. Rubber gloves ... I use them when I remember, but mostly, I can't be bothered. I have working woman's hands. So what?

While pimples can and often do accompany puberty, I cannot help but wonder if my complexion problem was compounded by my emotional angst, pent up anger and frustration, poison seeking an escape route. And could the intense pain I agonized through during my periods have had anything to do with the fact that I totally hated—resented—being a girl? It was, after all, my female parts that were causing me all my pain.

And so, my childhood came to an end. I was headed into high school, Grade Eight, a whole new world, a much bigger, far more complicated world and that ... that was not going to be easy, given how disorientated, deflated, and desolate I had become.

There is no doubt in my mind that my Grade Eight year was the absolute worst year of my life.

21

YOU'RE A BIG GIRL NOW
From the Frying Pan into the Fire

R   *EALLY? Is that me? It can't be …*
      After attempting to look in a mirror, Rose would inevitably have to turn away—avert her eyes—in disbelief. Her nose was ugly and wrong. You could see inside her nostrils. She hated her hair. It looked stupid and her clothes … what could she say about her clothes other than that she hated them. And all that was before her pimple plague. Now, with her face as it was, Rose felt downright hideous.

For the first while Rose did her best to hide her shame. She used coloured Clearasil in an attempt to camouflage her craters until the boy who sat behind her in English asked, "Why do you put that crap on your face? I can still see all your zits."

With that, Rose was crushed, just crushed.

At its worst, there was not a square inch that did not present with a plethora of putrefying pustules begging to be picked and squeezed into oblivion. Rose would pick and squeeze at her face till it looked like raw hamburger.

Once, after hearing salt was a disinfectant, Rose rubbed table salt into the gaping wounds on her face. Holy shit, not only did it hurt like blue blazes, but it also made a complete and utter mess of the complete and utter mess she was already staring at.

Most nights, Rose cried herself to sleep only to have her eyes swell up so badly she would barely be able to open them the next morning. Sometimes they would even be glued shut. Then she'd have to use a warm face cloth on them before she could get them open all the way. With this, Rose would then start to cry all over again. She didn't want to leave her bedroom, never mind go to school, but Rose always had to go to school.

"No, Rose, you are going to school. The fresh air will do you good."

Rose had quite a sizable walk—maybe a mile—to and from high school every morning and lunch hour. Because there was never any arguing with her mom … Rose with resignation, went to school every morning, but the fresh air didn't seem to do her mood any good. It was so rushed at lunch hour that Rose would almost have to run home and back so as not to be late.

Ironically, Rose got an award at the end of Grade Eight for never having missed a day of school, not for the entire year. With that, Rose was not proud so much as she felt deflated.

The last thing the doctor suggested to help Rose's complexion problem was a diet.

"No fats, ABSOLUTELY NO FATS, of any kind."

Rose didn't remember how long she was on the diet, but it didn't help her face and her mom thought she was becoming far too sullen.

Sullen ... of course I am sullen. Look at my face ... look at my life! I am not sure my new diet has anything to do with my being "sullen."

Looking back, Rose always maintained that the lowlight—not the highlight, but the lowlight—of her Grade Eight year was being convinced by her mom to attend the school dance.

"It is completely normal for people your age to develop a few pimples."

A few ... are you blind?

"Don't worry about your face Rose. 'Looks are only skin deep.' Your friends don't even see your face."

What friends ...? Rose could not understand why her mom was not more sympathetic to her plight but then ... Rose realized her mom was never sympathetic. It wasn't her style.

Whenever Rose thought about her first high school dance, she thought about the Beatles. She was sitting alone on the steps outside the gymnasium listening to "Hey Jude" playing in the background, when a boy, a criminal type of guy with pimples all over his face came over and started talking to her. Rose could tell this young man was trying to be kind. She could tell he felt sorry for her. He too told Rose not to worry about her face, but as soon as he saw his friends coming, he bolted.

Rose had no picture of herself during her zit era. Prior to bringing school pictures home, Rose would draw a big beard and moustache on herself. She would ruin them. Sure, her mom would be mad, but her mom's annoyance seemed the lesser evil. Having her reality tangibly confirmed and placed into space was just a tad too painful for Rose to bare.

Rose felt so hideous that the mere thought of having somebody else's eyes on her was almost intolerable, so she was always hiding somewhere alone. With such self-imposed isolation, Rose's loneliness became palpable. She could feel her loneliness at a cellular level. It could be said that Rose's loneliness followed her everywhere, except ... Rose didn't go *anywhere* she didn't absolutely have to go.

Rose's only diversion ... sewing. With her home economics sewing class, and help from her mom, Rose learned how to sew, and she liked it. Not only did it temporarily distract Rose from her distress, but it also provided Rose with a measure of motivation because she had a plan. By learning how to sew, and sew well, Rose would be able to make her own clothes, clothes she actually liked. Able to pick out her own patterns and materials, Rose sewed whenever she could. She sewed every night and all weekend long. Weekends, when she was done sewing for the night, Rose helped her mom with jigsaw puzzles, sometimes till 2:00 am. It was good. At last, something Rose enjoyed, and her mom approved of. It was an anomaly but a sorely needed one. Mother and daughter got along better then, better than they ever had before (or would again).

As Rose continued sewing, getting better and better at it, her mom would hire her, pay her ten dollars to make her a dress for an event she planned to attend.

"Really, Mom? Sure, I will make you a dress!" Rose was delighted by the opportunity but confused by the fact that her mom always handed her new material with exactly the same pattern.

Huh! No wonder Mom doesn't understand why I do not like the clothes she made me. She does the same thing to herself as she did to me. Weird.

It wasn't till the winter of Grade Eight that Rose finally found a high school friend, Patty. In still having to go home for lunch every day, Rose didn't have much time to socialize, but she and Patty, in sitting next to each other in homeroom, began chatting. With this chatting, a friendship developed. Because Rose's mom seemingly approved of Patty's family, Rose was allowed to meet her friend at the skating rink. There they joined up with other girls from school and had a marvellous time skating round'n'round—playing crack the whip—singing along with the songs of the day. Rose was also allowed to go over to Patty's house on the weekend, provided her chores were done. No, Rose never asked anyone to her house. She hated being at home, so why would she want to have a friend over?

Once in a blue moon, Rose would be allowed to stay at Patty's on a Friday or Saturday night, so long as she was home by 8:00 am the next morning. Again, she would have to be up and out of the house before anyone else was out of bed, but for Rose, it had become a small price to pay.

Rose was itching to live. She was dying to figure out how to *be* without *being* miserable. Time, and time, and time again, Rose had tried venturing forth, but time, and time, and time again, she hit exactly the same brick wall: her mom.

"Mom, can I go see Woodstock? It's on in the afternoon?"

"No."

"But why?"

"Because it is not the sort of thing someone your age should be watching."

"Can I go to *Romeo and Juliet*?"

"No, and do not ask me about movies again!"

Rose was allowed to go to *The Sound of Music* movie with her dad and ... a few years later, she went to *Romeo and Juliet* at the drive-in with a friend's parents but ... that was a wrap. Rose never found out if her mom knew about the *Romeo and Juliet* thing or not. All she could remember was that both she and her friend had sobbed their little hearts out at that movie. It was so sad ... Rose so longed to be loved ... find someone who loved her like Romeo loved Juliet.

In 1968—when Rose was in Grade Eight—the first World Cup skiing event was being hosted at Red Mountain near Rossland—her dad's hometown—and all were abuzz about it.

"Mom, the school is going up to the ski hill during the first World Cup. Nancy Greene and Jean-Claude Killy will be racing. Can I go with the school and watch the races?"

With Nancy Greene, herself, being from Rossland, Rose's mom had a tough time refusing her daughter. As such, it was with grave reservations and the strictest of warnings that Rose was allowed to join her classmates. It was a great day for Rose. She had a fabulous time. She and her friends volunteered as gatekeepers. It was cold, lonely, and boring but … she could say she was there … she was at the ski hill during the first World Cup in skiing.

"Mom it was fantastic … so much fun. Can I start skiing … P L E A S E?"

For whatever reason, whenever Rose brought up the topic of skiing, Rose's mom got crabby.

"I do not want to hear another word about skiing, Rose. I am starting to regret having let you go up there in the first place."

"Mom, can I shave my armpits … my legs, like my friends do?"

"No … absolutely not. If God had not wanted hair there, he would not have put it there." Rose's mom didn't shave her underarms or her legs. Rose thought it looked gross.

"Can I get my ears pierced?"

"What's wrong with clip-ons like I wear? If God had wanted holes in your earlobes he would have put them there."

Whenever Rose got home from church camp, she would be full of questions, questions about this and questions about that. Some would be about God, but others would just be about life and the world. Her mom had no time for such nonsense.

"Why are you always asking such stupid questions Rose? There is no such thing as God, heaven, or hell. All there is, is what you make of this life. There is no point in asking—thinking —about things you will never get the answers to."

With this, Rose came to believe her mom only pulled "God" out of the closest when it served her purposes, when it might work as some sort of justification. Unfortunately, for Rose's mom, her strategy did not work. Rose didn't buy it. She didn't buy any of it.

Because Rose could not make hide nor hair of the nonsense her mom spewed and there was no talking to her mom about anything, Rose's frustrated anger began to dialogue with itself.

So, why then, do we brush our teeth? If God hadn't wanted gunk on our teeth, he wouldn't have put it there ... right? Rose was frequently creating op-eds in her head about how absurd, obtuse, and unfair her mom was.

I don't think Mom was intentionally trying to be cruel. She had wanted me—all of us kids—desperately, for a very long time, and most often mothers want—try—to do better than their own mothers, so ... I am thinking Mom, as her own unique self, had hopes and dreams, worries, and fears that had been informed by her ancestry, experiences, and interpretations thereof, just as we all do. Had my beloved gran been like my mom when her daughter was young? Even though Granny had always been my most favourite person in the whole world, she had been my mom's mom. I wonder what my mom's childhood was like. I am almost scared to imagine.

Gran was not at all like Mom when I was with her. Was that because she was old? In having lived almost an entire life—a hard life—had she come to understand things, understand life a little better? I think maybe she had ... Mom was only halfway through her life … perhaps she just hadn't—had not yet—thought things through.

22

THE GUILT AND SHAME OF SELF-BETRAYAL
She Should Have Zagged

No, Rose was still not officially allowed to do anything, but because Patty's mom was not nearly as strict as her own, Rose started to do stuff. Despite what happened after her cancelled softball game, Rose began doing things and going places she knew she would not have received permission for.

In needing to remain in the good graces of the world—or the woman around whom her world revolved—fortified by her friend Patty and Patty's family, Rose decided to do the only thing she thought she could. She decided to game the system. Instead of zagging, Rose decided to zig. She began gambling with her conscience. Instead of summoning the courage to face the storm—her mom—directly, Rose used lies of omission to do what she wanted. 'Twas here, with this, that Rose first began betraying herself, betraying her innate sense of right and wrong.

In doing so, however, Rose was constantly on edge, worried some mystery person would squeal on her and she would be called to account. Would she feel guilty? She didn't want to. She didn't think she ought to, but guilt-ridden fear became her constant companion, and it began feeding a barrage of internal indictments.

So, Rose ... how are you going to feel when Mom finds out? What are you going to say? You already feel guilty, don't you?

No, I don't. I am just doing what I have to do. Mom is at fault here, not me. It is by Mom's hand that I need to work a-r-o-u-n-d legislative authority.

But you do feel guilty, Rose. YOU know you feel guilty.

Who are you anyway? You don't know anything about me, so just SHUT-UP and leave me alone.

Despite the ever-increasing noise in her head, Rose absolutely refused to believe she felt guilty for anything. After an extended internal dialogue between herself and her conscience, Rose would declare victory despite her defeat. She would have no option but to secretly concur with her accuser while pretending not to care. This withstanding, Rose's internal critic never did shut-up and never did leave Rose alone. It, in fact, followed her everywhere, and as time went by, seemed to collect a heavenly host of friends.

What would Rose do when she got busted? She had no idea. She preferred not to think about it.

Rose and her friend would go here and go there. They would do this, and they would do that. They would meet new and old friends at the park and stay, just dickin' around, sometimes till after dark. One time her friend's parents even took them to Fiesta Days and let them walk around by themselves. Rose was over the blue moon about that.

"Mom, can I start taking my lunch to school, please?"

"Oh, for pity's sake, Rose ... I suppose ... but, if I ever see you, or hear of you, hanging around town during lunch, young lady, that will be the end of it!"

Rose was thrilled. No more dashing home and dashing back. She never did walk around town, too many spies, but she was able to spend time with friends. She went ice-skating and eventually roller-skating with Patty and other girls from school. It was by that means that a company of cohorts began to coalesce.

The summer between Grade Eight and Grade Nine, Rose tested out the whole motel thing ahead of time. She thought she'd give it a go, just to see, before she went. Sure enough, it would have been a *no-go*, if Rose actually still cared what her mom said.

"The answer is no."

"But why? It's her aunt and uncle's motel, all we want to do is swim in the pool?"

"NO! The answer is still no and do not ask me again."

"Oh, Mom, you never let me have any fun."

"FUN? Life is not about having fun, Rose."

Needless to say, Rose did not understand but she had a blast at the pool, and she went many, many times. They would meet up with Patty's cousins and they would all swim and sun themselves laughing, giggling and being silly the whole time. One day the girls met a road crew staying at the motel. That was a bit creepy.

"Why are you doing that" Rose asked, as the guy she was with kept thrusting his pelvis into hers while they were kissing.

"Oh, I just wanted to see what kind of a girl you were."

Rose had absolutely no idea what the guy was talking about. At fourteen years old, Rose was incredibly naive—understandably—but … her mom was never the wiser.

It was not till the winter of Grade Nine that Rose was finally allowed to go to hockey games, provided she stay within eyeshot of her dad, and that her dad drove her home afterwards. With this, Rose believed her mom was killing two birds with one stone. Rose's mom hated the fact that her dad went for beers and Chinese food with his brothers after games, but in having to drive his daughter home, she could get them both home early.

Rose followed the rules for the first couple of games, but upon realizing her dad had no interest in where she was or what she was doing, Rose sat in the section that housed all the teens. She and her friends walked the catwalk at the top of the bleachers so they could scope out guys. Sometimes, she and her friends even went outside, walked around town talking, giggling, and being silly. All Rose had to do was make sure she had enough deets on the game to pass the preordained pop quiz she would inevitably receive once home.

Rose's very first boyfriend had zits like Rose did but he was cute. Neither had the intestinal fortitude to approach the other at school, so their friends arranged to have them hook-up at hockey games. They didn't talk much. All they ever did was go out behind the credit union and smooch. Their rendezvouses came to a screeching halt when Rose's mom noticed a hickey on Rose's neck, a hickey Rose hadn't realized she'd gotten.

"Rose, is that a hickey on your neck? And you got it at the hockey game ... good God Rose, who have you become?"

Rose didn't say a word. With no defence to offer, Rose retreated to her bedroom and the privacy of her own head. Rose's boyfriend didn't break things off. Rose did. She never looked at or spoke to that young man again. Her shame had rendered him superfluous.

So, eventually it happened. It was only a matter of time. Rose got caught, and no—no one—had squealed on her. Rose had sabotaged herself, and because of that, she was shaken to the core. Rose's shameful guilt came not so much from what she'd done. It was more that her deceitfulness had been broadcast in a way she could hear, in a way she was forced to understand. In being untrue to herself, untrue to her conscience, Rose felt like even less of a person than she already did. This withstanding, Rose continued to do what she felt she must, believing her ever-accumulating shame and self-loathing was well worth its wares.

Rose could not help but wonder what her poor dad must have endured that night ... having not kept a close enough eye on his daughter.

Yikes!

Rose had been anxiously awaiting her fifteenth birthday, because at fifteen she would be old enough to learn how to drive. Her mom and dad had promised her so … they took turns taking their daughter out in their old Ford Fargo—three on the column—pick-up. The Chrysler was far too expensive for a novice. Whenever Rose's dad took her out, Rose came home angry. He always wanted her to drive far faster than she was comfortable with. But, whenever Rose went out driving with her mom, she came home crying. Her mom was so crabby, and she made Rose so nervous. Rose wrecked three starters before she could intuit just exactly how long to keep the key turned. Once she had her license though, Rose was off and running, or … off and driving.

Rose absolutely loved driving, feeling herself drive. She would drive all over hell and gone for no reason other than to just drive. It was kinda funny though … Rose got her first speeding ticket less than a week after she got her license. Rose got many speeding tickets. At one point she even had to take a Safe Driving Course to keep her license.

Instead of borrowing the truck to go to friends, as she would ask for, Rose would quite often borrow the truck to pick up friends and drive around. Sometimes there would be seven or eight girls in the bed of the pick-up. Once, someone actually fell out, but they didn't get hurt so … all was well. A couple of times when her parents were out, Rose took the truck without asking.

One Sunday morning, while her dad was washing his truck he said, "Rose … do you know anything about all these bugs on the windshield? I am just wondering how they all got there."

"I don't know, Dad." With that, Rose knew her dad knew, but Rose also knew her dad would be good for it. It remained a secret between them. Rose never took the truck without asking again.

Needless to say, Rose began shaving her armpits and legs. She started off with her pits and then moved on to her legs. Although Rose was sure her dad's Wilkinson blades became duller than a hoe in no time, her dad never said a word about it. Rose was sure he hadn't because if he had, she would have heard about it. To solve this problem before it got out of hand, Rose formulated a plan. The holiday season was upon them, so Rose decided to get her dad a cheap razor and blades for Christmas. She got them knowing full well he'd give them to her. Then she would have a razor of her own. Her plan worked perfectly, just as she had planned.

One Saturday afternoon, after chores, a bunch of girls snuck downtown so Rose could get her ears pierced. It hurt some, but Rose had already arranged to spend the night at her friend's place. Rose had been growing her hair out for a while by then—how that came about, Rose had no idea—so she just made sure her hair covered her ears when her mom was around. Rose didn't remember if her friend's mom was in on the teeny-bopper delegation's designated plan that day or not. Rose's mom did not notice her daughter's pierced ears for quite some time, but when she did, of course, she had an absolute haemorrhage. Secretly, Rose thought it was hilarious.

And so, it continued down a slope that saw Rose's complexion quietly clear-up as her internal landscape darkened. It was through the success of Rose's lies, deceit, and deception that she so skillfully and nonchalantly slipped into *stage two*. Through purposefully staged, brilliantly executed, intentionally corrupt strategies, Rose began honing her skills as a Grand Master in Machiavellian cunning and manipulation. She'd taken the next logical step on the slope whose pitch would descend into the hell that was to eventually become her life.

> There was a girl, who had a little curl
> right in the middle of her forehead.
> When she was good, she was very good indeed,
> but when she was bad she was horrid.[7]

When I was young, I was forever being forbidden from doing normal things, things that everyone else did. As I got older, however, I began abandoning my integrity and betraying my intrinsically intuited codes of conduct to achieve my ends. For these crimes, crimes against myself and others, I was most often reprimanded by only myself, but, boy, oh boy, was I ever reprimanded. Whether it was beforehand or after the fact, the little voice inside my head and its heavenly host of friends, could be depended upon to pass judgement, regardless of the judiciousness of my self-styled justification.

Did my complexion clear up because my anger, frustration, and resentment were what I employed to fuel my newly found sense of power? Perhaps in having found a new avenue of release I no longer needed to bear witness to the poisons I had spent years collecting and containing.

Eventually, I had to dismiss *out of hand* my theory that having been adopted was the reason that I was, as I was. If it had been the fact that I was adopted then ... there would have been absolutely no way that Tom, my oldest little brother, could be as he was. He too was adopted and given the same bullshit story, but he ... he would flatly refuse to do what he was told. He would fight and scream, pitch fits all over the place without giving one hoot about the consequences. He was forever getting whooped for something he refused to do.

For many, many years I thought I hated my oldest little brother for being such an unruly child, such a bad little boy, but now ... now that I have thought things through, I realize I was jealous of him. He never compromised his integrity or betrayed himself. He could, and did, stand up for himself, and I couldn't ... did not.

He never zigged when he should have zagged. He always just zagged.

23

PRACTICE MAKES PERFECT
Problematic Proficiency

"Just who in the hell do you think you are Rose ... the Queen of Sheba?"

Who the hell is the Queen of Sheba? wondered Rose, perplexed.

By the time Rose hit Grade Ten she was a new woman, a new girl. She felt good about herself—very good. She had fashionable, self-styled clothes, and cleanly shaven armpits and legs. Her ears were pierced, and her complexion problems were a thing of the past, so Rose understood why her mom may have felt as she did.

Yes, Rose had perhaps become a little more self-entitled, a little more belligerent in that she no longer passively pretended to embrace unequivocal acceptance. Confident amid a gaggle of girls, Rose began to engage her mom in defence of her beliefs and desires, and Rose's mom did not like it. She did not like it one little bit. During their mother-daughter tête-à-têtes, Rose was forever flabbergasted by the flimsiness of her mom's beliefs and the absurdity of her arguments. Logical consistency and congruence were apparently of no import to her mom. She thought what she thought, and she was always right, no matter what. If, at some later point, she was proven wrong, well, she would just pretend she'd been arguing the other side. It used to drive Rose and Rose's dad nuts.

Yes, Rose's mom still annoyed the crap out of Rose, but by this point, Rose's anger had become the sword she wielded in battle. With this, it was only natural that she also began using it as a prop tailored to garner additional support from her friends.

"Holy, Rose, your mom is so mean."

"Ya, I know, right?" Or, in other words: "Poor me, right?"

With this, Rose's friends became willing co-conspirators in her subterfuge. Was it support, or was it sympathy? Either way, it worked. Rose was happy.

Rose was still as insecure and self-conscious as she had ever been. It's just that as time went on, Rose got better and better at keeping her true self—her emotions—hidden, locked tightly inside. She got better and better at steeling her exterior so no one could tell how scared she really was. Because Rose was so deathly afraid of losing what it had taken her so long to manoeuvre into place, a measure of acceptance amid a modicum of peers, Rose could not risk appearing anything less than required or expected, anything less than perfect. Intentionally reaping laughs was one thing, but having people criticize or laugh at her …

As such, regardless of circumstance, Rose pretended to have all the confidence in the world. It was with this pseudo-confidence that Rose applied to become one of the school's cheerleaders, cute little outfits, pom-poms and all those hot, popular, older guys.

How hard can it be? All you need do is perform like a trained seal. And Rose knew she had been doing that her entire life.

As her mom always used to say, "Practice makes perfect."

To her great delight, Rose made the cheerleading squad, and it was cheerleading that eventually, rocketed Rose into the big-time, invites into the upper echelon of senior high, bus trips to tournaments, after game parties, and the like.

Yes, Rose had made it, but the stress had upped by a factor of ten. Each and every move Rose made had to be analyzed and debated by at least two or three objectively held stances within her own head, before she was even semi-comfortable taking public action. And then, that action would be scrutinized and evaluated, given a score between one and ten with follow-up corrective criticism on how her performance could be improved the next time. It was exhausting.

In any case, Rose would very often have to summon the courage of Abraham—whomever Abraham was—to carry through with what she thought her role and new-found status required. It was in an effort to follow through with such a self-perceived prerequisite that Rose summoned the bravado necessary to ask the star basketball player to a Sadie Hawkins dance. He was in Grade Twelve, believed to be the hottest guy in the entire school.

"But I don't even know you," he'd said coldly.

Oh God! Rose felt like such an idiot, but she carried on and on till finally she convinced him, despite by that time, her better judgment. All the Grade Twelve girls were so pissed at Rose for using one of the Grade Twelve boys up.

The night of the dance, Rose's resentful date got stuck in the snow several downhill blocks away from Rose's house, so he had to walk up in a foot of snow to get her. Once they got to the dance, Rose didn't see him again till the curtain was closing. Because he had no intention of getting stuck in the snow again, he dropped Rose off halfway home. Man oh man, Rose must have replayed that demeaning little series of scenarios a million times. Each and every time cringing.

Really? Did I really do that ... yikes!

No, Rose had never spoken to him. She was a cheerleader during games he played, but that was it. She didn't really even like the guy. She thought he was probably a conceited jerk because he always had girls hanging off of him. After coming off so many years of feeling like such a loser, all Rose really wanted to do was wear him like a feather in her cap.

In attempting such feats from nothing but artificial audacity, when things went south or even sideways, Rose would be hooped. There would be no escape, so she would do as she did during her disastrous musical debut. Completely paralyzed, Rose would soldier on. She'd leave part of herself out there hanging, while another part watched from somewhere across the room.

The reason Rose couldn't just apologize and politely excuse herself was because she'd told everyone what she was going to do, and ... if it didn't come off, she would be publicly humiliated.

At least in finally convincing the MVP to take her, she was humiliated, but she was humiliated privately. No one else knew about it.

At least that's what Rose told herself.

Yes, he took me to the dance . . . it's not my fault he's an asshole.

It was only a couple of months into the school year when boney protrusions began forming on the heels and outside edges of both of Rose's feet. The doctor called them bone spurs and said they were something that developed for no reason.

Really? No reason ... something, caused them. You just don't know what, right?

"All we can do is saw them off, after which you will be in the hospital for three or four days."

Into the hospital Rose went. It was such fun. Friends came after school to visit. She could smoke whenever she wanted. One time, a friend raced Rose in her wheelchair down a corridor. Needless to say, a nurse intervened. She was not pleased. A bunch of kids brought her up a program from a hockey game she'd missed. It had been signed by a bunch of kids who said they missed her. Rose was thrilled to think people actually missed her. Upon leaving the hospital Rose was given crutches she'd been instructed to use for at least a week, but they hurt her armpits, so she made do without. It took a while for the nerves on the back and outside edges of Rose's feet to stop being so sensitive, but eventually, Rose's feet were perfect, as good as new.

'Twas not till the approach of Christmas vacation that the topic of skiing came up again. Rose's best cheerleading chum, Ally, was going to be spending the Christmas vacation skiing with her family and she wanted Rose to join them. Rose was thrilled. She desperately wanted to learn how to ski.

"Ally skis ... all the cool kids ski."

"Well, I don't know, Rose."

"Please, Mom. Ally's family has old equipment I can use."

Rose's mom knew the family. Ally's dad was a doctor in town so ...

"I suppose."

Saturdays were her chores day but if she got everything done, she could go skiing with her friend's family on Sunday. Rose could not have been happier.

Most of Ally's skiing friends had been skiing since they were little so they could all ski really well. Because of this, Rose knew she would have to become at least an adequate skier, pretty quick. She would have to push past her fear and just do it because, if she did not, there was no way the other girls would stand around twiddling their thumbs waiting for the likes of her. She knew if she took too long coming down the hill her friends wouldn't want to ski with her anymore. It was hard and it was scary but Rose snow-plowed ahead till she could crest and descend moguls, albeit out of control.

Given the pressure Rose was under to perform for her friends, it was not too long before Rose was skiing, and ... once she got the hang of it, Rose loved it. When Rose skied, she could lose herself. She could let it all go—let the world and the laws that govern it take over for a change. With the sense of freedom Rose experienced from skiing, she wanted to go skiing every weekend, but this ... this troubled Rose's mom.

"Not skiing again ... do you intend to spend every weekend up at that ski hill?"

"Why not?"

Ally's parents were keeping the equipment Rose used in their locker up at the ski hill, so Rose could use it whenever she wanted. Rose couldn't understand what the problem was.

"Don't for a minute think I do not know what goes on up there!"

"What? WE SKI!"

Rose couldn't for the life of her figure out what in hell's bells her mom thought went on at the ski hill. Okay, so maybe that's where Rose and her girls first tried smoking. A couple of them took to it right away, probably because their parents smoked. Rose, however, took a month of Sundays practicing once or twice a day, prior to being able to inhale and exhale without coughing, sputtering, and feeling so dizzy she thought she was going to pass out. Even when Rose had a cold or bronchitis, which was almost all the time, Rose felt honour-bound to puff away. Sometimes Rose's throat would be so sore she could barely swallow, yet still she would force herself to smoke, smoke a cigarette or two.

Rose's mom wasn't happy about it, but Rose continued to go skiing every Sunday whether it was with Ally or one of the other girls who went skiing regularly. She went that is, until she had to stop.

Because Rose loved being out of control while skiing, she took some horrendous spills. On one such occasion, Rose crashed and sprained her ankle. She knew she'd sprained it but because her ski boot offered so much support, Rose decided to ski on it for the rest of the day. What a dummkopf. As soon as Rose took her boot off, her ankle swelled up like a balloon. She could barely touch her foot to the floor. Once back at her friend's place—Bev's home—Rose called her mom, told her about her ankle, and asked if she could stay the night.

Rose's mom was livid. Eventually she caved—let her daughter stay over—but of course, Rose was going to have to be home by 8:00 am the next morning. This was during Easter break. If it had been on a regular winter Sunday, if there had been school the next day, Rose wouldn't even have dreamt about staying overnight at Bev's place, because there would have been ABSOLUTELY no way she would have been allowed to.

Rose was totally mystified by the fact that her mom was mad at her for hurting herself, spraining her ankle. It's not like she'd done it on purpose. But then, Rose's mom would be furious with her dad whenever he was sick or hurt himself, so Rose guessed it followed. She didn't understand, but it followed.

"No! No more skiing and that is final."

Not much of a problem. Back in those them hills, ski season ended at the end of Easter break.

By the end of Grade Ten, Rose felt herself a rising star. What heights would she reach? Her school had even sponsored her—and a cheerleading mate's—attendance at a week-long

summer camp in Ellensburg, Washington. Rose was on top of
the world.

n having been far too big of a coward to do anything but
succumb to the self-objectification necessary to satisfy
mom's desires/needs, I began objectifying myself, seeing myself
as something I could premeditatedly manoeuvre so as to fulfil
my needs. Hence my being willing to perform like a circus
animal for attention and fame, my continuing—despite myself—
to coerce a widely coveted stranger to take me on a date.
Unfortunately, by practicing this strategy to perfection, I lost
sight of it. What started out as an illicit means by which to
fulfil my need for acceptance, eventually, became the only way
I knew how to get any of my needs met. I became my needs
and nothing more.

Ever since I can remember, during my most emotionally
taxing moments, be they were the result of life as it arrived, or
me moving my tokenized self around my own personalized
game of life, 'twas as if I would automatically jump out of my
body so as to see—grab a quick pic of myself—from afar. I would
dissociate. In so doing, I often lost forever what followed a
stressful scenario. My memories of outcomes are so very limited.

I eventually learned that many of those with whom I attended
senior high believed me to be nothing more than a stuck-up
bitch. Huh, nothing could have been further from the truth. If
only they had known ...

As such, I have come to realize that many of those who appear full of themselves, are in actual fact, often just terribly insecure and extremely self-conscious like I was. Do they too carry snap-shot stories of themselves? Were they able, like myself, to watch themselves cross the room. Was Carly Simon's mystery man (from her song "You're So Vain") able to watch himself so as to be able to adjust, at a moment's notice, any and all forms of social faux pas he may have been on the verge of committing? Given what I now understand, I make a point of gently trying to engage with those who I feel may need a bit of a hug.

24

THE NOT SO LITTLE SISTER
Fallout of the Fourth

Sometime toward the end of Rose's Grade Ten year, her mom called all the kids into the kitchen to explain something.

"Soon, you will all have a little sister. Not a baby sister, but an eight-year-old sister."

"What?" they all clamoured in unison. All were dumbfounded in never having heard a word about it before.

Now, for pretty much the whole of Rose's life she had wanted a sister or a pet of some kind, either a dog or a cat. Her guppies weren't doing it for her, and her big beautifully decorated bedroom was so lonely. Rose had so dreamt of having a sister, someone to talk to, laugh with, and tell secrets or stories to in the middle of the night. She'd so dreamt of having someone to hang onto when she felt so cold, empty, and alone that all she wanted to do was close her eyes and go to sleep forever. But this ... now ... when she was sixteen. Rose was flabbergasted.

"When ... ?"

"We don't know yet but soon."

How soon was soon? A week, a month ... however long it was, shortly after Rose got home from cheerleading camp, she was told that it was going to be she who would fly down to Vancouver to be met by a social worker who would take her out for dinner, and then settle her into a hotel room. In the morning, the social worker would pick Rose and her belongings up, take her for breakfast, and together, the two of them, would go to meet Rose's new little sister at her foster home in New Westminster's Queensborough area. After introductions and goodbyes, the social worker would then bring both girls to the airport where they would catch a plane back to Castlegar, to the airport closest to Trail, where their mom and dad would be waiting to pick them up.

"What? Me? Why am I going?" Although Rose felt puffed about flying to Vancouver and staying in a hotel room by herself, she couldn't figure out why it was going to be her picking up her little—not so little—sister.

"We all just think it would be cute if it was you who went to pick her up."

"Oh … okay … I guess so." And as far as Rose recalled, that was how it happened.

Rose's new little sister was thin, pasty, and had bluntly cut, short, blond hair. She was shy and very insecure.

Rose's dad had built two tall skinny dressers, that Rose's mom had placed on either side of the big picture window in Rose's bedroom. They were to be for her sister's things—of which she had dismally few when she arrived. And the girls were to be sharing Rose's double bed.

The first alleged hurdle that needed to be cleared was finding Rose's little sister a new name to go with her brand-new life.

"WHAT ... ?" Rose was freaking aghast. *She's not having a brand-new life. She's still in her same life ... she is just living in a different house, with different people!!!!!*

Rose's mom was throwing out new handles: Sandra, Louise, Judith ... when all of a sudden, it occurred to Rose.

"Okay, Mom, how about this ... her name is currently Anne-Marie, right? How about we just shorten it to Annie, so it is not too different, won't be too confusing."

"Hmm ... Annie ... Annie ... yes ... I think that will work. What do you think Anne-Marie?"

Rose's heart broke as she turned to the scared little girl next to her nodding, eyes trained on her new big sister.

"Okay ... Annie it is." Everyone was as happy as they could be, given the situation.

The sharing of Rose's bed did not work out so well. Rose was not used to having anyone in her bed and Annie was constantly wanting to cuddle.

"Mom, Annie needs her own bed. She is always scratching my legs with her toenails."

A single mattress was promptly placed to the right-hand side of Rose's bed. There was a bookshelf with teenage trinkets on the left so ...

At first, Rose thought it odd that her mom hadn't just changed the furniture in the room, replaced the double bed with a couple of singles or a set of bunkbeds as was in her brothers' room but ...

"Well Rose, you are sixteen ... will be leaving home soon so ... "

Oh, okay then ... I guess it's out with the old ... and in the with new. If at first you don't succeed, try, try, again. That's what Mom always used to say.

Rose had long intuited that she was not living up to the dreams her mom had for her as a daughter, so maybe her mom wanted to give it another go? Try again ... replace Rose with someone whose performance might be preferable. Rose wasn't sad about this. She simply accepted it as a matter of fact.

Rose didn't remember much about what happened the rest of that summer, but it did seem to Rose that once her little sister arrived, she was no longer on the hook. Her chore duties all but disappeared, and she was being allowed to spend a lot more time gadding about with her friends. Rose's mom's focus had shifted, and Rose could not have been happier about it.

Hey, this little sister thing may be the best thing that's ever happened to me.

Time went on ... the summer passed with Rose enjoying her freedom from servitude, and then Grade Eleven began.

'Twas not till then that Rose noticed how severely the atmospheric pressure within the family home had changed, and not in a good way. The air was so heavy ... the sky was always overcast, and storms were forever on the horizon. Why?

Well, Rose's new little sister, Annie, for whatever reason, had introduced a dramatically destabilizing element into the former fairly even-keeled environment. It wasn't that Rose's dad did not take to his new daughter so much, but rather, that he could not stand the sight of her. He'd flash her dirty looks, call her names when he didn't think anyone was around. With this, Rose's mom and dad were forevermore at odds, if not at war. It was not a good situation—not for anyone.

Many times, through the years, Rose asked her dad why he hated Annie the way he did. He never denied hating her, but he would never say why. Rose thought that if only she knew what the problem was, she might be able to help fix it, but ... there appeared to be no fixing the situation.

"Dad's being so mean to Annie, Mom. Can't you do anything about it?"

"Why ... why is he being like that? What has she done?"

As per usual Rose's mom did not say a word. Either she didn't know, or she knew and wouldn't say. Either way ... the degree to which the addition of Rose's little sister changed the dysfunctional set point of their family, changed all of their lives forever.

With tension constantly in the air at home, Rose plunged off the top of the world, hit middle-earth with a thud, and just lay there. As such, the school spotlight Rose had so enjoyed being under, all of a sudden, had become far too bright so ... she quit cheerleading. She quit because the whole endeavour seemed stupid, winners at the expense of losers, prancing around like an idiot in a daft little costume. Rose no longer cared much for the people she had been hanging around with either. They all seemed so fake and insincere, so shallow and self-possessed.

Once freed up from cheerleading Rose got a job. She needed smokes, booze, and pot money. During her first foray into retail at the local Woolworth's store, Rose completed a crash course in Marketing 101. Here's how it went. There was a bin of slippers that cost a dollar and fifty-nine cents, and a bin of slippers that cost two dollars and ninety-nine cents. Low and behold if the store didn't decide to throw both bins together and put the whole dang works on sale for the low, low price, of two dollars and sixty-nine cents. Rose was sickened by the dishonesty of it all. She worked at her first job till a co-worker—an older lady—made her cry about something. With that, Rose quit.

Rose's second job saw her working at the cosmetic counter of the local Eaton's store. Rose found that job most ironic given that she, herself, was not allowed to wear make-up. Rose bought her very first pantsuit from that store. It was a navy blue, machine knit ensemble whereby the pants were solid navy and the top had stripes that must have been vertical because according to Rose's mom, horizontal stripes made you look fat. How long she worked at that job or why she quit, Rose had absolutely no idea. All she knew was that she worked there till she worked at a drugstore, and she worked at that same drugstore till she left home.

Finally, with money of her own, Rose bought herself brand-new ski equipment and matter-of-factly informed her mom, "Just so you know … I will be skiing this winter as much as I possibly can."

Because she worked at the drugstore on Saturdays—all stores being closed on Sundays and Mondays back in those days—Rose knew Saturdays were off the table. Sundays however … Rose told her mom that she would be skiing every Sunday and every non-working day she had through both Christmas vacation and Easter break. Rose was done with her family's nonsense.

On weekdays, Rose would get up and go to school. On Saturdays she would get up and go to work, and on Sundays Rose would be up by 6:00 am to pack a lunch, then zip down to the highway with her equipment where she would hitch a ride up to the ski hill.

Rose would ski all day, eating her lunch on the chairlift, and then, would head home. She would catch a ride with a friend's parents, as far as she could, and then she would hitch-hike and walk the rest of the way home, once again with equipment in tow.

Upon arriving home, Rose's mom would be making dinner, listening to Cross Country Checkup on CBC radio. Joke night was Rose's personal favourite. Rose didn't remember if she and her mom spoke upon her arrival home on Sunday nights or not, but she did remember her mom's comment on Boxing Day, as she walked in the front door returning after a day away skiing.

"Don't you care AT ALL about your family?"

Did Rose care about her family? Yes, well, Rose figured she must. How could she not? It was just that her family ... being at home, had become intolerable. Everyone was always mad at someone about something, and as soon as she walked in the front door, she could not help but be smacked smartly by the choked chaotic cacophony of coming catastrophe. Once The Wrath of Khan had been unleashed upon whoever's turn it was next, everyone would be expected to retreat to their respective corner and repress their rage till the next time. Nothing was ever discussed and nothing—absolutely nothing—was ever resolved.

Periodically Rose's mom would say, "Oh, you kids ... I do not know what I would do without you kids."

But Rose dare not offer a comment, because ...

"Oh Rose ... you are always making such mountains out of molehills. Things could be so much worse."

Really? How ...? That was the quintessential question Rose could not bring herself to ask audibly.

find it interesting that when I quit cheerleading, I no longer cared for the circle of friends I'd worked so hard to become a member of, i.e., hot jocks, popular girls. 'Twas it not but for their acceptance that I agonized over every item of clothing, strand of hair, my very existence? With what was going on in my family, had I become temporarily awakened to the banality, the supreme superficiality of my previous concerns?

I cannot help but wonder ... was it both my mom and dad, or just my mom, who wanted to adopt another child—an eight-year-old girl who without a doubt, was going to need a lot of time and attention, not to mention love?

Is that why I was sent down to pick up Annie ... because Mom and Dad were not on the same page with things?

It has been said that to name something is to know it. When something is given a name, it is given a conceptual container into which an understanding of that *thing*, is placed. And so, when a child is given a name, they are given a conceptual container into which an ever-expanding understanding of that child is placed. In this way, a child is not simply a prototype but becomes an *individual* who can be known. Once a child begins to embrace and internalize the name they have been given, that name begins serving as the conceptual container into which that child, him, or herself, can begin to place their ever-expanding, experience of their self. Is this how children successfully separate from others, know *self* as a singularly distinct being across time and space?

I wonder what mom was thinking when she wanted/needed to give Annie — Anne-Marie — a new name for her *new life*?

I know my parents were the ones who named me but ... by then ... I was already ten months old. A child definitely knows their name by ten months old. Did I have a name prior to being adopted? If so, what happened to all the info I had, to date, collected and stored?

After meeting my birth family, I thought about changing my name to what it might — *should* — have been, had I stayed where I arrived, but, I eventually realized ... all my experiences and everything I knew about myself was stored under the name I had and it was going to take more — a hell of a lot more — than a name change, to change who I was or how my future life would unfold. For that, I would need to actively participate in changing who I was/am and ... the way I chose to live my life.

So often in families, a child or two are favoured while another child or two are targeted for victimization. Mom always said I was the apple of Dad's eye, but I never believed her. To my mind, Tom was Dad's obvious favourite. As far as Dad was concerned Tom could do no wrong. My Dad admired the hell out of Tom. Jerry on the other hand, sweet little Jerry, not so much. He was constantly being castigated for something. Was dad trying to toughen Jerry up or ... did Jerry hold a mirror up to my dad that he did not like looking into? And Annie ... what was Dad's gross mistreatment of Annie all about?

With us kids getting older, needing—wanting—less and less from Mom, was Dad in anxious anticipation of getting his wife back? With the addition of Annie, was Dad fearing an extension of the emotional unavailability of his wife? Did he hold my little sister responsible for that?

My gut says no, it had to have been something else—something more—but what? What was the enigmatic energy emanating from Annie's embodiment that catapulted my dad into such complete contemptuousness? Just what journey had Annie's arrival *called* my dad upon? Whatever it was, my dad was neither ready, willing, nor able—it seemed—to be led far enough *into* himself to find out.

This is not to excuse my dad or take anything away from the lack of support Jerry received or the cruel and unusual punishment my little sister experienced at the hand—voice—of my dad. It's simply an attempt to understand how and why things were as they were.

And then there was my mom—what mirror might Annie—and I, for that matter—have held up for her?

25

LOVE AND LOSS
The First Cut is the Deepest

Rose loved her boyfriend, Leonard, to bits. Rose and he were about the same height. He was so handsome with his light brown hair and blue eyes. Plus, he was smart. He was headed to college after he graduated that year. Rose didn't remember how they first got together, but she had admired him from a far for a while.

Rose's mom knew and approved of Leonard's mom, so Rose, at the beginning, had been allowed to go over to Leonard's place to visit or to watch television. Rose and Leonard had so much fun talking and laughing. Rose felt like she could be herself around him. He didn't make her feel nervous or insecure. He even took Rose fishing one time. Leonard loved to fish, just as her dad had. Rose and her brothers used to go fishing with their dad all the time. In addition to all of this, Leonard was really nice to Rose—nicer than any of the other guys she'd been out with. In fact, one of the things Rose liked best about him was that he didn't want, expect, or pressure Rose into stuff she did not want to do. Sure, they experimented a time or two—curiosity and all—but it was equal, and it didn't really go anywhere. They were on the same innocent page, so it was all pretty pure, you know? That's what made the whole *affair* thing so cruel.

Rose had no idea why her mom disliked Leonard as she did. She hadn't seemed to mind the other guys Rose went out with—some of whom proved to be dicks—but for some reason, the longer Rose and Leonard were together, the more her mom's animosity toward him grew. Sure, Rose had a bruise or two on her arms from tickle fights and the like, but they were nothing. And sure, he flipped out when Tom dropped a water filled balloon on the roof of his car and dinted it, but who wouldn't?

Anyhow, one night, the womenfolk were doing dishes. Rose's mom always washed while Rose and her sister dried.

All of a sudden, Rose's mom, in a snappish tone, blurted: "You are having an *affair* with that boy, aren't you?"

"An *affair*, what are you talking about?"

"You know damn well what I am talking about. Don't play dumb with me Little Missy."

Rose had absolutely no idea what her mom was talking about but eventually she was able to comprehend what she was driving at.

"No," Rose muttered as she started to cry. She was overcome by shame even though she wasn't guilty as charged. Rose had no idea what happened after that. It was all a blank.

Another time, Rose's mom met her daughter and Len at the front door. Rose had missed her 11:00 pm curfew by mere minutes. A big screaming match ensued, and Rose left with

Leonard in his car. He drove her to Patty's house because Rose knew and trusted Patty's parents, and she knew they would welcome her, even so late at night.

"Yes, of course you can stay here tonight, don't worry, but we need to call your mom, so she doesn't worry."

Rose knew that was not going to go well but … she supposed it was worth a try.

"NO! SHE CANNOT STAY OVERNIGHT. HAVE HER MEET ME OUTSIDE YOUR HOUSE IN TEN MINUTES."

"But she is so upset. She has been throwing up ever since she arrived."

"I DO NOT CARE! IF SHE IS NOT OUTSIDE IN TEN MINUTES I WILL CALL THE POLICE."

Needless to say, Rose was outside waiting for her mom when she arrived. It was a long, quiet ride home.

That night, Rose wrote her mom a letter not apologizing— but explaining—and slipped it under her mom's bedroom door.

When Rose got home from school the next day, she had a letter sitting on her desk. They were both going to try and start over. Did they start over? They may have tried, at first, but it did not work.

Rose defiantly went to Leonard's grad on a Sunday afternoon, but she was forbidden from going to his graduation party.

"But why …?" Rose was heartbroken.

He phoned from his party but that just made matters worse. Because he had to buy his grad date a gift, he bought Rose one too. He bought her a little gold ring with her initials on it. Rose was touched to tears. Her mom just rolled her eyes.

Rose and Leonard were still together when summer arrived. Because Leonard's family had a cabin at Christina Lake, he spent most of his time out there, swimming, boating, water-skiing, fishing and the like.

Rose asked many times if she could accompany Leonard and his family to the lake, but the answer was always the same.

"No," and continued to be no even after his mom called Rose's mom to assure her that the couple would be well supervised.

Nope. Rose wasn't allowed to do that so she and some friends who she had previously dismissed in lieu of her new boyfriend, hatched up a plan. A few of the girls—the girls who were allowed—would go to the very same lake, Christina Lake, camping by themselves. Believe it or not, Rose was allowed to do that. She was thrilled about it, but she thought her mom was completely cracked.

Exactly where does Mom think I will be spending the weekend?

Wouldn't you know it, but the first weekend the girls went camping was a weekend when Leonard was at the lake alone, without his family. Rose knew her mom would have probably had a stroke if she knew what was afoot but … she didn't so …

Once off work, gear all packed up ahead of time, Rose and four or five of her chums headed for the lake. Rose didn't remember if she was dropped off at Leonard's cabin, or if he came to pick her up at the campsite, or if she made her own way there. Whatever the case was, on that Saturday evening, Rose and her beau went to a local dance. After the dance, they went to a party, and then later, back to his place where they talked and laughed and slept on the sundeck under the stars.

Next morning they went boating with friends. For Rose it had been dang near as much fun as church camp used to be. No, nothing untoward happened, and as far as Rose knew, her mom never found out but ... sometime later, and Rose had no idea how much time later, she and her mom were at the kitchen table talking when her mom suggested that it might be best if Rose broke things off with Leonard.

"Really?"

"He is always out at the lake, and you are always here Rose. He is never here for you. What kind of a boyfriend is that? Don't you deserve better?"

"Maybe I do ..." So, Rose's mom helped Rose draft a Dear John—Dear Leonard—letter to her boyfriend that night. Almost before the ink was dry, Rose was encouraged to drop the letter, unannounced, through the mail slot of his family's home.

"Best just get it done Rose."

So, what did Rose do? She did it. Of course she did it. That night in bed, Rose was beside herself. Not only had she, for sure, hurt Leonard's feelings with the most vicious of accusation, she had betrayed the truth of her most piercingly poignant feelings.

I still love him, of course I do, but ... how will I ... ever face him again.

For what she had done, Rose was harassed all night long by her hollering harbingers of heartache. The only thing Rose could do, could think of doing, was re-live their relationship—

every single moment of it—over and over and over again—for years. And not to make herself feel better, but to make herself feel even worse. Rose hated her mom for what she had made her do and she hated herself for doing it.

I bet Mom has been reading my diary and that's why she hated Leonard so much. In reading my diary Mom would have known that I love him, and she simply couldn't have that now could she ... n o o o o!

Rose had been keeping a diary ever since she was able to scribble her thoughts. Every night, when first she got into bed, Rose would spill her heart—her fears, feelings, and fantasies—into her diary. Her diary had a little lock on it, but Rose never hid it. She never thought to. She always just kept it in one of the cupboards behind her bed, in her bed's headboard.

What's the point of keeping a diary if Mom is going to read it? Stupid me!

I went to the lake camping with the girls a few, if not several, more times that summer in the hope of seeing my heart's desire, but not once did I see him. But ... even if I had ... would I have been able to approach him? Talk to him? I doubt it. I carried far too much shame and pain for that. What I did to comfort myself, was take up with whomever would have me. I'd do that just so I didn't have to be alone, feel totally unloved.

I no longer think Mom's distain for Leonard was because of her reading my diary. If she had been reading my diary, she would have known how truly troubled I had forever been, how locked inside myself I was. I now believe that my mom's angst—ever-increasing distain for Leonard—must have been grounded in the fact that I had grown so attached to him. Could she feel herself losing me or was she worried I would get pregnant or marry young—too young—as she perhaps thought she had? Whatever the case may be, the flame on the torch I carried for Leonard never quite went out.

Even years later—married with kids—whenever I ran into him, he would always smile and say, "Hi" ... and I would say "Hi" in return, as I blushed and pretended to be busy or preoccupied.

Well, I guess, in a way, I wasn't pretending to be busy or preoccupied because I would be busy fantasizing about the life that he and I would be sharing had things gone differently. Yes, I knew the conjuring of my capricious contentment caused me nothing but pain, but it was a point of pain I continued to cherish.

26

PSYCHE AND SOMA
Partners in Life

When Grade Twelve started, Rose tried to give it a go. She'd signed herself up for so many classes—hard classes—thinking she would make up for lost time, make up for the year before. She had promised her mom, but she had neither the strength nor the will to make it stick. She no longer cared about sewing or her wardrobe. She had several projects on the go that her mom kept bugging her about, but she just didn't care … she didn't care about anything. She hated her parents, her life, and herself.

No, Rose didn't like the way she was feeling but she didn't know what to do about it so … early in the school year she went to see the girls' guidance counsellor, her English literature teacher, about feeling so down and out all the time.

"I don't know what is wrong with me. I am always so tired and sad. I'm smoking and drinking, not doing what I am supposed to be doing. I'm in Grade Twelve. I am supposed to graduate this year. Can you help me?"

The advice Rose received back was: "Just stop all your foolishness Rose. Buckle down and get back to work."

"Oh … okay … thanks … good chat. Bye now."

Rose promptly strolled out to the smoke pit for a butt or two.

The next day, having thrown the "counsellor" into the same category as her mom—"l" for lame—Rose dropped English literature.

The day after that, she dropped Italian.

Rose's first term report card read: "Rose would do a lot better in mathematics if she attended class."

And the Community Recreation class—a specialty sports-oriented class Rose had been selected to attend … she told the instructor she could no longer attend class because she had rheumatic fever. Rheumatic fever of all things! Rose had no idea why she chose rheumatic fever. She figured she'd just plucked it out of thin air.

What Rose hadn't anticipated, in all this, was her Community Recreation teacher calling her mom to offer her condolences. Rose had no recollection of how her mom took that news. However it went, Rose never went back to that class either.

The only class Rose never missed, save once, was biology. It was Rose's biology teacher who, after catching Rose about to skip class, looked her straight in the eye and said, "Don't worry Rose, if you have somewhere more important to be than biology, do not let me stop you."

And he wasn't being snide or sarcastic in the least. With this, Rose's biology teacher became the only adult in Rose's life that she respected. As such, she never skipped biology again. She did not want to let him down.

It was not too long into the school year when Rose took up with her second boyfriend, Sandy. She didn't remember how they first got together, but she thought perhaps she might have met him while with friends buying pot at a local park. Back in those days—the '70s—kids could buy joints, complete with seeds and stems, for twenty-five cents a pop. Anyway, Sandy had just moved to town from Alberta, so he was a new guy in town. He had brown hair and brown eyes. He was slim and about Rose's height. He wore glasses. He was not drop-dead gorgeous, and Rose had never had any sort of crush on him but ... he was a nice enough guy.

He had a job, a car, and he liked Rose a lot. Neither Rose nor Sandy had any interests or ambitions or plans for the future. Mostly they just hung out. Sandy would pick Rose up for school every morning. They would each attend their own homeroom and then maybe a class or two. Because Rose liked her biology teacher so much, she began attending Sandy's biology classes with him. The teacher didn't seem to mind so ...

The majority of Rose and Sandy's day was spent down at the Tastee-Freeze plugging the jukebox, smoking, drinking coffee and eating chips and gravy. Rose was sure the school knew where to find her if they had chosen to look. Sometimes, when a group could be gathered, they would go up to the hospital parking lot or out to the bush somewhere and drink beer or cheap red wine—Bon Red—during lunch hour. That was always a hoot. Was Rose happy and having fun? No, she was not. She was just passing time ... that seemed to be pretty much all she had the energy or drive for.

It was shortly after Rose and Sandy partnered up that Rose started to get killer headaches, right behind her eyes. She would get one every day, like clockwork, just as the school day ended and she had to go home. The school thought that perhaps Rose needed glasses.

"Maybe … everything has been a little fuzzy lately."

Rose's mom fought it for a while. "Rose, there is absolutely nothing wrong with your eyes."

But eventually, she took her daughter to an eye doctor. Sure enough, the optometrist said Rose's needed glasses, but those glasses gave Rose an even worse headache, so she pitched them after about a month.

As fall began to turn into winter things at home began to heat up rather than cool down. Social Services was going to be paying a visit to check on the status of the newly formed familial union. Rose's mom said it was routine. She'd said they always paid a visit a year or so after an adoption, just to make sure everything was tickety-boo. Only problem … things were not tickety-boo and everyone in the family knew it.

Rose so wanted her mom to tell the truth.

"Please, Mom … PLEASE! You have to tell the truth. You have to tell the powers that be that dad is not adjusting well … that he's being a complete asshole to Annie. We can't leave things the way they are! Can we? It's hurting everyone. Our family is falling apart."

Well yes, apparently, they could, and they did! Upon peering into the living room, Rose saw her parents sitting there, smiling their faces off. With that Rose knew—just knew—they'd lied—

lied with their best freaking faces on. Rose couldn't stand it. She couldn't be in that house one minute longer, so she left; she left heart-broken, disgusted, devastated, and aghast! She left feeling like her head was going to blow off.

Rose ended up at her old friend, Rosie's house. Rose and Rosie were no longer that close, not since Sandy had arrived on the scene, but they were close enough, close enough for Rose to find herself at her front door at 7:00 pm at night. They chatted for a while. Rose never told Rosie why she'd come for a surprise visit that night. She likely couldn't have even if she had wanted to. She was far too horrified.

With this—with the truth NOT out—Rose was done. She was out. She did not give a rat's ass about anything. As far as Rose was concerned … neither the world nor anything in it made a lick of sense.

'Twas around this time that Rose started having a new re-oc-curring dream. Every re-run would be the same. Rose would climb a steep flight of cement stairs only to be sent backwards down the same stairs after someone—person unknown—opened and then quickly shut the door at the top. Every time, waking up, Rose would be thrashing around in bed, as if she really were falling backwards down a flight of stairs. Rose would be aston-ished. She couldn't figure out how or why her body could be—would be—responding to something that was only happen-ing in her mind.

Early to mid-December 1972, Rose's mom, her sister, and she were in the kitchen cleaning up after dinner when Rose's mom accused Rose of not cleaning the stove. With that, Rose turned around and left the kitchen. She went into her bedroom and threw herself on her bed. After lying there a while, Rose decided she'd had enough, and she wanted out. She snuck back into the kitchen and took all the 222s they had. The painkillers were always kept in the kitchen, in the cupboard to the left of the kitchen sink, easy access for Rose's dad because he was always in pain. Was there one bottle or two? Rose believed there was a half-bottle and a full bottle. However many there were, Rose took them all. Did she take them while in the kitchen or after she'd gotten back to her bedroom? Wherever it was, Rose remembered it being tough getting them all down. They made her gag, but she persevered.

Once they were down, Rose lay back down on her bed and began waiting for the end.

So ... I wonder how it's going to happen. What's it going to be like. I guess I am just going to have to wait and see ...

While she lay on her bedspread—huge faux pas—Rose heard the phone ring. Then, she heard her mom calling her. It was Sandy.

"Do you want to go for coffee or something," he'd said.

"Sure," Rose said. Even at the time, wondering why she'd said yes.

However it went, next thing Rose remembered, was she was being helped onto a stretcher in the emergency ward and getting a huge tube stuck down her throat. It scratched and scraped all the way down. Nothing after that ... till Rose woke up in intensive care puking her guts out and crying her head off.

It must have been the next morning before Rose saw her mom. While telling Sandy how much she hated her mom, Rose looked up and saw her mom standing in the doorway.

"OH MY GOD, WHY COULDN'T I HAVE JUST DIED!" Rose screamed as she proceeded to lose every last bit of composure she had.

All Rose's mom did, as Rose recalled, was stoically walk over to Rose's bed and whisper something about sending her to Vancouver, if that's what she wanted.

Had Rose heard her mom correctly? The words rang hollow. Rose did not understand. *What ... why would I want to go to Vancouver?*

Rose did not understand. Part of Rose was baffled by her mom's cordially bestowed consolation, while another part was in complete hysterics over what her mom had just heard her say. Rose had no idea how long she had been crying uncontrollably before a nurse came in and asked if she would mind folding serviettes for the hospital.

"It would be really helpful. It needs to be done and I am way too busy, so if you don't mind ..."

"Sure," Rose said. And it was just what Rose needed. Rose folded box after box of serviettes that day, truly believing she was helping that nurse, when in reality, it was that nurse who had helped Rose out immensely. Such a silly little thing, but it worked ever so well in calming Rose down.

The next morning, Rose called her mom asking if she could come home.

"No Rose … you are crazy, you need help, and you're not coming home till you get it. I can't take it! I don't know what to do with you anymore."

Rose was devastated. To Rose's mind, the problem was her family, not she, herself. Later that day, Rose was transferred to the psych ward, Rose's home for the next what … week, ten days, two weeks. Rose didn't remember.

Rose was assigned a room with a girl around her own age but she left after the first night. Thereafter, Rose was alone. It was a bit freaky at first because everyone else was a lot older than Rose, more like Rose's parents' age. They all looked completely nuts, completely whacked out, glazy-eyed and vacant. Everyone, that is, except for this one guy who looked fairly normal, until, all of a sudden, he'd twitch out. He'd start screaming and yelling and flailing around like a lunatic. Then he'd get locked up in a padded room. With all of this, Rose kept to herself.

Although it may sound strange to say, Rose rather enjoyed herself in there. It was peaceful and quiet. She could do what she wanted, so she made everyone a homemade Christmas card out of old Christmas cards and little scraps of coloured paper, foil, string and what have you. The unit had its own kitchen so Rose could make herself a snack whenever she wanted. They had Cheese Whiz. Rose loved Cheese Whiz, but her mom never bought it. It was too expensive.

Rose had no idea how long she was there before she saw her psychiatrist. Did she see him once or more than once?

She had no idea. All she remembered was that he was a *nutcase*. He was short, stocky, and rather unkempt looking. He had long, scraggly hair, extremely bushy eyebrows, glasses, and a long, scraggly beard. He also had an exceptionally monotone voice.

"Well Rose, I hope you know you've hurt your family a great deal."

"Yes."

"Are you ever going to do this again?"

"No."

"Right then, I want you to continue taking the happy pills I prescribed you, morning and night, and you can go home, spend Christmas with your family."

And that was it! Rose was apparently cured. A little break from her family, some pills that did nothing, and Rose was given permission to return to the loving embrace of her family for the holidays.

The story, according to Rose's mom, was to go something like this: "Rose took a drink while on medication and it made her sick. Silly monkey."

Nary a word was ever spoken on the topic, or about the incident, again. The sardonic story to be given was to disguise, disfigure, and discredit Rose's failed suicide attempt, which filled Rose with everything from rage to resentment.

Lies, lies, lies ... nothing but lies ... ever! Two emotions Rose did not experience, however, were regret and remorse. Rose knew what she was doing. She knew what she wanted but she had failed ...

I can't even kill myself properly. Rose found this particular failing of hers most ironic. *People who don't want to die, do, and people who do want to die, don't. What's up with that?* Rose didn't get it but in accepting fate's decree, in accepting that it was not yet her time, Rose got on with it. She kept on keeping on.

Annie eventually told Rose that their mom thought she had attempted suicide as a result of her inability to get over her boyfriend.

Now, why would she have thought that?

Rose knew her mom couldn't have read her diary because she no longer kept one. Writing in it had become far too tedious and … if her mom was reading it … what was the point. Did her mom have a guilty conscience? What else could have made her mom think what she did? Rose's only satisfaction came from the fact that her mom thought her actions had come back to bite her in the ass.

Rose herself had, more than once, wondered over the years why she had done what she had done that night. Yes, she'd caught hell for not cleaning the stove when she was sure she had, but she was always catching hell for something … nothing new about that night. Maybe that night was simply the last straw, the straw that broke the camel's back. Maybe it was a combination of everything including the fact that she had not gotten over—never did get over—her former boyfriend.

Christmas came and went. Rose didn't get the whole Christmas thing. What was the point? Everyone sitting around in their best duds pretending they liked each other, pretending they were grateful for all the stupid, pointless gifts they received. In an attempt to avoid the possibility of verbal unpleasantries, some cheesy Christmas movie would be blaring away in the background so ... Rose couldn't see Christmas as anything but a fanciful but feeble farce.

"It's about family, Rose ..."

To that, all Rose could do was roll her eyes at her mom, YET AGAIN.

No, there was no skiing for Rose during that winter. Her new beau, Sandy, didn't ski and after everything that had happened Rose barely had enough energy to get out of bed in the morning never mind propel herself to the ski hill for a day of extreme sports.

The only noteworthy thing to have happened ... Rose had sex for the first time. Her boyfriend wanted it and he had been so very kind to her. It was a token of appreciation more than anything else. The unfortunate reality to this being ... a precedent had been set. After that first time, sex became an expectation. Rose hated it but what could she do? She tried to pretend boyfriend number two was boyfriend number one but that didn't work. It didn't work because Rose knew her first boyfriend would never have forced her—expected her—to do something she did not want to do.

There was a stretch when Rose thought she might be pregnant. She didn't know whether to laugh or cry. If she was pregnant, she knew she would never be able to tell her mom, what with her mom never having been able to have her own kids. What would she do? Well, Rose figured she would have to run away from home. Sandy said he would go with her so … 'twas all for not however. 'Twas a false alarm.

Thank God!

Rose and Sandy were so relieved not to be pregnant. Shortly thereafter, Rose went to a female doctor—not their family doctor—to get herself on birth control pills. Luckily, she didn't need parental consent. That would have been a whole new, a whole different rock-faced cliff to climb.

Once Rose started having sex regularly, she started having trouble with her legs. Her thighs began to ache something terrible. The ache was so intense Rose could hardly walk. At school she needed help to climb or descend stairs. She needed someone to help her bare her own weight as she lifted and lowered her body. Eventually, Rose's mom brought her daughter to the doctor. After writing a script for her current—latest—bout of bronchitis, the doctor advised Rose and her mom that Rose's leg problem was probably due to Juvenile Arthritis.

"It may get worse, but it may not. Either way there is nothing we can do for it."

By the time grad season rolled around, Rose's achy legs were a thing of the past. Clearly it had not been Juvenile Arthritis. Rose's faith in doctors was failing fast.

Only one more bottleneck of tiny, tangled tales left to round out the state in which Rose went into the world, and they all surrounded her long-awaited graduation from high school and escape from Dodge.

Rose was in Grade Twelve, so yes, it was her grad year. Pictures, picnics, dinners, dances, and ceremonies were being planned by the school's student counsel while a proliferation of parties and pancake breakfasts were being planned by parents.

Was Rose excited? Eh! Not so much.

Given her efforts and how much school she had missed, Rose thought it would be a damn miracle if she graduated. Rose never did her homework, never handed in assignments, and never studied. With the exception of biology, Rose did not attend any of her classes regularly, and when she did, she was often drunk or stoned so she knew her grades had to be in the toilet. She also knew she was going to have to write the math final. None of this mattered for the moment though because all the festivities, except for the ceremonial handing out of diplomas, occurred prior to anyone knowing if they actually graduated. As such, either way, preparations had to be made.

In order to find a novel pattern and material for her dress— something special—Sandy agreed to take Rose to a giant fabric store in Colville, Washington—a small city just across the border—so Rose could pick out exactly what she wanted. Rose's mom was having her daughter's dress made by a seamstress—a neighbour lady—as a special treat. As it turned out, the dress fit perfectly, but Rose hated it. She thought it was hideous.

"I don't know why, Mom ... I liked the material when I saw it on the bolt, and I liked the picture on the pattern package."

The afternoon before the big event—grad dinner and dance—a group of girls, Rose included, all arranged to have their hair done at the same salon at roughly the same time. Just for fun, a few of girls brought a big bag of vodka spiked oranges. 'Twas easy enough to do. All you needed was a syringe. Pull juice out. Shoot vodka in. It was fun and all the girls ended up a little bit on the tipsy side. This was of no help however when it came to Rose's fancy new do. Rose had expected to look like the model in the picture she'd brought as a guide for her hairdresser. Instead, she believed she looked like a freaking idiot, stupid roller sized bubbles piled atop her head. No amount of vodka spiked oranges could have helped that situation.

After the big ten-course spaghetti dinner, that luckily Rose did not slop on her hideous dress, the tables were cleared away and the dance began. Rose had no idea whether she had the first dance with her dad or not, 'twas a blank. That's what was supposed to happen, but Rose had no recollection of it whatsoever. Whether Rose had the first dance with her dad or not, shortly thereafter, she, Sandy, and two other couples took off in Sandy's car. They were off in search of a party, somewhere they could have fun doing what they enjoyed doing. Unable to locate a venue worth venturing into, the four of them drove around self-medicating until 7:00 am, when a pancake breakfast was due to begin. The breakfast was nothing special. To Rose's mind the whole grad thing was very anti-climactic, a big ta-do, about nothing.

No pictures exist of Rose's high school graduation. And down the line, Rose would not remember if she destroyed her grad pictures the same way she'd destroyed her zit era pics, by penning in a beard and mustache, or if she'd just tossed them. Whatever the case may be, there were none to be found.

Next came exams. Rose had tried to study for her math final but gave up because she was way too far behind. She couldn't make hide nor hair of all the notations and formulas she was supposed to have memorized, so when the time came, Rose just put an "x" in whatever box seemed most appropriate at the time. She had been told that the correct answer was more often than not, the third option—"c"—so she took that into account. With no work displayed, it would have been patently obvious to the marker that Rose had guessed her way through the exam. This withstanding when the marks came back …

Well, look at that … I got exactly 51%, exactly what I need to pass, exactly what I need to graduate. Rose burst out laughing. *Are you kidding me? What a crock!*

Sure, Rose was happy. She was ecstatic but she also knew there was no way—absolutely no way—she had passed that exam, so she knew—knew for sure—her mark had been fudged, fudged by someone or a group of someones.

Now, why on earth did they do that? Was it because they felt sorry for me or was it because I was such a pain in the ass, they didn't want me back?

Either way, by doing everything she could not to graduate, Rose graduated. As if Rose wasn't already disillusioned enough with the world … as far as Rose was concerned the whole graduating from high school thing was exactly the same as Christmas … nothing but a giant farce.

Sure, I've had had a hard year. Everyone at school—students and teachers alike—are probably aware of it. I had after all attempted suicide. But graduating me? Seriously? After all the bullshit I pulled? Why didn't anyone call me on my pitiful behaviour?

Rose knew she was behaving badly so … what message did having such behaviour ignored or dismissed send? The message it sent to Rose was that … nobody really gave a shit.

Rose's mom was delighted to learn that her daughter had graduated. She had been so worried.

"See Rose, you passed your math exam, you graduated. Just imagine how well you would have done if you had applied yourself."

To that, all Rose could do, again, was roll her eyes. Little did her mom know how truly disgraceful her daughter's performance, her daughter's behaviour, had been.

Of course, Rose's mom was disheartened that her daughter would not be going to university or college, as she had hoped, but she did take comfort in knowing that her daughter had a plan, sketchy though it may have been.

Rose and Chris had been planning their escape for months. Rose got a bunch of stuff from the gas station where Sandy worked: dishes, silverware, towels, etc. They were always having some sort of promotional program, pieces of which Sandy assisted Rose in procuring. In thinking she would tick off everything on her wish-list, Rose also picked up a kitten, a kitten she named Willie. Yes, you read this correctly. Even though Rose's parents had forbidden her from getting a kitten, Rose decided to get one. That first night, Rose secreted Willie away in the furnace room, but sad, lonely mews drifted up the airducts. Needless to say, a scene ensued.

"No, I did not get him to purposely defy you. I got him because I wanted him. Besides, we'll be gone tout de suite. Failing permission, Rose did not seek or expect forgiveness, all she needed was a tiny touch of tolerance and she got that. Willie was in the furnace room for a week or so.

Between the two of them, the girls had about a hundred dollars, not nearly enough, but they weren't worried. They would make do.

And so it was, a mere two days after school was out, Sandy arrived at the crack of dawn, to pick up Rose, Willie, and Rose's household wares. As they headed down the hill from Rose's family home to pick up Chris and her stash, Rose turned around to see her mom standing on the porch. Rose believed her mom would be overjoyed to see the ass end of her eldest daughter. She had been such a pain in the ass. This withstanding, Rose's mom looked like she could have been posing for a Norman Rockwell original, as she stood there wistfully waving goodbye.

Not even once, did it occur to Rose that she might miss her mom ... silly monkey.

I believe that suicide is none of anyone else's business. It is a personal decision, an agreement made between a single solitary self and the universe. I have, however, come to believe that suicide, in the grand scheme of things, is pointless. The only real way out, being *through*, all the way through one's *Dark Night of the Soul*.[8] Only through living the life we are given are we able to undo that which binds us to our suffering. Only in living my life—meeting my destiny head-on—have I been able to look back and see—truly appreciate—how miraculously orchestrated the course of my learning has been. Had I been allowed to quit, had I found a way to quit, to my mind, I would be back to try again—again, and again, if necessary—until I could get 'er done.

Was an attempted suicide always in the offering for me? Is that why I used to dream about my own funeral, dream I was watching it from above or afar, paying attention to who came and who didn't, what was said and what wasn't?

Was my grad dress truly as hideous as I remember it being? Without any pictures it is hard to now know but ... was it the dress that was hideous or was it myself, in a perfectly fine dress, that I thought hideous? I felt hideous on the inside so perhaps I saw exactly what I needed to see.

I was so unhappy, and in having no idea how to undo my unhappiness, I began to get headaches—horrific headaches—every day prior to having to go home from school. Then, right after having to choke back the fact that my parents did not tell the truth about our situation at home, I started dreaming about having a door slammed in my face, a slammed door that sent me tumbling down ... down ... down in both mind and body. Yes, I'd dreamt of my funeral many times previously, but it was only after I was really down and flat out that my suicidal gears caught, and I attempted to put a permanent end to my pain. Failing that, I turned the screw even tighter by beginning to have sex I did NOT want to have. With that, my legs, my thighs began to ache.

Was this my psyche attempting to relay its pain—my transgressions against self—through my body? Was it trying to send me a message I was not yet able to interpret? The reason that I ask is because 'twas not till George and I were exploring the cause of my grave unhappiness, that my thighs, once again, began to ache, began to ache something horrible.

"You know George ... this feels like a really old pain. I remember it from when I was a teenager."

"Oh ... that's very interesting Rose. What was going on in your life during that time?"

My bone spurs returned prior to blowing up my life. I did not want to have them sawed off again. I wanted to figure out what was causing the disfigurement of the anatomical structures upon which my movement through life depended. By coincidence, while shopping for shoes, I discovered that I had been wearing shoes that were a whole size too small. I had thought that shoes were supposed to fit snuggly—as protection—around your feet, but no, this is not the case. Feet, apparently, need room to expand, move around. Once I had the correct shoes, my bone spurs went away, and never came back again. Were the walls I had erected around my fear preventing me from giving myself enough room to relax into life?

With regard to the headaches that I used to get prior to going home from school ... for a month or two prior to blowing up my life, I would get migraines, excruciating migraines that started at the back of my head and fanned out in every direction. I thought going to the chiropractor was helping a bit, but mostly, I would have to retreat to my bedroom—ALONE. After shutting the blinds and the door, I would take to my bed, lay flat on my back with eyes closed till sleep relieved my suffering. It's been over thirty years and I have never had another migraine; I'm not even sure I've had a headache since.

I had a dog once—a black Chow Chow named Sasha—whose legs, while asleep and dreaming about chasing a squirrel, or whatever dogs dream about—would be running and running. Her little legs would be going a mile a minute in response to whatever was happening in her mind.

Psyche and soma. I have come to believe that our bodies are the physical manifestation of our mind. And so, my relationship between mind and body has continued to be, with my body acting as an interactive encyclopaedia offering messages sent by my inner most self about the way I am thinking or the way I am living. That mind and body are inexorably connected ... I no longer have any doubt.

Much like my starry, starry night memory, I am now unable to determine if what follows actually happened or ... it was a dream. At some point, either in *real* life or in some netherworld, my mom told me that, eventually, as things became increasingly more difficult between my dad and my little sister, she came clean.

She laid the facts out to Social Services who responded, saying, "Well ... at least she has you. She does not have anyone else."

Whether reality or merely a dream ... that was the truth of it so ... does it really matter which it was? In the symphony of being, I guess the situation was our family's fate—karma—to fix if we could or carry forward if we must.

27

FROM TRAIL TO RED DEER
The Long-Awaited Escape

So, two days after school was out, Rose, her new kitten Willie, Chris, and Sandy as the taxi driver at the helm of his red Chevy, left town. Just as an aside, taking a free ranging kitten on a road trip it not the easiest of things to manage. Willie's favourite spot, for whatever reason, was down near the gas, brake, and clutch pedals.

The complement headed east. Why east? Well, Sandy was originally from Alberta and Rose was hoping to use his connections to help her and Chris land a place to live and find jobs. It worked. Through a friend of Sandy's grandmother, the girls found a basement suite. It was a horrifically dumpy place. It was filthy dirty, stunk of mildew, and had a giant, dirt-bottomed hole in the bathroom floor, but at fifty-five dollars a month … the girls could afford twenty-seven fifty each per month.

Through Sandy's oldest sister, Chris landed a great, high-paying union job in the kitchen of the local hospital, but in only having one opening at the time, Rose was SOL. She ended up as a combo cook/waitress/dishwasher at Boston Pizza. The girls were so happy to finally be out on their own. At first, it seemed a dream come true.

One night, after leaving Rose a huge tip—five bucks or something—a creepy but friendly sort of a guy showed up staring through the girls' basement bedroom window. Chris was horrified. Rose didn't remember giving him her address, but yes, she decided she would go to a party with him. It turned out to be a biker party in a run-down house out in the bush somewhere. All Rose remembered about being there was seeing a stark naked pregnant woman leaning against a wall under a flight of stairs. All the woman did was stare blankly into space. Rose figured she had to be stoned out of her gourd. In thinking, knowing, she was out of her depth, Rose asked to be taken home. Luckily, Rose was taken home and she never saw the guy again.

Mid-August, Sandy moved to town to begin attending college that coming September. In wanting their son to get a business degree, Sandy's parents were footing his tuition and living expenses. Little did they know their son had no intention of staying in residence. As far as Sandy was concerned, he would be living with his girlfriend, Rose.

Prior to Sandy's arrival, Rose and Chris had shared the double bed. After Sandy arrived, they took turns in the double bed. Chris one night, Rose and Sandy the next. When Rose and Sandy had the bed, Chris slept on a cot in the dingy old storeroom off their suite. When Chris had the bed, Rose slept on the cot and Sandy slept on the couch.

Rose's job at Boston Pizza only lasted a couple of months because the manager kept hitting on her. She'd gone on drives with him—as friends she thought—but Rose was still so very naive.

As far as Rose knew, Chris was fine. She seemed happy enough, till, shortly before Rose quit her Boston Pizza job, Chris, in missing her boyfriend too much, decided to move back home. Her mom sent her enough money to get herself and her stuff back home on a Greyhound bus. Rose was alright. She still had Sandy.

After a brief stint at a real estate office that let Rose go due to a lack of work and a single day at the local Woolco—they had wanted Rose to climb a ladder in a dress and she was not having it—Sandy's sister was able to get Rose on at the hospital. She was hired on as a housekeeper in the emergency ward. Her shift was from 3:00 pm till 11:00 pm which Rose really liked because she could sleep in and still do something fun after work. The money was great—a union job—but Rose didn't much care for the work. Some of the messes she had to clean up were beyond anything she could previously have imagined and slinging a mop for five or six hours a day was not fun. She did, however, like the people she worked with. She worked with three older women: two named Ewin and a Margaret. Rose had never heard the name Ewin before and to be working with two of them ... at the time, Rose thought the name odd, so it stuck in her mind.

With her new, far better paying job, Rose would finally be able to find herself, and her cat, Willie, nicer digs—a new and improved basement suite—and she did. It had a window that opened onto the lawn so Rose could let Willie in and out with ease, and there was access to a washer and dryer, which was really great because Rose and Sandy would no longer have to lug their laundry to and from the laundromat. Rose was thrilled. *Woohoo!!*

With Sandy starting college in September, Rose thought that she too might like to go to college. She went to see one of the college admissions counsellors who told Rose that she would need to do some upgrading, and if she wanted a student loan, she would have to get a signed letter from her parents stating that they could not afford to send her to college. Well, there was no way Rose was going to do that. She did not want to ask her parents for anything, ever again. As consolation, Rose registered for a single class, an introductory level biology class. She had always loved biology and it was perfect because the class was in the morning. She and Sandy would get up in the morning and go to school. Sandy would be at school all day, but Rose would go home and get ready for work. It was great.

Rose was so impassioned about her class, and she worked so hard at it. She was forever doing homework, studying, and telling Sandy about all the neat things she was learning. With a routine, someone to keep her company, and something fulfilling to occupy her mind, things for Rose were good. She was calm and stable. At night, after Rose got home from work, she and Sandy would chat, play cards, or maybe watch TV, hand firmly on the horizontal hold because the screen rolled almost continually.

On weekends, the couple would go over to Sandy's sister's place or go to the movies. The one time they did go to a bar, they ran into Rose's mom's long-lost hero. They ran into "What's His Face," the accordion player, who had performed on *Starlit Stairway*. Rose was astonished.

Okay that's weird. What are the odds ... of all the people in the world to be in the bar?

Out and about one day, Rose found the most beautiful three-quarter-length, dark brown, suede parka. It had fur around the hood and embroidered trim around the fur of the hood, down both sides of the zipper and around the bottom. It was so nice, and it fit so well. Rose thought she looked terrific in it, but it cost eighty dollars. That was almost an entire paycheck. After a brief bout of deliberation, Rose decided to take the sales lady's advice and buy the coat on layaway.

"Yes, let's do it." Rose was hatching a plan. If she put twenty dollars down and then paid twenty dollars every payday, she would be able to pick the coat up, and call it her own, by Christmas. Then, she could go back home for Christmas and show everyone—show her mom—how well she was doing. Rose could almost see her mom's eyes welling up with tears of pride as she gazed upon Rose's new, top-of-the-line, winter coat.

In order to cover the cost for both her new coat and a plane ticket home, Rose picked up a Saturday morning job cleaning for a well-to-do family in a ritzy neighbourhood. Every Saturday then, for four or five hours, Rose would be given the most unpleasant of tasks to do. The last and by far the worst job was stripping a tile floor of its yellowed plastic coating. For that job, her tools were a pair of rubber gloves, a scraper, a box of Chore Boys, and a can or two of goopy malodorous solvent.

Chemical inhalation was not yet a thing, so a mask or respirator were not even considered. Sure, it was a tough job, but Rose eventually got 'er done. The lady of the house was ever-so pleased, and Rose was exceptionally proud of herself.

Whether Rose blew off biology before or after she picked up her coat it matters not, after all the hard work she'd done, she failed to show up for the final. There is no doubt she would have passed as she'd have gone in with a B+. Rose knew that, but she was so dang proud of herself for acquiring such a flashy new coat, she was sure she no longer needed biology—or college—to prove anything. With such a coat, Rose was convinced she had proof enough to demonstrate her inherent worthiness to those whose approval she so desperately sought.

For whatever reason Sandy wasn't going home for the holidays and that suited Rose fine. He could watch Willie while she was away. And it could also serve as the perfect opportunity to get Sandy out of her place and into the college residence his parents had been paying for since September. 'Twould be just as easy for Sandy to care for Rose's main squeeze—Willie— from his residence as it would be from her place.

Why did Rose want Sandy out? Well, as was mentioned earlier, sleeping with Sandy had always been a bit of an ordeal for Rose. Actually, it wasn't so much the sleeping. Rose rather enjoyed sleeping next to someone. It was the sex. From the very beginning Rose had hated it, but it was something she felt she had to do because she was his girlfriend. Lord knows Rose couldn't tell Sandy the truth. To Rose's mind, the truth would hurt his feelings far too much.

Better to just ease and appease him out by telling him that it would be far easier and less lonely for him if he stayed in residence while she was away. Once she was back ... she'd find some excuse to keep him where he was.

There was only one more problem to sort out before Rose could revel in the reclamation of her dignity and respect during a Christmas respite. Rose had not yet told her employer that she had planned a Christmas getaway because she did not yet have any holidays. She'd only been working at the hospital for a few months, and holiday time was not awarded until one had a year's worth of service. In order to circumvent this complication, Rose told her boss that she had to go home because her dad was sick—really—sick. Sandy's sister and brother-in-law offered to drive Rose to and from the airport in Calgary—a couple of hours away—so she was set.

Had Rose's mom or dad met her at the airport when she arrived back in town? Did her mom say anything about her coat when they first re-united? If she had, it hadn't been what Rose had hoped to hear because she didn't remember it. The only reaction Rose remembered getting was from a Dianne "Someone or Other" ... someone whose appearance and poise Rose had envied—during her old cheerleading days.

"Wow, Rose. That's a great coat." Apart from that ... nada.

And the only memory Rose had of her Christmas trip back home that year, was from one night after being out with friends. Upon entering the basement door—sporting her new coat—Rose was alerted to the fact that her mom was hosting one of her ladies' church club meetings. Rose's mom wasn't in sight but there were other ladies everywhere, one of which being Sandy's mom. As Rose was taking off her boots, one of the ladies—a woman Rose had known for years—approached her.

"So, Rose ... how are you enjoying your job as a lab technician at the Red Deer Hospital?"

"...
....
....
....
....
...."

"Oh, I like it fine. It's going really well. I am as happy as the dang dickens." Rose did not want to embarrass her mom by pointing out her LIE!!!!!

Despite her cavalier attitude, Rose was crushed, absolutely gutted. Not only had her mom NOT been impressed by her coat, but she was also ashamed of her, so ashamed of her that she'd felt the need to lie to her church ladies about her daughter's job ... and who Rose was. Rose remembered nothing further about that night or the remainder of her trip. All she remembered was that one incident and as excruciatingly painful as it had been, it remained a secret. Rose never told her mom, or anyone, that her mom's jig was up.

Once back in Red Deer:

"But WHY ... why can't I come back?" Sandy was confused.

"I'm not really sure Sandy. I just feel like being alone for a while. We can still hang out if you want to." Sandy wasn't happy but he didn't argue.

Rose's performance at the hospital, after she got back from her Christmas catastrophe, was dismal to say the least. She no longer cleaned the way she was supposed to. She began going through people's belongings and she sat around reading magazines. Was she trying to get fired? What else could she have been trying to do? 'Twasn't long before Rose quit the hospital. She quit because she didn't want to be there anymore.

By that time, Sandy was working as a taxi driver. Man, sakes alive, what a motley crew at that taxi stand—unbelievable oddballs and fringe dwellers, but they were nice, and they had their own curling team.

One night a group of them travelled to a small town, close by, for a bonspiel and a few beers. It was fun.

Given her ability to mix with the crowd it wasn't long before Rose, too, was working at the taxi stand. They wouldn't hire her on as a driver. They didn't want female drivers—too dangerous they'd said—so she was hired on as a dispatcher. Holy, was that ever a hairy job, phones ringing off the hook and then trying to figure out who was closest to what, who to send where. The drivers would get so pissed at Rose if she sent them somewhere she should have sent someone else. They would yell and scream at her when they got back to the shop.

Rose would have nightmares about phones ringing, and if her phone, per chance, ever woke her up, the first thing out of her mouth would inevitably be, "Blankity-blank Taxi." All for minimum wage—whatever that was—and the worst possible hours you could imagine.

Sometimes, depending upon how busy it was, Rose would have to work straight through the night. As hellish as it all sounds, Rose rather liked it ... she thought it was fun. Most often she and Sandy worked the same hours, so they spent time together, were together in every way but the biblical. All was well, or well enough, till Rose met a guy, a guy with whom she was ever so enamoured.

Sandy and Rose had a couple of girlfriends they had met through Sandy's roommates. Sandy dated—pretended to date—one of the girls, in an attempt to make Rose jealous.

Ya ... not working!

And the other, well she and Rose hit it off so well that she asked Rose to accompany her home to her parents, in a neighbouring town. She was going to attend an NDP rally and allied house parties and hoped Rose would join her.

"Sure ... why not? Something different, it sounds like fun."

Rose carried, in her mind's eye, a pic of herself, noticing Will for the very first time. She was standing inside the front door and Will was standing in the doorway of the kitchen.

Oh my god, he took Rose's breath away. He was beautiful. He was tall with long brown hair and brown eyes. He was sporting a full-length white sheepskin coat, that, as it turned out, he'd made for himself. He was English—from England— and had the dreamiest accent. After staring at each other for a bit, and chatting for another bit, the two of them decided they should get together the next day. Rose gave him her friend's home number. He said he'd call.

Rose and Will spent the next day and night together. Will lived in his sister's basement in Edmonton, two hours north of Red Deer. Will's sister and her husband had come from England a few years earlier and Will thought he would check Canada out while he had the chance. Rose and Will talked on the phone and visited back and forth for several weeks or a couple of months, Exactly how long it was, Rose hadn't the foggiest. She'd bus up to him or he would drive down to her in his cherry red MGB.

During one of Rose's visits up to Will's place, Will's sister made her impression of Rose quite known at the breakfast table.

After looking at Rose, she turned to her brother and said, "So, would you ever marry someone who had sex with you right away?"

Ouch! Rose felt like she'd been slapped in the face. It hurt but …

"Oh … I don't know … I haven't given it any thought."

Ouch! Rose carried on as if unfazed by it all.

On Rose's final trip up to visit Will, she took the bus up on Friday, as usual. The two of them spent Friday and Saturday together, as usual, but then, Rose was going to meet up with Sandy late Saturday afternoon.

Sometime earlier, Rose had heard that the band Three Dog Night was going to be staging a concert in a nearby city, and Rose longed to go. For most of her life, "One is the Loneliest Number," had been her theme song. As it turned out, the nearby city was Edmonton, Will's city, and Sandy had tickets, one for Rose and one for himself. Sandy wanted to take Rose to the concert knowing full well she was going to be spending the previous day and night with some other guy. Rose was surprised that Sandy was up for such a thing but … good. If he was in, she was in.

The concert was fabulous. Rose and Sandy had a good time but later that night in their hotel room … not so much. Rose had no recall around how it unfolded, but as you may guess, this was the end of it for Sandy. Finally, after all the abuse Rose had dished his way, Sandy was done. He packed up his stuff and went back home to Trail.

After Sandy left, Rose got sick. She got really, really sick: fever, nausea, achy all over. For at least three dog-gone nights, Rose was dazed and disorientated—so dazed and disorientated, that she once again dealt herself a most crushing blow. While in bed, sleeping on and off, the phone must have rung. Rose didn't remember the phone ringing, but it must have rung, and she must have answered it, because when she finally came-to, when she was finally consciously aware of what she was doing, she was holding the phone knowing—just knowing—that she had been screaming at whoever was on the other end of the phone. Dumbfounded and speechless, Rose straightened her arm, held the phone as far away from her ear as she possibly could and hung up. That was the only thing she could think of to do so … she hung up. Did the phone ring again, right after that? Maybe it did. Rose thought it might have, but she didn't answer it. She couldn't answer it. She knew—just knew—it had been Will. She was destroyed, distraught beyond measure, so she promised herself she would never—ever—think about Will or what had happened, ever, ever, again.

Rose could barely believe what happened but … it had happened, and she had done it, so all she could think of to do was call her mom. Despite thinking, believing, she would never need her mom again, Rose called her mom …

"Mom … can I come home?"

Rose's mom said she would get her dad to come and pick her up. "He'll be there in a day or two."

"What about Willie?"

"Yes, Rose, I will somehow convince your dad to pick up your cat as well."

"Okay good. Thanks, Mom."

Rose's dad arrived a day and a half later. Rose was going to have to put Willie in a cardboard box in the trunk.

"But he'll be so sad back there all alone …"

"He will be just fine, Rose. That is the only way he is coming with us."

They had Rose's stuff—cat included—packed into the car in no time. It was a breeze getting everything into her dad's honking big, bronze Chrysler.

Before leaving town, Rose wanted to go say goodbye to her employer and friends down at the taxi stand. Rose's dad refused to go in with her. He stood outside the car across the street and waited for his daughter to do what she needed to do. With this, Rose couldn't help but wonder if she embarrassed her dad as well … it sure seemed so. Once Rose said her goodbyes, they were off. Less than a year after Rose arrived in Red Deer, she was headed back home to Trail.

So, what was the synchronistic significance of running into my old accordion playing nemesis, "What's His Face?" Was the message intended to reaffirm that *it's a small world* ... or was it that ... we never really leave the past behind. We bring it along with us wherever we go.

It mattered not to me that I was interested in biology, loved learning about the mechanisms of life. My life was not about that. It was not about finding myself, attempting to find out what I enjoyed doing, what interested me or what I wanted to pursue. It was about acquisitions and appearances. I wanted—needed—to externalize what I had internalized. My life was about delivering or possessing what the world—my world—had advocated as mattering most, and I thought a prestigious pelt would do.

Had my mom lied about my job because she, herself, was embarrassed, or was she embarrassed for me? I wasn't a professional, but I had a job, a good job. And what about Sandy's mom? As Sandy's mom, she most certainly would have known I worked in housekeeping, and not as a lab technician. How did she feel about my mom's misrepresentation of her daughter? Poor Mom ...

28

FROM TRAIL TO KELOWNA
Land of the Illustrious

*H*ome again, home again, jiggety-jig.
That's what Rose's dad always said whenever the family returned from some sort of outing. He would say it when he was in a good mood. If he wasn't in a good mood, he wouldn't say anything. He would just get *that* look on his face. Rose was home from Red Deer and happy about it, so that was the line that ran through her head.

Because Rose's little sister had overtaken what had once been her bedroom, Rose had to move into the rumpus room.

Rose returned to Trail sometime in May, and by June, she had a new job. The smelter in town always hired summer students, so Rose told them what they needed to hear, and it was a go. She ended up on the gardening crew.

With Sandy still around and Chris going to the local Business College, the three of them fell back in, relations between Rose and Sandy being greased by the fact that both Sandy and Chris were now part of a much larger group, a group that included one of the girls Chris was going to business college with and her fiancé; both of them lived downstairs from Chris and her mom. Alas, Rose had found her footing once again. She found some footing and she found a new young man, Don, with whom to be enamoured.

Don was tall, dark, and handsome and worked as a photographer for the local newspaper. All the girls in town loved him. Rose thought him quite the catch. The only problem … Don was Chris's youngest older brother, and Chris was NOT pleased that her friend—Rose—was dating her brother.

"But why, Chris …?"

"Because you are WAY different when you are around him …"

Whatever …

Rose was hopeful her friend would come around, but until then, she was happier than the dickens hanging out and going on dates with her new beau. Unfortunately, Rose's mom was not happy with her daughter's new situation. In fact, Rose's mom was becoming ever-more unhappy with her daughter's behaviour.

"Rose, you are never home before midnight, and often times you arrive home inebriated. You are a bad influence on your brothers and sister."

With this, Rose roared laughing. Was she kidding? Rose knew her brothers got home a lot later than she did, especially Tom. Sometimes it would be 3:00 am, before she heard him, and his car get home.

Whatever …

'Twas shortly after Rose blew her mom off that her mom told her that both she and her cat had to move out, and she was to go nowhere near her younger brothers and sister.

"Fine ..."

So ... for lack of anything better to do, on such short notice, Rose carried her cat and her stuff, load by load, over to Don's place. He wasn't home at the time, so Rose just piled her boxes on his porch and sat with her cat waiting for him to get home. Yes, he let Rose move in. And yes, he let Rose borrow his car every day to get to and from work, but Rose intuited Don was not overly happy about the situation because she did not feel all that welcome. No, they had not discussed Rose's moving in beforehand. It just happened the way it happened and it unhappened in a fairly similar fashion.

Nary a week or so after moving in, Rose was advised that she would have to move out for the long weekend because the young man with whom she had just begun cohabitating, had a friend coming to visit for a few days.

"Is it a girl?"

"Yes." Although utterly heartbroken Rose remained as cool as a cucumber. Heaven-forbid he learns how shattered she was.

"Well ... I guess I better get looking for an apartment then," Rose said, before chuckling resignedly in response.

It took only a day or two for Rose to find a reasonably nice place. It didn't allow cats, but it had a kitchen window that opened onto the roof of the first floor suites so ... Rose would make it work. Having to walk to and from work every day wasn't fun, but Rose coped. And even though they were forbidden from doing so, her youngest brother and sister came to visit quite regularly.

One night, upon arriving home from somewhere, she found her recent betrayer sitting on the stoop of her apartment building waiting for her. He said he was sorry and wondered how she was doing.

"I'm fine," Rose responded with counterfeit cheeriness.

She and Don's relationship recommenced without another word. He didn't offer, and Rose didn't ask, because at that point, she already had her own apartment.

Walking to and from work wasn't that bad. Rose had gotten used to it. The couple carried on as a unit until a career change took Don out of town. He wanted to become a forest ranger, so he moved to Manning Park. Yes, he was going to be ever so far away, but they agreed to stay in touch and visit when they could.

With Rose's summer job rapidly coming to an end, Rose knew she had to find another source of income pretty darn quick. She'd heard about a program where if you were out of work, Manpower would sponsor job training, so she thought she would give that a go. It worked.

While collecting Unemployment Insurance (UI), Rose took a business course. Her UI cheques were to be tied to her attendance. Rose did not want to go to the Business College in town. She wanted to go somewhere fun—somewhere exciting. Rose felt she belonged in a place where beautiful people lived, so she wanted to move to a resort town in the Okanagan. There was a college that offered a business course in Kelowna, so she decided to move there. Little did Rose yet know, however, that she would eventually consider the coming year the second worst year of her life—the worst year being her year in Grade Eight and her second worst year being her year in Kelowna— and these were the only years in a near lifetime of years that Rose had bookmarked.

How was she going to get herself, her stuff, and Willie there …? Sandy.

Once Don left, Rose reunited with her old crew. Chris had since moved away but Sandy and the rest of them were still there so … while explaining the logistical dilemma she faced in taking advantage of her new opportunity, Rose wondered aloud if it might be the perfect opportunity for a road trip, bit of a holiday.

"What do you think, guys?"

Sandy, Chris's friend, and her fiancé, were in. And so, it was. Off they went in Sandy's car. Yes, having Willie in the car was a huge pain in the ass yet again. His favourite spot still being down by the foot pedals, but they got where they were going.

After a few stops at a few different motels close to the college, Rose found a cute little self-contained one-bedroom unit—lakeside—that was rented monthly to students.

"Yes, I'll take it. It is perfect."

After getting Rose's stuff unpacked and then going out for a few supplies, all was well, till it was time to hit the sheets. Then, all hell broke loose. For some reason, it was assumed that Rose would sleep in the same bed as Sandy. Had they been drinking? Oh, there is no doubt, but there was absolutely no screaming way Rose was going to get into the same bed as Sandy.

"NO! I am NOT doing it," Rose screamed hysterically.

With that, both chauffer—Sandy—and accompaniment—Chris' friend and her fiancée—drove off. Either they found another place in Kelowna to stay for the night, or they spent the night driving back home to Trail. Either way, Rose was glad they were gone.

Rose remembered nothing further about that evening or the following day(s).

The week before school started Rose hooked up with a couple her own age who was staying at the same motel. The three of them had a few beers and a chat most every day. Rose had just started getting her bearings at school when her beloved Don called and said he would be coming for a visit. Rose was so excited she couldn't stop talking about it, not to her new friends or herself.

All decked out in a new outfit, just for the occasion, Rose started cooking dinner at around noon. She wanted to make the best dang dinner she could think of ... spaghetti, meatballs, and a green salad. In order to do that, she would have to cook the sauce all day.

At 6:00 pm, thinking her dinner guest would be arriving soon, Rose thought: *Let's see ... he's off work at four. It's a two hour drive ...*

Rose put the water on for the pasta, and instantly, her inner demons were off and running.

He's not coming Rose. You know he's not coming, right?

By 7:00 pm ... *where is he? He should be here by now!* By then Rose had refilled the pasta water thrice. *Maybe I should just cook the pasta now ... yes ... why not? Hopefully, he will arrive soon, but if he doesn't, I can cool the cooked pasta in cold water, so it doesn't all stick together and then just reheat it once he's here.*

But Rose . . . he is NOT coming. You know he is not coming. Why would he visit a loser like you?

By 8:00 pm, Rose was starting to lose it, pacing back and forth attempting to fight off an obsessional self-loathing that refused to relent.

Eventually, Rose went over to her new friends' place and asked them if they would like to have dinner with her.

"Sure," they'd said carefully avoiding Rose's eyes. "We'll be there in a minute."

"Great, I'll go heat-up the food," said Rose to her friends as her many voices conversed among themselves.

They know ... they know Rose. They know he is not coming. Aren't you humiliated? You should be humiliated.

You are SO pathetic.

Yes ... maybe I am pathetic but ... he still might come.

Once Rose's friends arrived, they had dinner and a couple of beers. After spending some time speculating on what might have happened to Rose's boyfriend, Rose's friends left. They said they had to get up early the next morning. Rose did not believe her friends. She figured they just wanted to escape. As soon as they stood up to leave, Rose began to dread having to be alone with her thoughts ... her voices.

Eventually, come 10:00 pm, Rose's Prince Charming arrived.

Rose never asked why he was late. She pretended his arrival had unfolded as expected.

The only thing Rose remembered from the entire weekend was him dropping her off at school on Monday morning. She had wanted to skip, to spend more time with him, but he said no. He insisted she go to her classes as she was supposed to.

Shortly after Don's visit, the young couple Rose had befriended suggested they introduce her to a friend of theirs.

"He's really good-looking and he has a convertible. Maybe he could take us for a ride?"

Totally ignoring the fact that she already had a boyfriend, Rose said yes.

Come Saturday, a preppy, surfer-looking dude pulled up in front of Rose's friends' place in a very expensive-looking white convertible. Rose didn't find the guy all that attractive. He was blond, and not her type, but he did have a dreamy car, so Rose headed over, intros were made, and they were off.

It was a beautiful, sunny day, so they drove in the open air, all over the place. Sitting atop of the backseat, wind in her hair, Rose fancied herself a movie star, doing what movie stars did.

After an afternoon of driving around, they went to a bar for a few. After that, it was decided that they would all go skinny dipping.

WHAT? Rose silently screamed, taken aback at the suggestion. *What should I do?* And then it began.

Of course, you should go, Rose. Everyone else is going. What's wrong with you Rose?

Why are you even thinking about it?
Movie stars go skinny dipping all the time.
Are you too shy? Are you too insecure?
You are too fat, Rose. You will look ridiculous. Don't go.
Well ... it's not like they are perfect, and they are going.
What's the big deal? Just go ... don't be such a chicken shit.
You're right ... I will go. Who cares if I am fat? Who cares
if I look hideous. They asked me to join them so I will join them.
Everyone else is going to, so why not, right ... right?

So, despite herself, Rose stripped off her clothes—all of them—and went running into the water, but she did it in a huge flurry. She did it quickly, between breaths, so she didn't have time to experience what she was doing. The water was freezing. Did she stay in long? Rose didn't remember. All she could remember was that by going skinny-dipping, she must have given the guy the wrong impression, because the four of them ended up back at his place, some big house he was staying at. Rose didn't really want to go—be there—but she had no way to get home and she did not know where, exactly, she was.

Rose did not sleep a wink. Sickened and dialoguing with herself non-stop, Rose just lay there trying to pretend she was dead, but it wasn't working.

No, Rose, it is not rape unless you've said no. You have to
say no first.

You are such an idiot, Rose.
Fine ... I hate myself. Is that what you want to hear?

Rose didn't recall how or when she got back to the motel. All she remembered was how bloody disgusted she, and everyone else in her head, was with what had happened. But, in having done such a thing to herself ... after that she avoided her friends, and whilst avoiding them, they moved away.

Rose kept pretty much to herself for a while after that. She went to school regularly. She was doing okay in her classes. She'd taken typing in high school, so it was just a matter of getting her speed up. Rose found the accounting course a little confusing. It took her ages to get the whole credit and debit thing straight. She didn't much care for Pitman shorthand, far too much memorization. The girls Rose went to school with were nice enough. She didn't befriend any of them, but she didn't dislike any of them either. She went to a school dance by herself, but she would never do that again. She'd felt far too conspicuous.

In time, Rose began chatting with a random selection of girls staying at the motel. They didn't do much, mostly they just hung out, had a few drinks at the motel or at a nearby bar. One night, after a few, Rose called her mom—collect of course—from the bar. She ended up crying and carrying on, about what, Rose wouldn't remember. All she remembered was that her mom suggested she should get in touch with an aunt and uncle—one of her dad's sisters and brother-in-law—who lived close by. Lonely as she was, Rose got in touch with them.

From then on, every Sunday afternoon, Rose's cousin—the same age as Rose's oldest little brother—came to pick Rose up. Rose would spend the afternoon there and then after dinner her cousin would drive her back to the motel. It was always so peaceful and calm at their house. Rose could relax, be herself and not worry about anything as they chatted and had a few laughs. Rose enjoyed it a lot. Her cousin tied his own fly-fishing flies, and he turned one into a brooch for Rose. Rose wore it until it broke.

With the exception of her calling her mom from the bar, all was relatively calm and quiet until Christmas was around the corner. Most everyone at the motel was going home for the holidays. Rose had no interest in doing that. Instead, she thought it might be fun to spend Christmas with her boyfriend.

"What do you think? Can I come?"

"I live in a residence and my room is really small, but I guess, if you really want to ..."

It was set. Rose had a plan: a very exciting plan she got busy making plans for. She bought her boyfriend the most awesome ski sweater for Christmas. She wished they'd had two sweaters, so she could get one for herself, but they didn't so ... she gave it to him. She brought her skis, poles, and ski boots with her so she could go skiing while her boyfriend was at work. She had been carting her skis, boots, and poles around since she left home ... *probably for this very occasion*, Rose mused to herself, self-assuredly. Yes, Rose had everything worked out.

She'd catch the Greyhound. She and her Don would spend Christmas together, and then they would travel back, in his car, to visit relatives. By New Year's Eve they would be back. A giant New Year's Eve party had been planned and the two of them certainly couldn't miss that. Rose was convinced everything was going to be perfect, turn out just like it did in the movies ... What about Willie? Someone at the motel agreed to feed him while Rose was away.

On the afternoon or evening when Rose arrived, all was good. Their first overnight together, not so good. The room was very small, and Don felt really weird about everyone knowing Rose was in there with him. As such, for the rest of Rose's stay, they lived in a friend's place who was away. It was a nice place, but it was so far away from everything and everyone. All Rose had for eight or nine hours a day was a TV. The one day she decided to go skiing, Don was livid. Manning Park was an hour east of Hope and an hour west of Princeton so ...

"Now there is no gas in the car? Great! How are we going to make it to the gas station?"

Rose felt horrible, full of shameful remorse. She hadn't given the gas thing a moment's thought and she hadn't even gone skiing. Upon arriving at the ski hill, Rose didn't even get out of the car. All she did was sit and cry till she turned around and went back to the house. She did not want to go skiing alone.

Christmas morning was nothing special. It was just the two of them. Don liked his sweater, so that was good. Rose got a handwritten gift certificate to a weekend anywhere in B.C. that she wanted to go. Rose had offered to cook them their own Christmas dinner. She would have so loved to impress Don with her cooking, her homemaking skills, but he had said it was a waste. They might just as well have their Christmas dinner: turkey and the fixings at the resident lodge with everyone else. And so, it was.

Their trip back home was a little too exciting in that they were driving in a blinding snowstorm and nearly plunged off a cliff on several occasions. Once back in their hometown, they couldn't find a place to stay. Either there were no vacancies, or the owner wouldn't rent a room to them. Everyone knows everyone—and everyone's business—when you come from a small town. The couple ended up having to backtrack until they found something. After that first night, they stayed at a friend's place, Don's friend, not Rose's.

Rose called her mom while she was in town. Rose was surprised when her mom sounded glad to hear from her as opposed to mad. Rose said she'd probably pop by for a visit, but she never did. When push came to shove Rose couldn't go visit her mom. She just couldn't. How could she look her mom in the face after all she'd done? Rose was convinced her mom was better off without her, so she let her no-show go.

Once back to Manning Park, it must have been a wait till the New Year's Eve party, but all Rose remembered next was being at that frigging New Year's Eve party, going into the kitchen and catching Don smooching it up with some other girl. Rose saw them but she did not say a word. She turned around, grabbed her coat, and in dire, desolate, despair walked three miles in the freezing cold, back to where she and Don had been staying. There, she packed up her stuff and went out to the highway to catch the 3:00 am Greyhound back to her motel. All this Rose did while softly crying.

'Twas not till she boarded the bus that Rose began to cry uncontrollably.

Once back at the motel, Rose was demolished. She lay in bed crying inconsolably for weeks. She managed to get out of bed and go for wine and smokes, every now and again, but school ... no can do. Eventually, Rose wrote her boyfriend a searingly poignant—pathetically pity-inducing—letter and for effect, she charred the edges around the paper her letter was written on, expensive vellum writing paper Rose bought specifically for the purpose.

The only reason Rose went to school was for the money, so it was no surprise when she had to pay a visit to the manager of the motel.

"I am so sorry but ... I have no idea how I am going to pay this month's rent."

In response, the manager suggested a roommate. A young girl, Rose's age, had arrived through the holiday to start school at the beginning of the semester, and the manager thought it might be more affordable for them both if they shared a two-bedroom, rather than each pay for a single.

The girls became roommates. It was party time.

Neither of the girls went to school much but they sure did go to the bar a lot. Once, when they were out of toilet paper and only had five dollars between them, they went to the bar for five dollars' worth and stole toilet paper out of the women's can. And once again, totally inebriated this time, Rose called her mom—collect—from the bar. Even as she hung up the phone, Rose had no idea why she'd called or what had transpired.

Next morning …

Why Rose ... why do you do such stupid shit?

I don't know ... I really don't know.

Well STOP! You really have to stop!

After a good internal-dialogue-thrashing, Rose promised herself she would not call her mom from the bar ever, ever, again. Yes, Rose's little voices could always be depended upon to critique and condemn.

Rose's roommate was only in town a couple of months before she quit school and went back home. When that happened, the motel manager arranged for Rose and Willie to move in with three other students who were sharing a unit that slept four. The master bedroom was occupied by a male student, and the kid's room containing three single beds, accommodated three girls of which Rose was one. It worked out. While it probably goes without saying that the party of four and assorted friends partied far too much, apart from not attending classes on a regular basis, Rose did not get herself into trouble. She'd gained a lot of weight. Her complexion, once again, had deteriorated, and she'd gone on a few dates she should not have, but, by and large, given friends to keep her distracted, she was okay.

At some point Rose's family came to town to visit the aunt, uncle, and cousin she had grown so fond of. With that, her aunt was bound and determined Rose should reunite with her family.

"Come on Rose, you haven't seen your family in a very long time and your mom has already said that she really wants to see you."

"Oh, I don't know, Auntie ... I don't really want to."

"Your cousin is leaving now. He will be there in twenty minutes to pick you up."

"Okay."

"Good then dear. I'll see you in a little while."

"Ya, see you soon but ... are you sure Mom isn't mad?"

"Yes, Rose, I am sure. She is not mad at you."

Rose was so scared ... so freaking scared to see her mom. She hadn't seen her mom in ages, and she knew she looked far from her best. As it turned out, however, the visit went fine. Nobody talked about the past or anything hard. They just shot the breeze. It was good. Rose and her mom were back in touch. Every so often Rose's mom would phone Rose and Rose would phone her mom from the motel, not the bar.

As the school year was ending, everyone was packing up and getting ready to go back home. Rose did not finish her business course, so she did not receive a diploma or certificate of completion. The whole exercise, once again, had been a gargantuan waste of time, and Rose had no idea what she was going to do next.

Now, what am I supposed to do?

The answer to Rose's question arrived in short order. The manager of the motel asked Rose if she would be interested in working at the motel for the summer. Because the summer season was always so busy, every summer the motel manager hired an assistant manager to help her. If Rose agreed, she would move into the house with her—the manager—a woman in her early forties whose husband was chronically ill—in the hospital—and her two kids, an eight-year-old boy and a five-year-old girl. Her room and board would be free, and she'd pay Rose four hundred dollars a month.

"Are you kidding me? Of course I am interested. I'd love it. Thank you, thank you so very much." Rose was ecstatic. Summer was right around the corner, and she could see herself be-bopping around the motel looking all tanned and svelte, meeting all those tanned good-looking guys with money— enough money to be staying in a motel on the beach of such a party town.

The first thing Rose felt she needed to do in preparation for the upcoming summer influx of hot guys, was get a tan. Because she worked all day, Rose decided her best bet was to buy a sunlamp. That way she could get a decent tan in the evening after she'd retired to her bedroom for the night. Personal sunlamps have long since been banned, but back in the day, in bold letters, a warning appeared:

CAUTION: **Do not use for longer than 10 minutes**
Do not use without eye protection
DO NOT FALL ASLEEP WHILE LAMP IS IN OPERATION

'Twas good advice. Rose had been using the lamp for a while and she was beginning to develop quite a nice little glow when she got just a little too comfortable with the process. She fell asleep, face side up for … however long she fell asleep.

Rose believed what finally woke her up was an unconscious attempt to move out of the way. Whatever woke her up, and

THANK GOD SHE FINALLY WOKE UP, the front part of her body was burnt to a flaming crisp and … with eyes wide open, she could not see a gall darn thing. She was blind. And so, it started.

Oh GOD, Rose, how can you be so freaking stupid?
Now you are going to get fired because you can't see.
Your boss is going to be SO mad at you.
Heartbroken, Rose moved the light out of the way and decided to go to bed.
Maybe my eyes will be better in the morning.

Ever the optimist, Rose shut her eyes and willed herself to sleep much as she did when she was young. She pretended that she was dead.

Upon opening her eyes in the morning, Rose thought that maybe her eyes were a bit—emphasis on the bit—better but she still couldn't see. Instead of everything being black, as it was the night before, everything was white, completely white. Rose heard voices down in the kitchen, so she got up, got dressed and then, using geographical memory, managed to go downstairs.

In the doorway of the kitchen, Rose sheepishly fessed up to whoever was present. Was Rose's boss pissed? Rose thought so. To Rose, she had sounded pissed, but was she really or did Rose just interpret her as being pissed because she had expected her to be pissed?

Rose carried on as best as she could and slowly, very slowly, over a matter of weeks, her vision was back. The only difference for the next while—the next few years—was Rose needed to wear sunglasses for function rather than fashion.

Rose's job at the motel had not turned out as Rose hoped. It was neither glamorous nor exciting. The manager was always out with her doctor boyfriend, so Rose was always home alone tending to the manager's kids while she tended to all her many other tasks, like answering calls, taking bookings, showing and renting out rooms, cleaning the house, doing laundry, cooking meals, and cleaning up afterwards. Rather than being the assistant manager, Rose felt she had been hired on as servant, slave, and babysitter.

If nothing much was happening at the motel and Rose had something she wanted to do, she could usually get the day off, but she did not have any regular days off. She was on duty twenty-four seven unless other arrangements had been made. Arrangements were rarely made because everyone Rose had known had moved once school was out. Rose was friendless, sad, and lonely. Mostly she just watched TV and ate junk food in her bedroom, after she had gotten the manager's kids to bed. Rose didn't remember if she continued going to her aunt and uncle's on Sundays, after she had started at the motel, or not.

In needing something but not knowing what it was … Rose had a rendezvous or two, with a guy or two, staying at the motel, but they'd been temporary lapses in judgement and Rose hated herself for them both, paid dearly for them by way of self-addressed scorn.

One morning, after a late-night tryst, Rose woke up with her entire face covered with tiny red bumps that itched like crazy. She could barely stand it. Her manager thought it was swimmer's itch, but Rose hadn't been swimming so ... Rose thought it was either . . . she was allergic to the guy she'd been with, or she had got it when she lay in the sand. The weirdest part ... it was only on her face. Rose got exactly the same rash on her face a couple more times that summer but had no recollection of what those occasions were connected to.

One day, in wanting to snap herself out of her funk, Rose decided to go to Vernon, so she asked for the day off. No, Rose did not know anyone in Vernon, and she had never been there, but she had heard it was a nice place so she thought she would go check it out. It was only about an hour, by car, away.

Maybe there will be something fun for me there?

Rose got herself fixed up as best she could and then took the bus to highway 97, the main drag out of town where she stuck out her thumb and began hoping for a ride. Everyone hitch-hiked, all the time, back then. It was usually no big deal. This time, however, Rose was picked up by a guy who had no door handles on the inside of his car. The only door handle in the entire car was next to him, by the driver's seat. He said he'd removed them to prevent his kids from opening the doors, but Rose didn't believe him. She was freaked out. She thought for sure he must have been a rapist, murderer, or serial killer, so she asked to be let out at the next gas station. Rose was so surprised when he did. The gas station he'd stopped at was beside a Dairy Queen, so Rose, disappointed that her planned excursion to Vernon had been kiboshed, stopped for a chocolate sundae before making her way back to the motel.

Can't go to Vernon ... may as well have a chocolate sundae.

'Twas around about this time that Rose decided if she was going to do anything about her lackluster life, she needed a car, a car of her own.

Since Rose and her mom had been doing okay as of late, Rose thought, *Maybe Mom will lend me money to buy a car. Why not? I'm working?*

There was no way, however, that Rose could ask her mom for money over the phone. No way. Rose was far too afraid to do that. What if her mom gave her a hard time, or worse yet, she said no? Rose didn't think she would be able to handle that so ... she decided to write her mom a letter saying how bored and lonely she was, how she had no friends and how a car would really pick up her life. Rose was so excited after she mailed that letter. She could see it all now.

I'll be like a star. Everyone will be so impressed.

It didn't take long for Rose to get a response to her letter.

"No, Rose, I will not lend you money to buy a car. You are working now so I think you should save up your money like everyone else has to." Rose's mom also advised her daughter that in sounding so down in the dumps, she should perhaps seek counselling.

Rose was furious, furious, and very, very hurt because she thought that she and her mom had been getting along very well as of late.

What a bitch! Can't she see I am at least trying?

Once Rose fully accepted the fact that her mom was not going to help her, Rose had to figure out a new strategy. With an advance on her paycheque—for the down payment—Rose financed the purchase of an older Vega station wagon—red—through a local credit union.

"Guess what, Mom ... I bought myself a car and ... I was thinking ... if I drive over, I can show you it and maybe visit with my friends while I am in town."

Although Rose did not find the appearance of her car ideal, it was still a car—a fairly impressive acquisition.

Rose made several trips back home that summer. It was so nice to be among friends, people she knew who knew her. She felt so isolated and alone in Kelowna.

Almost every night, with her own car, Rose would cruise the empty roads at the edge of town—Kelowna's urban interfaces—instead of lying on her bed eating junk food and watching TV. The roads were wild and dark, but Rose loved it. She was forever seeing faces in the clouds and feeling invisible animals run past her. Rose even bought herself a camera in the hope of capturing her nightscapes. She took millions of pictures and that was back when you had to develop an entire roll of film prior to being able to see what you'd captured.

I wonder why my camera won't pick up what my eyes do.

Rose would be very disappointed that her pictures didn't reveal what her eyes did. She wanted to show people what she saw, what came alive as everything else slept. Unfortunately, Rose never took note of how happy she was while out on her own, fully engaged in something curiously interesting, something she enjoyed, and Rose *really* enjoyed taking pictures.

It was because Rose finally had her own car that she decided it was time she started to cruise the beaches of the swanky tourist town she had moved to, so she took an afternoon off, to scout the public beach in town. Rose was sure—absolutely sure—that it would be there, if anywhere, that she would meet *the one*—someone who could—would—sweep her off her feet, take her away and forever love her to bits.

In the hope of reaching her ends, Rose got herself arranged on a beach mat with suntan lotion, a couple of magazines and her shades. Lying there, looking gorgeous, a guy around her own age, wandered up beside her.

As they chatted, Rose could tell by his comments that he was sizing her up.

"Ya, you are not bad. You're cute enough, but you are a bit fat. You'd have to lose some weight if you wanted to be my girl. You could work on that though, right?"

Yes, his comment had hurt Rose's feelings, but she knew he was right so …

He then asked if Rose was interested in getting together later that night.

"Sure," Rose responded all googly-eyed, thinking that this could be it. He could be the one. He picked a time and a place, so on the way home, Rose stopped to buy a new outfit and some new lipstick. Although fat, she wanted to look her best. She was so excited.

Rose and her fantasy man met at a bar he suggested, at a pre-arranged time. During the date, they sat with a group of people Rose didn't know, but after a beer she was fine. She actually won a beer guzzling contest. Then, after plans were made to hook-up again the following evening, Rose drove herself home.

Upon arriving back at the house, Rose knew she was far too drunk to go through the front door. She didn't want to wake up the household, so she decided to go in through her bedroom window. After carefully removing the screen and sliding open the window, Rose hoisted herself through the window. Only as she slipped, with her wrist coming down on the sheered shard of glass in the bottom right-hand corner of the frame, did Rose remember that a large piece of the sliding glass window was stuck in the bottom right-hand corner of the frame. There was blood everywhere because blood was gushing from the corner of her left wrist. In her drunken stupor, Rose wrapped gauze tightly around and around her wrist to stop the bleeding.

Oh well ... I will deal with it properly in the morning.

Needless to say, by morning the gauze was glued solid to Rose's messily sliced wrist. There was no way the gauze was coming off for an inspection. Totally humiliated, Rose had no option but to slink downstairs to the kitchen and tell her tale of woe, totally leaving out the fact that she had been drinking. With this, her boss's doctor boyfriend drove Rose to his office where he removed the gauze and stitched up her wrist. He didn't freeze it because ...

"It probably already hurts as much as stitching it up will."

He was right, and Rose ended up with a wack of stitches. The scar lingered on, as a reminder of her daftness.

Sometime during the day, Rose's new prospect called to say he was staying in a tent at some park and wanted to know if Rose wanted to meet him there. Any trepidation Rose may have experienced was more than abated by her collection of concerned commentators.

Why not, Rose? It will be fine.

Off she went. This time, however, Rose actually managed to say: "No," and she kept saying no until he stopped.

"What do you mean NO! Why else would you have come here?"

Rose felt so stupid—so incredibly stupid—and humiliated, yet again. This time, at least, she had said no and had a way to escape. Rose did not go to that beach—or any other beach—again.

After that, Rose relegated herself to nighttime drives only. She needed to keep herself out of harm's way till she could get herself out of that god-forsaken place. Kelowna had neither been fun nor exciting and it was definitely not full of beautiful people. It was the same old, same old.

Thankfully, Rose's summer motel job was coming to an end, and as far as Rose was concerned, it was none too soon. She couldn't wait to leave it *all* behind—again—but how was she going to do it this time …?

Rose didn't want her leaving to look like she'd failed, once again, so she had to come up with a plan. After putting on her thinking cap, she came up with what she thought was a brilliant idea. She would invite Jerry and Annie to come for a visit during her last week at the motel. It could be like a little holiday for them, a week away from Mom and Dad. She had a little money saved so ...

"I'll take them around, show them a good time."

Rose figured they could hang out at the beach while she was at work, then she could take them out to do fun stuff. The motel was pretty empty by then, so Rose's boss said they could use one of the rooms for free.

Why not, thought Rose. *It'll be fun for us all. They can take the bus up and then I will move back home when I drive them home.*

Perfect, Rose. That's a perfect idea.

Rose called her mom to share the idea. Her mom was skeptical, but eventually, with a little help from Jerry and Annie, she consented. Rose's mom and dad would drive them up and then Rose would drive them home a week later. It was set.

Other than a fight between Jerry and Annie that resulted in a screen door being slammed so hard it cracked, Rose believed Jerry and Annie had a pretty good time. They went to the beach, ate in restaurants. Rose took them shopping, got them each a new outfit and a haircut. Rose had to store some of her stuff at the motel, but she told the manager she would be back to collect things in fairly short order. They had fun, and then they packed it all up and headed home.

A year and two months after Rose arrived, she was headed back home again.

A long time ago, one of my male friends said, "Rose ... you are like a rock."

For the longest time, I had no idea what he meant. I didn't know if he was complimenting me or insulting me. I do know now, however, exactly what he had meant. Rocks, in not having emotions, are incapable of expressing them. Although I did have emotions—very strong ones—I never, ever, allowed my painful ones out. Allowing myself to appear vulnerable was something I just could not do.

When I think about all the delusions of grandeur that I indulged in, I am given to wonder where it all came from. Had I, indeed, been Queen of Sheba in a past life? Rumour had it that my birth mother, to a degree, suffered from similar delusions. Could I have gotten it from her or ... had I watched too much television, read too many issues of *Cosmopolitan* magazine? Maybe I got it via osmosis, from the dreams and aspirations of my mom ... Mom for herself or for herself through me? Whatever it was, my believing I should live and love among rich, famous—beautiful people—sure did a number on me.

I was frantic—spinning like a top—trying to find someone, something, anything, that would take me where I wanted to go, so I could be happy. I thought what I needed was "out there" and I had to find it, or stumble across it, somehow, somewhere. Not once, did it ever occur to me that what I was looking for might be inside of me. If only I had pursued myself as hard as I pursued everything but ...

Thinking back on Mom deciding not to lend me money to buy a car, I cannot now help but think that she did exactly the right thing. I needed—desperately needed—to learn how to do things for myself, by myself ... and even though the car thing was the infamous coat thing all over again, I was very proud of myself for having gotten it all by myself.

Were those wild dark energies that I could neither classify nor comprehend but soulfully savoured on those lonely roads at the edge of town, trying to tell me something? Were they calling to the frightened little voice inside of me, asking me to please open the door and face my ghosts, stand firm against—fight—that which I couldn't see, that which haunted me?

The longer I ignored the meek little voice inside of me, the louder, more insistent my hungry, scared, self-serving, self-loathing voices became. Back and forth, back and forth they argued until there was such a cacophony inside my head, numbing myself out was my only source of relief. And so ... I drank. I drank a lot. It wasn't the booze that led me to my ridiculously misguided—harmful—decisions and behaviours. I drank in order to cope with the consequences of the ridiculously misguided—harmful—decisions and behaviours that continued to drive me to remain so lost, alone, and terribly confused. In not knowing what else to do with myself, using and losing myself in time seemed to be my only option. Are people who party all the time happy? I sure as hell wasn't!

Below is an old memetic legend attributed to an unknown Cherokee elder. To my mind, it says it all.

A fight is going on inside of us all.
It is a fight between two wolves.
One is evil—he is anger, envy, greed, arrogance,
resentment, lies and ego.
The other is good—he is joy, peace, love, hope,
serenity, humility, kindness, empathy, generosity,
truth, compassion and faith.
The wolves are fighting to the death.
Which wolf wins?
The one you feed.

29

FROM TRAIL TO VANCOUVER
No Matter Where You Go, You Bring Yourself With You

*H*ome again, home again, jiggety-jig.
      Rose's homing device knew of nowhere else to go when she needed to regroup. It was her starting point. She had partners in pain there, so once she was back … it was on with the show.

Rose was only in her parents' rumpus room for a day or two before she was off and running again. Although she and her buddy Chris had been on the outs since Rose started dating her brother Don, being the friends that they were, they sorted it. They sorted it out enough to decide that together, they would accompany their flatlander friends during their bi-annual trek back to the prairies.

Rose knew she needed to go back to Kelowna, from whence she had come, in order to collect and fill out her unemployment insurance cards, but after that, she'd be free and clear for two whole weeks. You see, after Rose was laid off from the motel, she was once again eligible for UI benefits. All she had to do was fill out her cards every two weeks. That way, she would have minimal income till she found a new job.

"It's okay, Mom, Annie said she would look after Willie for me."

And so it was, a quick detour to pick up and sign Rose's UI cards, and the girls hit the road.

It was a long, long way to the prairies. They did an overnight at a friend of Chris's whose place was empty as they were passing through. Yes, they'd received prior permission. It took two full days of driving to get where they were going, but Rose and Chris had a dandy time laughing, crying, eating in restaurants, and drinking beer en route.

The reception the girls experienced upon their arrival could not have been more hospitable. Everybody's families were so nice. The girls—Rose and Chris—had such fun during their wild and crazy time in a small prairie town. The only downer was that while Rose was away, her beloved Willie went missing. It was suggested that a racoon might have gotten him because, one night, he did not make it home and he hadn't been seen since.

"Poor guy. I hope it was quick."

Rose was sad about losing her Willie but … never mind, the show must go on, and so it did.

Upon returning from their adventure, Chris decided to move to the big city—Vancouver—where her boyfriend's new job had taken him, and so, *what the heck*, thought Rose, maybe I should move there too.

"What think? Can I come with?"

"Why not? That's where we should have moved in the first place … right?"

"Right."

"To the future!"

Rose was once again full of hope as she and Chris cheered with their friends in the bar on the eve of their departure.

The girls moved in with Chris's boyfriend and his room-mate. Once they had jobs, they would find a place of their own. Chris and her boyfriend shared the hide-a-bed in the living room, and Rose took the single bed in the bedroom that Chris's boyfriend had vacated. Only problem … the boyfriend's roommate hated Rose.

One day, he packed up all of Rose's stuff, put it in the elevator and pressed the button sending it all down to the lobby. Everyone laughed but … Rose got the message. It hurt, but Rose had nowhere else to go, so she stayed.

While Chris lay on the couch, smoking cigarettes, eating bonbons, and answering ads in the newspaper by telephone, Rose charged around town, job interview, after job interview, like a lunatic.

Chris got a cushy government job with fabulous wages and Rose got squat. As a result, Rose was available and getting desperate when her mom called about a job at a finance company in her hometown.

"What with your new secretarial skills, Rose, you'll be a shoo-in."

No, Rose hadn't briefed her mom on her failure to receive a diploma or certificate of completion. She couldn't see the point in telling her mom how big of a failure she was. Her mom already knew. Although Rose hated to do it, she packed up her stuff and moved back home. What option did she have? She'd tried like a mad woman to find a job but … it just wasn't happening. And so, Rose's big city adventure was over. Roughly a month after Rose's third attempt at moving away, she was headed back. 'Twas short but not sweet.

Home again, home again, jiggety-jig.

W hile treading water, while being aimlessly pushed and pulled from here to there, and back again by my swirling eddies of unfulfilled needs and desires, I coped or kept myself occupied via one of three things: I worked on some half-baked plan that needed my time and attention to execute; I self-medicated; or I willed myself to sleep. Those were the only things I knew how to do, so I carried on doing them, hoping for the best.

30

LOVE AT LAST
Dashed Dreams

Rose got the office job with the finance company in town that her mom had alerted her to. She was at the front desk fielding calls, typing up paperwork, and calling delinquent clients. Rose liked it okay. Her boss was really nice.

This time around, Rose found her own place posthaste. She needed to live on her own. Nobody said anything, but then, nobody had to, everybody knew all too well. She ended up renting a rundown, old guesthouse at the back of an older Christopher Walken looking guy's yard. It was a tiny two-bedroom place that needed work, but Rose fixed it up to her liking. The basics were already there: fridge, stove, table, and chairs. She made lace curtains for the kitchen and her dad helped her with laying old indoor/outdoor carpeting wall to wall. She painted three walls of her living room black and installed red flocked wallpaper on the fourth. Her mom gave her an old sectional. The bed in the main bedroom was already there, and the bed in the second—spare—bedroom was one she pinched when Don helped her collect her stored stuff from the motel.

Why had it been Don that helped her retrieve her stuff? Rose figured it probably had something to do with the gift certificate (to go anywhere in B.C. that she wanted to go) that Don had given her the Christmas before.

Rose was happy in her little place. It had the same sort of eerie atmosphere as the drives she loved to take on the empty roads at the edge of Kelowna. She could hear—but not see—critters scurrying around in the walls and the attic. Very often at night, while walking through her landlord's yard to get to her little house, Rose would feel something watching her, standing, or passing near her, but instead of continuing to marvel in the magical, mystical manifestations she could feel but not see, Rose started to become nervous ... she began to question the inherent benevolence of her unseen world.

Who ... what ... are you?
Show me yourself.
What do you want?

Rose had become unsure of whether, or not, who or whatever was watching her was intending to do her harm. She'd glance back at her landlord's house, but as creepy looking as the guy was, no, that wasn't it.

Rose had heard her name called from undisclosed locations many, many times since that first time, when she was a child. Most often, she would casually look around for an answer to her quandary. If there were people about, she would look deeply into their faces in an attempt to determine if it had been they who had called her while pretending not to, but Rose could never figure out from whence the voice arrived. By this stage of the game, Rose had gone from hearing her name being called to feeling as if she was being watched. And while Rose had never liked to be in bed without light streaming in, Rose could no longer sit in her well-lit bathroom's claw-foot tub without the door open. Rose always needed an escape route, an escape from what Rose did not know. She just needed one.

And at night, if tangled up in her bedclothes or sheets, Rose would wake up flailing around in a panic. If she happened to get stuck while putting on or taking off a shirt or dress, Rose would be like a wild animal till she freed herself. It got to the point where, in elevators, Rose would have to hold her breath and shut her eyes. Closed stairwells were even worse. Rose would move as quickly and quietly as she could to get the hell out of there. Rose's fear of being watched, of having some-one—something—jump out at her, became almost overwhelming. She'd have to talk herself down every time.

One night, as Rose was about to jump into bed, she glanced in the mirror above her bed and saw the face of a dark bearded and mustachioed man staring at her. Rose thought she should have recognized him, but she didn't. She was so freaked out. 'Twas as if her apparition knew her, saw right through her. Rose was so shaken she could not look in the mirror again that night. She just slid into bed, under the mirror and went to sleep, willed herself to sleep as quickly as she could. In the light of day, Rose took the mirror down and stashed it in a big blue trunk in her spare bedroom. She had wanted to toss it, but she couldn't. It had been her gran's.

Rose wondered if maybe something bad had happened in her little house. Maybe her little house was haunted by someone that had died or lost their mind there. It was weird and crazy, but Rose made peace with it, she made peace with her poltergeists because it was her own little house. It was her little hide-away and she loved it.

Rose worked by day, partied by night. Chris, of course, wasn't there, but all the other members of her former contingent were, so Rose had comrades with whom to casually commune. Things were humming along nicely until … Rose found out she was pregnant. Who was the father? It mattered not because—whoever it was—they were long gone.

With Chris no longer around and Rose not having been back in town long enough for the cement to have dried on her current contacts, who could Rose tell? Tell her mom? How could Rose tell her mom she wanted to undo something her mom and dad had tried so long—so hard—to do? Rose was alone, completely alone.

Shortly after, Rose was admitted to the maternity ward where she could hear all the new babes crying. She was sobbing almost uncontrollably by the time her doctor came to wheel her away.

"You know, Rose, it is not too late to change your mind."

But Rose shook her head, unable to get any words out. And so, it was done. Rose did not recall how long she was in the hospital, or for how long she was off work or what she had said her problem was. All Rose remembered was her feeling of emptiness—complete and utter emptiness—as if part of herself had been surgically removed. Well, in a way ... it had.

It wasn't long after Rose's abortion and she was back to work when Clifford, the Samoyed dog, Rose's canine sidekick, arrived on the scene. One morning, a young girl came into Rose's office carrying a huge ball of fluffy white fur with big brown eyes begging to be appropriated.

"Anyone want a puppy?"

How could Rose refuse? He was so cute and all the little furball needed was a home, someone who wanted—loved—him. Rose knew she could do that.

Clifford loved car rides. He loved visiting. He was a little too fond of leather shoes, but given his other attributes, Rose was able to overlook that. Rose and Clifford became inseparable. He was the only one Rose trusted, and she trusted him implicitly.

Every so often, the credit union offered its members an opportunity to have a family photograph taken. One year, Rose made an appointment for herself and Clifford to have their photograph taken. To Rose's mind, Clifford was her family. The photographer was not pleased when he learned Clifford was a dog, but after some sweet-talk, he consented. Rose cherished that photo. She had so many good memories of she and Clifford, she, and her big white dog.

Clifford even accompanied Rose on a business trip. Rose's employer had asked her if she would be willing to fill in at their office in Merritt—a tiny community a couple of hundred miles west—until they could find a replacement for their old receptionist.

"Why not? Might be kinda fun … something different."

Rose felt like such a hotshot, travel expenses and a living allowance. Rose couldn't bring herself to chain Clifford up outside while she was at work because it was the winter and far too cold. Instead, she left him in her motel room where he ended up chewing the legs off one of the upholstered chairs. That had cost her a few bucks, but it was worth it. They kept each other company. As a treat, Rose would bring home a Styrofoam cup of gravy every night to pour over her dog's food. Clifford loved it and Rose loved doing it for him.

One day, out of the blue, Rose's manager invited her to come to his parents' place for dinner with him. He still lived at home, and for some reason, wanted Rose to meet his father. It wasn't till after dinner that Rose realized why. His father was a minister, and Rose surmised that he must have wanted to convert her. Whatever the reason, as soon as the Father started talking to Rose about God, Rose started to cry. Not only was the Father astounded at Rose's response, so was Rose.

"Gee whiz … I've never had anyone start to cry on me before."

Rose was so confused. She wasn't religious. By that time Rose thought the whole concept of God was totally ludicrous.

Ya, right, some old guy sitting in the sky passing judgement …

So why had her tears come? Rose didn't get it but from then on, Rose was terribly uncomfortable around her temporary boss. And even though she knew she hadn't revealed anything, she felt like she had revealed far too much.

Rose's first stint at the finance company only lasted about six months. The girl whose place Rose took wanted to come back, and all had been so sad to see her go, they took her back and asked Rose to transfer to a larger office, either east or west, for the same pay. Rose wasn't interested in leaving town. Not for the same money.

Rose's next gig was to be one of the first female labourers hired on by the smelter in town. Due to the conditions and nature of the work, they only hired hefty women to do men's work. Rose was thrilled when she lost fifteen to twenty pounds in the first couple of months. As a shift worker Rose rotated through days, afternoons, and nights as she worked seven on and two off, with an additional day every four rotations.

Her first placement was as a loader operator, someone who loaded zinc slabs onto tiny, specially designed, railway cars. After that, she was a pusher operator. Someone who drove a machine that pushed the little specially designed railway cars to where the zinc slabs would be picked up and shipped. After that, Rose got her forklift license. It was official looking and laminated. Rose was impressed and she loved driving the fork-lift. She felt so powerful and cool as she be-bopped here and there, picking up this and dropping off that. It was great until she accidentally backed over three or four of the carpenters' chainsaws. So ended her forklift career.

"Sorry," didn't cut it. She was transferred to the tank rooms as a tester. This job entailed Rose ensuring the correct chemical composition within each tank—in her many rows of tanks—making sure they were appropriate for the laying of zinc on the aluminum cathodes. Rose thought it was an okay job. The tank rooms were sopping and often very steamy, sticky, stinky, and there was a lot of downtime—which often made the job a trifle boring—but, all in all, how could Rose complain? The money was amazing at thirteen something an hour. For a girl, during that time period, 'twas as if she'd hit the jackpot.

With that job, Rose's life changed considerably. She had to be up and out the door by 6:00 am, so she was forced to cut way back on her partying. Her days off were still pretty much the same: out all night, asleep all day. But that too ended abruptly nary three months into her new job.

Rose met a man whom she adored. A man she knew also adored her. It was love at first sight for the both of them, and it was a miracle, nothing short of a miracle at last. Nick was tall, had dark blond hair, blue eyes, and sported a fairly substantial mustache. He was a Sam Shepard looking type of guy who worked in the tank rooms, like Rose, but he was a puller, he sheered zinc slabs from the aluminum cathodes upon which it formed.

It began with long looks and shy avoidant actions that gradually worked their way into casual, but not so chance encounters. Full consummation occurred after the couple unsuspectedly ran into each other at a nightclub. From that evening forward, Rose and Nick were as one. They were forever together taking Clifford for long walks every night and holding hands as they fell asleep every night.

One day, while Nick was at work, Rose thought she would take Clifford to a park out of town for a run. Prior to doing so, however, she decided to stop for Chinese food. While in the restaurant filling her face, a huge bang rocked the restaurant. As the other patrons started jumping up to see what was afoot, Rose decided she too best see what was going on.

"HEY ... that is my car on fire! It must have been my car that blew up."

HOLY! Thank God, Clifford wasn't in the car!

Rose felt blessed, like she had an angel on her shoulder, because if Clifford had been in that car ...

The fire was attributed to faulty wiring but Rose knew it was probably the dozen or so Bic lighters she'd dropped down the front dash heater. All those lighters in conjunction with the blazing hot sun under which Rose had parked her car, a disaster waiting to happen. After thinking about it for a minute, Rose thought it a miracle her car hadn't blown up earlier. The whole affair turned out to be giant windfall for Rose because she'd paid eighteen hundred for her car and her comprehensive insurance paid her twenty-two hundred.

With cash in Rose's hand, and Nick's little pick-up as a trade-in, the couple bought a used van. What sold them was the white fur rug in the back ... it would be great to sleep on when they went camping.

After the landlord entered Rose's apartment one day and saw the way Rose had decorated the living room of "his" rundown old guest house (three black walls and one with red flocked wallpaper), Rose was evicted. It wasn't that big of a deal because Rose and Nick were planning to move in together anyway.

After much looking, a perfect place was found. It was a modern two-bedroom split-level suite with huge windows over-looking a big, beautiful valley. In love, as they were, Rose and Nick were so excited about their lives together. There was very little drinking, very little doping. Rose left her job so she could throw herself into the Suzy Homemaker scene: cooking, clean-ing, making preserves and fixing their place up. They made a few trips in their van, but with those trips, it soon became appar-ent that the white fur rug they had so loved, was infested with fleas. No matter what the couple did, and they tried everything, they could not get rid of those fleas, so they had to get rid of their van. The van was traded in for a brand spanking new, forest green Honda Civic, which back then cost only seven grand, taxes in. The couple could not have been happier. They were both sure they would be married, together forever, and so did their respec-tive parents. All was well … all was perfectly well until that following spring when Rose got pregnant … again.

Nick did not want another child. He had been married once before and already had a five-year-old son so …

"No, Rose … not now!"

What did Rose want? Well, in order to be happy, Rose needed to keep Nick happy so … she didn't want the new life she was carrying either. Who was Rose going to tell this time? Well, she had let all friendships from her past lapse, as she basked in the throes of near matrimonial bliss. Tell her mom? She couldn't do that.

This time, instead of being placed in the maternity ward, Rose ended up in some sort of pre-op holding tank with one of her uncles—her mom's youngest brother, with whom she hadn't spoken in over a decade.

ARE YOU KIDDING ME?

Rose couldn't believe it. She looked away as fast as she possibly could. Heaven forbid he recognize Rose, his niece, and then run around town trying to figure out why she'd been in pre-op.

The next morning, prior to Rose's release from the hospital, her old boss from the finance company and a trainee he had in tote, spotted Rose in her room as they walked by. Of course, Rose was recognized, so her boss came in and asked her why she was there.

"Oh ... just woman's problems you know."

"Ohhhhhhhhh ... you're having an abortion," he'd said jokingly and laughed.

"Ya right ..." Rose responded as light-hearted as she possibly could, wishing she could morph into one of those stone figurines on Easter Island. *Oh, my freaking God ... how and why does this shit happen?*

Once back home, Rose was greeted with a potted fig tree in the living room. Nick bought it as a means by which to cheer Rose up. She pretended it did. It was a beautiful little tree and it had probably cost a fortune but ...

A fig tree ... a freaking fig tree is supposed to replace our baby?

Rose had no idea that she was going to have the response she had to the taking of her second child's life. She was angry.

Rose was so angry and so sad. She had a terrible time being around babies since her last abortion, always compelled to figure out how old her first would have been had she actually had him or her. But now, after her second, every time Rose heard or saw a baby, her eyes would well up with tears and she would have to look away in order to figure out how old her two babies would be if she'd had them.

No more! The next time I go into a hospital, it will be to have a baby, not kill one.

Thereafter, things stopped working. Rose and Nick were ruined. Less than a year after moving in with the man of her dreams, Rose, Clifford, a fig tree, and the newest addition, Callie the calico cat, packed up and moved out. Rose fell apart.

In hearing my name called from undisclosed locations, was I throwing my voice, was I attempting to jar myself into paying more attention to the fight, the discord, inside of me? Why else would I, or at least a part of me, call myself from inside my own head?

And what of the growing foreboding I began to experience in the ineffable wild dark energies I used to relish, the energies that, in Kelowna, used to call to me. Suddenly these energies had begun to carry a sense of foreboding; I felt watched, trapped, ready to be pounced upon. Why? In refusing to heed their call to self-recognition, had they leapt out of me, hoping that if I felt—saw—them from afar, I would then recognize them, realize them as part of myself—the pain of my self-betrayal? All in due time I suppose, all in due time.

I have marvelled at the twists, turns, and temporary entrenchments that typified my former life. I moved all over the countryside chasing fantasies, but when an employer offered me a tangible new start ... I refused it. Was it the money or ... was it, unfinished business?

Like the synchronicity of randomly seeing "What's His Face" in a bar four-hundred and seventy miles away, six or seven years after the fact, how about finding myself next to an uncle as I awaited an operation? And then having an old boss see me in the hospital after said operation? With the last two, it would not so much be about carrying our world around with us, as it would be ... the eyes of truth are always watching you. There are no secrets ... not really.

The type of fig tree Nick bought me after having our unborn baby aborted was a Weeping Fig. I wonder if Nick knew at that time the type of fig tree that he was buying me or ... was that just another one of those crazy coinky dinks?

Had I truly loved Nick, or had I just been in love with his idealism, his ability to provide me with what I felt I wanted, needed? We were the same in that we were both lost and alone in a world we did not understand. In our disorientation, we indulged in flights of fancy such as living off the land, travelling via Volkswagen van to and through South America, and while doing that, life was good. Once reality set in, however, once our youthful yarns were yanked from us, once our union created a reality neither of us were yet ready to live up to, we were finished. We tried and tried again, but nothing ever stuck. My sense of loss was just too great.

31

A FOUNDATION IS LAID
Still Lost, Alone, and Terribly Confused

This time, there was no *home again, home again, jiggety-jig,* but Rose was, once again, without a job or a place to live.

In desperation, Rose and pets moved into a miniscule hut, a row of which had been built years ago to house army recruits. It was five-hundred square feet, tops, squishy for the three of them but it did the job. And … as luck would have it, the finance company Rose had previously worked for, was once again hiring.

"We would be delighted for you to come back and work for us Rose."

Yes … Rose was once again set, and it was back to the same again. All Rose had missed was a year.

In having done far too much damage—purposeful hanging of shelves—in her tiny little army hut, Rose was evicted after a mere month. What Rose did next—late spring of 1977—was … drumroll please … buy herself a small, very old, and dilapidated house.

"What do you think, Mom and Dad? Will you come look at it with me? It's only ten-thousand dollars"

"Okay, Rose, but … are you sure? It is a huge commitment."

"Oh yes, Mom. I think it is just what I need, something to focus my attention on."

"Okay then, I'll get your uncle to have a look. He's an electrician and can tell us if the house is safe … livable." This was not the same uncle Rose found herself next to in the pre-op holding tank, it was a different uncle—Rose's mom's oldest brother.

After agreeing to assess the home, he said, "It is very old Rose. The electrical is knob and tube, but it looks safe enough. It needs a new roof, and you will have to cut all the vines down and make some repairs before it's painted. The creek running through the basement doesn't seem to be causing a problem. It will make a great root cellar. Yes, I think it's fine."

After paying off two cars, Rose thought the credit union in town would be her best bet for a mortgage, but Rose's mom said her uncle offered to finance the house for her. She would need to treat it as a mortgage—pay one-hundred dollars a month till she had it paid off. That would take her eight plus years, but she hoped she could pay it off earlier.

"But why is he doing it? I hardly know him?"

"Oh … he probably has the money and wants to help you out a bit."

Days later …

"Guess what, everyone? I bought myself a house! I am a homeowner!"

Upon moving in, Rose had to give the house a good cleaning … it was filthy. The basement too, was in a very sorry state but she loved the little creek that ran through it. Rose thought that eventually she'd like to turn her basement into a little grotto, of sorts. Rose knew it was going to take time to fix her little house up—make it her own—but she was in no hurry, she figured she had all the time in the world. With the purchase of her little house ... both Rose's mind and Rose, herself, were fully occupied and entertained.

"Dark brown? You can't paint your whole bedroom dark brown Rose ...?"

"If you don't want to help me, Dad, that's fine but I am painting it dark brown."

Rose's dad helped her paint the bedroom dark brown. Her mom helped her hang wallpaper in the hallway even though she hated the paper Rose chose. It was ceiling to floor pictures of trees.

"Rose it will make the hallway look so narrow ... so dark."

Rose liked the wallpaper because it was going to make her hallway look like the wild and dark, like the empty roads she used to drive. Once it was up, Rose loved it. She thought it looked perfect. She thought her little house was perfect. She loved it.

At some point, Rose tried to re-snag Sandy, but lucky for him, he didn't bite. He had gone off to train for his dream job, and then worked in the bush for a while prior to arriving back in town with a new girlfriend. That didn't stop Rose from trying though. Sandy was working an afternoon shift for the railway in town when Rose thought it a good idea to sit in her car and wait till his shift was over so she could accost him—talk to him—without his girlfriend present.

Problem … Rose got her car stuck in the snow before she could park it next to his in the staff parking lot. After her own efforts proved pointless, Rose went for help. She rounded up a security guard who grabbed a shovel and headed back to Rose's car with her.

"But WHAT are you doing out here by yourself at this time of night?"

Rose was stumped. The truth was out of the question, so all Rose did was smile. Tired, wet, and grossly humiliated, Rose went home to bed knowing that this time, the universe was against her. After finally resigning herself to the fact that Sandy was no longer an option, bygones became bygones, and all became the best of friends. Sandy even ended up as best man at Rose's wedding.

Once Rose found out that her old friend Chris and a friend were planning a backpacking trip through Europe that included an eight-day guided tour—September 1978—Rose wanted in, but in order to afford the adventure, Rose knew she would need a second job. So, Rose worked by day for the finance company, and by night, as a waitress in a nightclub. What a job … having to dash around in sexy attire and four-inch heels for five or six hours a night. Rose knew the girl cashing her out at the end of the night was stealing tip money from her but … she needed what she was bringing home for her trip, and even with the theft, she was bringing home darn good money. The tips were terrific.

Rose knew there was no way her day job was going to give her a month and a half off to go on vacation, but she knew she was going to have to leave that job soon anyway. The district supervisor had begun giving Rose the gears for not soliciting customers the way she should be.

"Why are earth would I try and get them to borrow more money when they can't afford to make their payments now? No, I am sorry. I cannot do that. I will not do that."

"Well then, I am afraid, Rose, you are in the wrong job. You should be looking for another line of work."

Rose's mom was very worried about her daughter quitting yet another job, especially now that she had a house and a mortgage.

"Don't worry, Mom. I have paid all my bills two months in advance, and I have more than enough saved to cover my trip and all my expenses. I will get a new job when I get back."

Rose's little sister said she would drop by Rose's house every day after school to keep her plants watered and her animals fed and cared for.

"Everything will be fine, Mom. I promise."

Rose's dad was going to remodel Rose's bathroom for her while she was gone. Rose had bought fake pine planking wallboard that she wanted installed horizontally on the bathroom walls. Her dad was aghast.

"You can't install it horizontally, Rose. It will look like an outhouse."

Rose laughed. "I know, Dad … that's the look I am shooting for." Rose knew her dad would do it the way she wanted it. Her dad was good that way.

The Europe trip was grand. The girls laughed and cried, ate, and drank. They had a few squabbles but made up and carried on.

While the other girls penned postcards to their boyfriends, Rose penned hers to her dog Clifford. September through October: London, Paris, Nice, Rome, Venice, and Florence. Rose wouldn't remember the exact itinerary of visiting the eight countries in twelve days, but after their tour, they were in Edinburgh, Scotland, and Llandudno, Wales, before going back to London for their flight home.

In order to celebrate her trip and more closely match with the world traveller she'd become, while in Wales, Rose decided a new hairdo was in order. She wanted a perm. The hairdresser suggested that Rose might want to get her hair layered first, but no, Rose was adamant. Well … Rose might have thought she knew what she wanted but it turned out … she should have listened to the hairdresser. Rose's hair came out looking like she'd stuck her finger in a light socket. By the time Rose left the salon she was in tears, and once back in their room, Rose locked herself in the bathroom. The girls were trying their best to be supportive, but Rose could hear their giggling.

"It will calm down in time, Rose …"

"Really … are you kidding me? Look at it!"

Best part, Rose's mom was to meet her at the airport, but she walked right past Rose. With her new do, Rose's mom didn't recognize her daughter.

Even Rose had to admit: *Now that's funny!*

Post-European adventure, Rose settled back into her house and commenced job hunting. She ended up as a cocktail waitress in the lounge of an upscale hotel. It was permanent full-time work so she would be fine financially. Fundamentally, however, not so much. It was a bad environment for Rose. Waitressing in the nightclub was Rose's second job. She had to get up early in the morning, so there were strict limits to her capacity to carry on in a crazily manic fashion. After a shift at the lounge, however, Rose was dressed up, amped up, and ready to go. Working from 11:00 am to 7:00 pm, Rose was always out painting the town red with friends, lounge lizards, contract workers, or businessmen of every description.

Since Rose and Chris's excursion, once again, they had become close, so every couple of months Rose would zip down to the coast for the weekend. Rose enjoyed partying with pristine prospects because she believed her permanent passion would probably present himself amidst places and personalities as yet unexplored. Yes, always on an adventure, always with the same aim, looking for love in all the wrong places.

Rose, during this time, would drop in on her mom every now and again for a visit—a coffee or something—and she would always attend her mom's Sunday night family dinners.

"It is Sunday night dinners that hold this family together, Rose."

Even though Rose would roll her eyes in response, she always went. No matter what Rose did—or had done—whenever she went calling, her mom welcomed her in.

When Rose experienced her very first card reading, she'd had it with her mom. However it came to be, Rose and her mom had back-to-back appointments with a local psychic, who, it was said, was very good.

This woman did first-come, first-served readings in her house, and the living room was full of patrons when Rose and her mom arrived. When it was finally their turn, Rose went in first. As the fortune teller began reading the cards drawn and laid before Rose, Rose began to cry and could not stop crying. This time Rose knew why she was crying. She was crying because every single thing the woman said was true. Rose was miserable and had been miserable for a very, very, long time. She was wasting her life, not doing anything, and she needed to do something, find something. The only hopeful tidbit the card reader threw in was that there was someone *out there* meant for her. There was just someone else in the way at present.

Once done, Rose's mom went in.

Later, as Rose's mom exited the reader's little room, Rose could read nothing on her mom's face, no emotion whatsoever. As far as Rose recalled, neither she nor her mom said a single word on the way home. Both were lost in their thoughts.

'Twas after the unadulterated accuracy of her card reading that Rose decided to leave the lounge. Yes, the money was good—great—but maybe, she considered, she should try and find something a little more grown-up, some sort of a career. Apart from the soliciting thing, which Rose refused to do, she had enjoyed her job at the finance company so when she heard about an opening at a local insurance agency, she applied.

Back in those days, Rose's ability to morph on a moment's notice into whatever was necessary was quite astonishing. Like a chameleon, Rose could transform her presence, poise, and persona, as well as prompt the prerequisite passion in a flash, so long as she felt it aided her pursuits. Rose got the job. She was hired on as a car, house, and commercial lines insurance agent trainee. With this job, in her new house, Rose calmed down some. Her new job required focus and effort, and her house and its garden needed tending so ... this is not to say Rose quit going out with friends. Heavens no. She just went home earlier and stayed home more often than she used to.

Time went by, and save her constant disappointment *looking for love in all the wrong places*, Rose was fine. She had her friends—her roommate Petra—to fall back on and fall back on them, she did, perhaps a little too much so because .... on the night of January 25, 1980, when a bunch of them ended up at Rose's house after leaving the bar ... Rose allowed herself to fall into the arms of a friend she barely liked anymore, she fell into the arms of Lois's fiancé, Randy.

I t never occurred to me at the time, but I bet it was Mom and Dad who spotted me the cash for my house. Mom probably just didn't want me to know it at the time.

From the time I was young, I would always — always — get hung up on the principle of the thing. In always having had a very clear sense of right and wrong, I had a really tough time understanding my world, when I was looking outward. I never, however, applied the same principles of right and wrong to myself, to my own behaviour. Even when I knew—knew—I was doing something wrong, it never occurred to me that I was being the same hypocrite I accused so many others of being. Rather than listening to the truth of my own little voice, I allowed my battalion of coercive abusers to formulate rational justifications for whatever I deemed best for myself at the time. In principle then, I expected everybody else to be good and honourable, stand in their integrity, while I, due to need, desire, or circumstance, felt righteous in doing my own bidding regardless. It wasn't a winning strategy as I was to eventually learn. Oh, what a tangled web we weave, when we practice to deceive. Could it be that my eventual learning was the point of everything I put myself through? I have come to believe that it was, yes.

I was convinced I did not need my mom, but in reality, I am quite certain I did. What other adult did I have in my life who, year after year, despite my shifty serpentine shenanigans and paralyzed sense of purpose, always, whenever I went calling, welcomed me in.

I still remember having my tarot cards read for the very first time. It was amazing. How on earth had my card reader known how desperately desolate I was? And ... how did she know about Randy, the one who was *out there* for me that had someone—a fiancée—in the way at that time? I have had some pretty amazing card readers in my life, but I have also had a few terrible ones, ones who I knew were complete frauds. It's hard to pass judgement on them though ... after all ... I'd spent a lot of my life as a huge fraud ...

Speaking of fraud, we now return back to Randy and Rose, to that day in 1992, when the shit hit the fan—when everything for Rose would change.

THE END OF THE BEGINNING

32

THE PENNY FINALLY DROPS
By Grace We Are Freed by Truth

Rose and Randy were in a state of shock after Rose's tremor of truth callously tore its way through their lives, so each were alone with their thoughts until their kids were tucked in for the night.

Then it was their turn. Stabilized by alcohol, they would talk.

Rose had no memory of how the minutes, hours, days, weeks, or months thereafter flowed exactly. All she could remember was the general gist, and the particularly peculiar, profoundly ponderable moments that preceded the dissolution of her former life.

Having come as far as she had—albeit against her conscious will—Rose thought it best to come clean about everything, so she told her husband what had caused her eruption. She told Randy that she invited their bank manager to lunch and that she thought she loved him.

Upon getting home from work the next day, Randy informed his wife that he had called the bank manager and given him shit for destroying his marriage. He told him, in no uncertain terms, to BACK RIGHT OFF.

"For once," barked Randy, "I decided to do something with my anger."

Rose was horrified, humiliated, and heartbroken. The bank manager had not done anything wrong. By his mere existence he was the inspiration, the push Rose needed to realize how terribly unhappy she was. She was the guilty party, not he.

And Randy ... well, he hadn't dealt with his anger, he'd sent it downstream, thrust it upon someone else to deal with. Needless to say, Rose never heard back from the bank manager, and she began using a different bank branch. Thankfully, Rose's next appointment with George was only a day or two in the offing. She was ready. She could hardly wait.

Rose gave George the run down, right down to Randy's call to their bank manager. George listened intently, no judgement, just a grimace or two acknowledging the unpleasantness of it all.

In response to the results of Rose's newly formed commitment to complete honestly, all George had to say was: "Well, yes, Rose, honesty does have consequences."

"No shit Sherlock" mumbled Rose prior to them sharing a chuckle interpretable only through the intimate therapeutic relationship they had forged through Rose's years of psychotherapy.

George suggested Rose and Randy begin seeing him together once again in an effort to talk things through. "... the only time a marriage really needs to end, is when someone is being abused."

And because Randy had never raised a hand, or spoken an ugly word to her, it was Rose's sincerest hope that she and Randy could somehow overcome her deceitful beginning and start anew on an honest, far happier note. They did, after all, have three wonderful children whom they both adored.

It was mindboggling to Rose that Randy had been experiencing matrimonial bliss while she had been suffering—in silence—to the point of near destruction.

"What is wrong with me, George? I have everything I have ever wanted. Randy and I have good conversations. He has his jobs, and I have mine. We do fight about money but ... mostly I just hate having sex. I hate being touched and the like when I don't want to be and ... I never want to be."

Having to express her disdain for sex while her husband was in the room was just about the hardest thing Rose had ever had to do. It felt so mean ... almost cruel, but Rose knew if they were ever going to get through this mess, she was going to have to be completely honest ... for once.

"I just want to be able to enjoy sex that's all."

The day after a particularly revealing and/or productive session with George, Randy came home from work terribly upset.

"While thinking about you as a little girl who may have willingly submitted to her own sexual abuse," Randy said, "I suddenly knew, deep down inside myself, it was true. Somewhere deep down I have known, all along, that you are a stuck little girl whose fear and lack of self-worth would let me do whatever I wanted. It made me feel good, powerful. I liked it.

And as soon as this thought came, I started to cry. The tears came and came and would not stop coming. It is me, Rose. I am your abuser. You need not look any further for an abuser because it is me. It has always been me."

Randy's truth had so devastated him that Rose's heart could not help but bleed with his. She had never felt closer to Randy than she did in that very moment.

Maybe there is hope for us after all.

That night, the strangest thing happened. Upon getting into bed, Rose's heart began to race, and she began to gasp for air. Randy said he felt like he might throw up and his face was getting hot, really hot.

In crawling into the same bed, after the day's revelation, Rose's body responded with panic and fear, while Randy's responded with nausea and shame. And so … both Randy and Rose got up. They both needed a drink, maybe two. With nothing but their minds intertwined, their bodies laid bare the truth. They were both blown away.

The next day Rose began researching mind-body connection.

After a session or two with George, discussing his newly uncovered truth, Randy suggested he no longer needed to attend the counselling sessions. As far as he was concerned, he had gotten to the bottom of his issue, and so now, he believed it was up to Rose to sort herself out.

With this, Randy turned to Rose and said, "Once you get over the suppressed anger I feel coming from you Rose, I am sure we will be fine."

And so, Rose continued going to counselling alone.

George began encouraging Rose to follow her stream of consciousness. He stopped her only to discuss further what he felt needed fuller investigation. When Rose got stuck, George would tell her to close her eyes and tell him what she saw. All she ever saw was a strip of negatives or a filmstrip running backwards through a projector.

"Roll the film back, Rose, look at it."

Rose's mind was trying to help her, but everything went so fast ... flashes of thoughts too jumbled to make hide nor hair of. With this, George suggested Rose begin journaling. He recommended Rose set aside an hour or so every day—morning—to record her thoughts so as to organize and make sense of them.

At first, Rose's thoughts unravelled so fast she could barely get them down. Sometimes she didn't. They would disappear before she could record them. After a bit of practice, however, what Rose ended up with astonished her. Themes and patterns began to emerge. Through capture and consideration of her memories and thoughts, Rose was able to peer into the interpersonal dynamics of the world she had grown up in. She was beginning to understand things, understand why she was the way she was. Rose marvelled at how *it all* was starting to make sense. Hence journaling—expounding on her thoughts—became a passion Rose never lost.

With her journaling, Rose and George's discussions were upped an enthusiastic notch or two. In exploring a variety of topics upon which to speculate and muse, Rose was led to novel insights and things to ponder. She and George had the most wonderful chats about all kinds of stuff.

With all her thinking, and discussing, Rose began seeking out all manner of deep psychological, philosophical, metaphysical, and mystical books to complement her growing understanding of herself and the world. She was beginning to deeply regret the fact that she had not attended university when she had the chance. Her mom and dad would have proudly sent her to any university she wanted, but by Grade Twelve, all Rose was interested in was getting away from her parents and the hell-hole she believed she lived in.

"I so should have gone to university, George! That is who I am. I love learning, learning what I am learning, understanding." But Rose knew she was too old; she had missed that boat. She was the mother of three young children who needed her.

"Going back to school now would just be selfish. I will have to be content journaling and learning what I can on my own."

Just for fun, Rose signed up with distance education for an introductory psychology class. She loved it, buried herself in it.

Little did either Rose or Randy realize, Rose was indeed slowly but surely getting *fixed*. By then she had been seeing George every two weeks for years, so she had a pretty good handle on why she was feeling the way she was. The suppressed anger Randy felt coming from his wife came from the fact that he refused to leave Rose alone physically but that … that was what Rose was still hoping George would be able to help her fix … she could not imagine having to raise her three children without the help of their dad. As such, Randy and Rose were still in the same bed having sex when absolutely necessary for familial harmony.

One night, after the deed was done, Rose lay silently steaming.

I HATE you, Randy. Why won't you just leave me alone! I do not WANT to give myself to you. I never have! We do not connect. You ask for directions but there are no directions to give you. No matter what you do, you cannot make me want you in that way. Don't you know that? CAN'T YOU FEEL IT, YOU STUPID MORON?

Once Randy was asleep, Rose got up thinking maybe writing in her journal would help her calm down enough to go to sleep. Tomorrow, after all, was another day. As Rose's thoughts began to arrive, she began to transcribe them: *First it was Mom controlling me, now it is Randy. I am sick of it! As an adult I should be the boss of my own self, thank you very much!*

With those thoughts, things began to unwind, quickly. Rose remembered a question George once asked her.

"If you do not want to have sex with Randy, why do you do it?"

At the time, Rose had said she did it to keep the peace, but *... whose peace was I attempting to keep? Certainly not my own ...* With that thought, Rose's psyche finally released the hidden agenda that since childhood had been fuelling her silence and her duplicitousness. *The real reason I have been having sex with Randy is so I can continue to carry him around like a security blanket—like my stuffed rabbit Bugsy—so as to never feel alone.*

Rose came to understand that she needed Randy as she had needed her mom. Neither her mom nor Randy had ever really controlled her. She had been CONTROLLING HERSELF so as to guarantee proximity, if not the affections, of those she needed most. With this realization, Rose was literally undone. Not a comforting realization but there it was ... finally ... the truth of the matter.

When the penny finally dropped, Rose had no option but to finally face the cold hard fact that it was she, and she alone, who was responsible for the mess she had made of her life. It was no one else's fault. There was absolutely no other conclusion to be made. She had done what she had done, and she had seemingly done it all ... ON PURPOSE!

Rose's monumental breakthrough arrived during the early hours of November 2, 1992, a month and a day after the shit had hit the fan. And although exceptionally unpleasant, the truth of the matter did provide Rose a margin of deliverance, a smidgen of salvation. What she had done—had been doing—was horrible—almost unforgiveable—but she'd had no idea what she'd spent her life doing. With her realization, Rose better understood the phrase: "Father, forgive them, for they know not what they do."[9]

What she could not yet get a handle on was: *Why ... why don't we know what we are doing?*

B y the time Randy had his moment of clarity at work, I was quite certain he was not the source of my prob-lem(s). He had merely married a broken woman—me. A woman he hadn't known was broken because I had lied to him. With his revelation and the evident pain of it, I was filled with hope. With Randy's revelation, I was convinced that soon we'd be at the bottom of things, and we could fix our life together.

With *the truth of the matter*, I came to realize that my life—all along—had been my own, my own to approach with the nature and temperament I had been given. The nature and temperament I had come into the world with. I had unknow-ingly been born into an intergenerational prison from which I needed to free myself.

For as long as I can remember, I was afraid of not being good enough, not being accepted. When I was alone and not thinking about it, I was fine, but I never reflected on that. 'Twas only after I was no longer able to tolerate the torture of my fear-avoidance tools and tactics that I sought out George, who taught me how to reflect on things. It was via deep reflection then, that by a bolt of inspiration lightning, my lifelong fear revealed itself as the mysterious force driving the cycle of pain that was my life. In finally shaking myself awake, my darkly subservient, darkly subversive deeds became visible in the light of conscious awareness. In finally coming face to face with myself, in such a way, I promised myself that I would suffer fear no longer. The truth had set me free, free enough to voluntarily—consciously—decide which wolf to feed from then on.

Toward the end of my time with George, I remember saying, "You know George ... I feel like I have been doing this for eternity."

To this, George neither agreed nor disagreed, but nodded his understanding of my meaning in his usual way. Had those who'd come before me been submitting, submitting, always submitting? Perhaps.

In deciding to listen—fully commit—to the voice of my tiny little self, the voice that all along had been trying to get my attention, trying to call me to *the good*, be true to the nature I carried within, in time, with practice, I was able to fully exit that which had kept how many generations captive?

33

THE DARK BEFORE THE DAWN
Breaking Free

Although Rose continued to share a bed with Randy, she declared a marriage moratorium.

With firm conviction Rose finally said, "Randy, I am sorry, but I no longer want you touching me. I hate it and I will no longer tolerate it."

Even though Rose had tried to lay down her new law, more often than not, in the middle of the night, Randy would slowly crawl over to Rose's side of the bed and try to start something up. Feeling totally disrespected Rose would get angry and tell him to stop. On more than a few occasions she even got up and crawled into the other side of the bed because Randy would not leave her alone.

Randy would always half wake up and say, "Oh, sorry I was asleep ... dreaming."

Rose did not buy it, neither did George. This withstanding, Rose was still not ready, willing, or able to leave the marital bed.

The plan was to go back to the prairies, to visit Randy's parents for Christmas that year, but Rose couldn't imagine it, being with Randy's entire extended family for ten days or so. She refused to go.

"Sure, take the kids, they are dying to go but I need to be alone."

Rose hated Christmas anyway, such fuss and feathers about nothing. Although Rose would have preferred everyone be told the truth, the story was that she stayed home to look after her mom, who was still recovering from her cancer treatment.

Lies, always lies ...

Instead, Rose went skiing with friends. It was glorious. She had not been skiing in years. Rose had all but forgotten the sense of freedom to be had while zooming downhill at a million miles an hour. It was fantastic.

Mornings were spent journaling to her heart's content. She was making huge strides in unwinding the strip of clips that ran backwards through her mind's eye. Afternoons were for household chores, short outings, or a nap if the mood struck. Rose spent her evenings soaking in their giant jacuzzi bathtub and reading. She could sit in that tub sipping wine and reading for as long as the hot water held out, and they had a very large hot water tank. She'd be like a prune when she finally slipped between the sheets of a bed SHE DID NOT HAVE TO SHARE.

Well rested and firmly placed—centred—after two weeks, Rose was ready to give it another go, ready to welcome her family home with arms wide open. There was still not to be any connubial bliss, however. To this, Rose remained steadfast.

January turned into February and as you might guess, Randy was getting increasingly obnoxious through the night.

In response, Rose suggested Randy move his sleeping quarters into the basement rumpus room. Randy wasn't happy but he complied. With this, questions were being asked but not answered.

"They are not stupid, you know? They know something is wrong. We need to tell them the truth." Rose believed the kids needed to be told what was really going on. She would take all the blame because well … she was to blame.

"Mommy isn't sure she wants to be married to Daddy anymore."

At first, the oldest didn't say a word. She just started to cry. Her little sister got extremely angry and began throwing a crying fit. Their little brother … well … he didn't know what was going on, but he could feel what was in the air, so he started to cry along with his sisters.

The event was horrendously painful for both Rose and Randy, but as they sat and listened, the most amazing thing started to happen. For the very first time, Rose and Randy's children began sharing their innermost thoughts and feelings with their parents. In allowing themselves to become real in front of their children, they had given their children permission to become real in front of them. It was magic.

"Why didn't you come to Grandma and Grandpa's with us at Christmas, Mom?"

"I can tell when you are mad at Daddy. You pretend not to be, but I can tell."

"I knew there was something wrong. I always know when something is wrong."

"I know when you say you are tired you are not really tired. You are just sad. Why are you always so sad, Mommy?"

"Would it help if we did more chores?"

"Are you going to get divorced? I—we—don't want you to get divorced. Suzie's mom and dad are divorced, and she hardly ever gets to see her dad."

Once the conversation was over and the kids had been tucked into bed for the night, Rose slithered her way to bed for a huge cry regarding the mess she had made of her family's lives.

Rose and Randy were living as roommates when on Valentine's Day, Rose opened a box containing an obscene looking black and red negligee, far lewder than the black and white French maid outfit she'd received the year before. With that, Rose knew—just knew—Randy did not love her. He loved the resentfully subservient contorted monstrosity Rose had spent the last decade plus showing him. At that moment, a light bulb came on—something in Rose changed. She realized that what she needed to do was only in a matter of time, but … for whatever reason … the time was not yet.

On the night of Rose's thirty-eighth birthday, February 1993, on her way out to an evening group therapy session that George had recommended, Rose happened to glance up into the night sky. What she saw took her breath away. It was a star, twinkling its little heart out from within the crest of the moon. It was the most breathtaking celestial configuration Rose had ever seen, and it was exactly like the symbol that appeared on a locket of her Granny's that her mom had given to her years earlier. Apparently, Rose's mom had cut her teeth on that locket. Her bite marks were etched into the back.

Rose was thrilled to bits. She was so thrilled she called Randy and the kids out to have a look. It was enchantment made manifest. Not since childhood had Rose experienced such a prolonged sense of joyful wonder.

"What does the symbol mean?"

Rose asked George and everyone she knew. No one seemed to know. All she could ever find out was that it appeared on many Middle Eastern flags, and it was prominent in Islamic cultures. Her question as to *why* was never answered.

At one point Rose even bought a software program—Guide to the Galaxy—for her computer so as to ensure she had not dreamt the whole thing up. The closest Rose could get to her location was Vancouver, Washington, but even then, when she typed in her birthday, there it was, a star—the planet Venus shining like a star—in the crest of the moon.

Rose felt like she had been privy to a most magnificent heavenly marvel ... and on her birthday no less. What did it mean?

'Twas not but a day or two later that Rose became convinced that what she had experienced, what she had seen in the heavens was an omen, an omen that foretold of a bequeathment she was about to receive, because suddenly and without warning—during one of her morning journaling sessions—Rose received a gift; she had a vision.

People throughout history have used the word vision to describe sudden flashes of clarity, but it wasn't like Rose saw anything with her eyes. It was more like the world disappeared and her mind opened to the workings of the universe. She travelled deep into time ... back, back, back to the beginning, while at the same time travelling deep, deep, deep into the nature of reality where everything—absolutely everything—was suspended in a dynamic matrix of energy ... everything exchanging particles.

From her new vantage point, Rose's life felt completely different. She was not alone. She had never been alone. She was and would always be a bit-player in a grand and utterly profound symphony of being. She understood that her manifold miseries were not miseries at all. They were unspeakably beautiful in both purpose and design. Psychic pain had been her predestined primordial precursor. Her ancestral line had travelled eons—generation after generation—to arrive where she was at this very moment. Wherever the hell that was ...

Tears broke as Rose leapt out of her chair in delirious delight and began to dance. Despite *The Cloud of Unknowing*[10] that still blocked Rose's vision of a future, she rejoiced. By means of an event Rose could neither understand nor explain, a veil had been lifted. Rose was transformed. She didn't know exactly how she had been transformed, but she knew that she was.

Rose spent the rest of the day writing like a mad woman in an attempt to gather, grasp, and articulate all she had gleaned from her glimpse into the secrets of the universe.

Whilst out and about the next day, Rose couldn't shake the feeling that she was in the world differently somehow. Was she more self-conscious ... less self-conscious, or had her state of consciousness just shifted—expanded—somehow? It wasn't a bad feeling. She just felt different, better. Rose felt more like herself.

Rose tried to explain her experience to Randy and to her mom. Randy suggested Rose had lost her marbles.

"I have never been more in control of my marbles in my entire life," Rose responded.

Rose's mom didn't say a word—as usual—but then went on to tell all of Rose's siblings that their sister was having a nervous breakdown.

Rose couldn't help but laugh because she knew nothing could have been further from the truth. She'd had breakdowns in the past, but none had provided the clarity and insight this event had provided. For the first time in her life, Rose felt like her feet were firmly planted on the ground of her being.

Upon telling George what she had experienced and how it had made her feel, George said he was proud of her.

Rose beamed! She could not remember anyone ever telling her that they were proud of her.

"But what was it, George? How did it happen?"

He said he didn't know. "Does it matter?"

"No," responded Rose. "I guess it really doesn't."

Rose and George then shared one of their little chuckles.

It was not until April, a day in April 1993, that Rose was finally ready. Once Randy was home from work, Rose told him she wanted a divorce. Not only was the premise upon which Rose built her life false, the wife and life Randy thought he had, were fantasies being feigned by a fraud, and Rose could not, did not, want to be a fraud any longer.

Yes, Rose had hoped that they could start over. And as hard as it was, she had tried her best to be honest and hold her newly found boundaries, but she was not yet strong enough. She was not yet strong enough to shoulder the near constant expectations she felt coming from a husband who wanted nothing more than this old life, his old wife back.

"She's not coming back, Randy. I am telling you, she never existed!"

With this, Rose thought both she and Randy deserved better. She deserved to have her boundaries respected and Randy deserved to be loved the way he wanted to be loved. Rose knew she could not do that.

Yes, George had said, ". . . the only time a marriage really needs to end, is when someone is being abused."

And okay, so maybe Randy had never abused Rose but … Rose had been abusing herself. She had been abusing herself for years, if not her entire life, and she wanted—needed—it to stop. What Rose felt that she needed was to be alone—away from all expectations—long enough to sit in her centre and allow it to become strong.

'Twould be hard, Rose knew that, but she was not afraid. She finally had someone on her team. She had herself.

Through a most mystical or transcendental transference of truth, I came to understand things from a completely new perspective, a perspective that transcended both time and space. Via some instantaneously illuminated set of inspirations, I understood that I, and everything else in existence, was, is, and would always be intrinsically connected, all is but part and parcel of a singular whole, an infinitely complex totality of components functioning as one, toward its *final cause.*[11]

Whatever the antiquated significance of a star—a planet lit by reflected sunlight—in the crest of the moon, I have come to believe that it was the cryptic precursor of a transformative truth to come, a transformative truth that would continue to deliver time, and time, again. Not only did it precede my awakening, but the alchemical magic inherent in my mystical moment has become my touchstone. It has given me a time and place to which I can return when life becomes a struggle. There, I am restored. My sense of balance returns because just as a book that contains layer after layer of complexity can only reveal its totality through multiple readings, with every visit, my vision has continued to offer me ever-more inclusive, ever-more expansive understandings of the reality in which I am immersed.

Clearly Randy had not been shaken awake by his momentary revelation. Although gaining a momentary glimpse into the truth of the energy that animated him, he was, seemingly, not ready, willing, or able to recognize his behaviour deeply enough to accept and alter what drove him. With him continuing to so adamantly pursue something so wrong, I came to realize that

Randy, on some level, must have always known he had married a broken woman, that he had somewhere, in a deeply hidden part of himself, voluntarily consented to being a co-conspirator in my trauma re-enactment, the trauma re-enactment that would finally—eventually—wake me up, help me connect enough dots to finally see—so as to finally stop—what I was doing. No, of this he was not consciously aware but ...

As George may have said, "He is not there yet, so ..."

Are people brought together, or do people come together as part of an agenda intended to advance something far larger than a need for companionship? Are we all called by an other or others to attend to our own particular journey? As I look back on the pals with whom I used to party my pain into the past ... did we have things to teach and learn from each other? And what about families, be they of origin or placement ...

I can now see how Sandy—my second boyfriend—and Randy, were, although not the same person, both calling me to the same lesson, in exactly the same way.

Are all relationships secretly synchronized to offer specific opportunities for growth? How else can you explain the joint journey, the darkly disturbed but devoutly dedicated love shared by my Mom and Dad? How else can you explain the road my ex-husband and I travelled?

With this I wonder ... despite the seeming absurdity of it all, was I purposely picked up from a place of poverty and placed in prosperity, perfectly placed in the arms of a woman whose personal privation, whose drive toward self-understanding could—would—be reflected in my own?

Finally, out from under both myself and my situation, the only truths I carried were my children. They were not lies. As pieces of myself, I had sought them out my entire life, and as my mirrors—the continuation of my line through time—I knew it would be they who could—would—show me what I needed to see. I knew it would be they who could—would—help me to become the person I was intended to become. Besides, I loved them. I loved them unconditionally. In a life that had never had anything else in it, they were my everything.

34

WHEN ONE DOOR CLOSES ...
New-Found Freedom to Explore

Everyone was aghast at what Rose was about to do. Rose's mom wouldn't—perhaps couldn't—say a word, not a single solitary word, but Rose could feel where she was. She was angry, resentful, and scared for her grandchildren, if not for Rose herself.

Rose's biological mother gave her a very strict warning. "Rose, you have relived my life in just about every way, please do not leave the father of your children. It was the worst decision I ever made."

"But I am not doing what you did, mother. I am not leaving Randy for another man. I am leaving him for myself, a self that until now, I did not realize I even had. Besides, it would be grossly unfair to Randy, the kids, and myself to continue trying to live a nightmare of lies that I know would eventually kill me."

Rose's friends were as surprised as all get out. They had no idea how unhappy Rose was. As such, they didn't know what to say.

May 1993, ten days after what would have been Rose and Randy's twelfth wedding anniversary, Rose and Randy were legally separated.

On the way home from the courthouse Randy said, "Well, Rose, you have what you wanted ... you are now free."

"Yes, I am, *finally*," was all Rose could offer as the car radio belted out U2's "Who's Gonna Ride Your Wild Horses."

Now, how's the playing of that particular song, at this particular moment, not indicative of a world—a reality—in constant communication with cognizant constituents?

Randy was not handling things well and Rose did feel bad. She felt terrible in fact—horribly guilty—but she could not, would not, go back to faking it. Rose had finally closed the door on her dark night in anticipation of a new dawn.

Neither Rose nor Randy could afford to keep the house, so it was put up for sale. They would go their separate ways once it was sold. Rose would have full custody of the children, but she and Randy would share guardianship. Once living apart, Randy would pay child support but no alimony for a couple of reasons. Number one, Rose did not feel she merited alimony. Number two, Rose did not want to remain dependent upon the man she had used as a meal ticket for the past twelve years. Enough with the guilt already; she knew if she was ever going to stop feeling guilty, she would have to stop using people, stop doing things that would make her feel guilty. Given the situation, Rose realized she would have to become a lot more gainfully employed in very short order.

In an effort to give Randy some time and space to get his shit together, Rose decided to take the kids down to the coast, Vancouver, to visit Chris and her family. Their kids had grown up together, so were like cousins, and Rose could use a good commiseration with her oldest, dearest, friend, the maid of honour at her wedding. Rose also had something else in mind. She wanted to go skydiving. Rose had so longed to feel herself free as a bird to soar the open skies and ... that is exactly how she now felt. And so, it was set. Both families would spend Saturday at Stanley Park, and on Sunday, everyone would accompany Rose as she tested her wings.

As Rose was completing her lesson with the instructor to whom she was to be attached for a tandem jump, Rose noticed Chris waving her over. Her youngest daughter had a question.

"Mommy, I am afraid we are going to watch you die."

"Oh sweetheart," said Rose, "this is something Mommy has wanted to do for so very long. If I die, at least you will know I was happy, but I am sure I will not die here, now, doing this. I am just now learning how to live."

With that, Rose handed each of her daughters one of her crystal earrings and her little son her pouch of lucky stones to hold while she fell through the air with the greatest of ease.

Rose could see the kids watching as the plane slowly climbed to the 10,000 feet it needed to be. She was so happy and excited she had to choke back tears of unmitigated joy. Once they were where they needed to be, Rose, her tandem partner, and the cameraman Rose had engaged to film her flight, got out onto the wing strut.

"One, two, three," the instructor yelled and … they all jumped. As Rose began to fall, her eyes were shut until she had a quick word with herself.

Rose you have wanted to do this forever. You paid a lot of money to do it, and you are doing it now, so OPEN YOUR GOD DAMN EYES!

With that, with eyes wide open, Rose's breath was taken away. Tears cascading down her cheeks, Rose revelled in the freedom she experienced flying weightless, wind in her face, the whole world visible below her. After forty seconds of free fall, the chute opened. Then, a few spins and twirls, over here, over there, all followed up by a perfect four-point landing.

"I did it! I did it!" screamed Rose in jubilation.

She waved to the cameraman who was still filming and said, "Hi, Mom and Dad," completely forgetting her dad was dead. She hugged and kissed everyone on the landing field and then offered to buy everyone lunch. It was lucky no one asked for a car, because at that moment, Rose probably would have bought them one.

On the way back to Chris's place, Rose's oldest daughter wanted to know how old you had to be to go skydiving.

"Well darlin' you have to be way older and a little bit crazy."

Once back home, all sat and watched Rose's videotape. The jump had been set to Van Halen's "Jump." It was perfect.

Life in the house with Randy was getting progressively uglier. Randy wanted things to go back to the way they were but Rose assured him they never could, never would.

One night he even told Rose he would rather see her dead than to see her leave him. Rose knew things had to change, but the house had still not sold, and Randy refused to move out. He continued to refuse until Rose called his bluff by threatening to find an apartment for the kids, dogs, cats, and herself.

"Fine," Randy finally agreed. "I will be out by the time you get back from Disneyland."

You see, after recovering from her cancer treatment, Rose's Mom wanted to pay for each of her kid's families to go to Disneyland. A trip to Disneyland was something her mom wished they—she and Rose's dad—had done for their own kids, but it never happened, so she wanted to send her grandchildren. Given the situation, Randy refused to go ... not even for his kids' sake, so Rose invited her mom to come along with them.

It was a great trip. Yes, her mom drove her crazy and the kids missed their dad—most especially her little son—but in all, everyone had a fabulous time. Rose's favourite ride was Space Mountain, zipping around full blast in the pitch dark, nothing to trust but the universe itself. The kids enjoyed the San Diego Zoo, but Rose knew she would never go to another zoo. All the animals look so sad, caged, and staged, as she had once been. At Universal Studios, Rose put her name and the kids' names in to appear in a mock Star Trek video. She had been a Star Trek fan from a ways back, forever praying Scotty would somehow just beam her up. Finally, by way of a fun video, her prayer was answered.

Although Rose could not help but feel that her husband had cut off his nose to spite his face, having her mom accompanying them turned out to be quite opportune. Although no one knew it at the time, her mom—the kids' granny—would not be around for much longer.

Thankfully, Randy was out of the house, had moved in with a friend by the time they got home.

Rose tried relentlessly to find more work, more bookkeeping jobs, something, anything, but no luck. She even applied at the old lounge she used to work at. Nothing was appearing. While haggling with her frustration, a not-so-novel idea popped into Rose's head.

Maybe I should go back to school after all.

By this time, Rose had completed three distance education courses and had done very well, so she applied at the local community college located half an hour away and applied for a student loan to supplement her income.

If I can't do what I should, maybe I should try and do what I want.

Everyone—absolutely everyone—was aghast again.

"What … you are thirty-eight years old? You have already made your bed. What are you thinking?"

Well, yes, that was true. Rose realized she was a middle-aged woman of three, but she had made her bed wrong the first time and it was her mom who had insisted the whole bed had to be remade if it was not done properly the first time.

Believe it or not, Rose was accepted as a full-time student at her community college. Thankfully she applied as a mature student because there is no way she would have been accepted based on her high school transcript. As was mentioned earlier, Rose had not been a stellar student. It was a miracle she even graduated. Next bit of synchronicity ... Rose qualified for a student loan. She was set. In having set her eyes on a new beginning, a new door had opened. Rose started college full time in September 1993.

Rose was in love with her new life.

In the evening, after the kids were in bed, she would sit at her desk, strewn with books and papers, reading, and thinking, as tears rolled down her cheeks. As of late, Rose had found herself shedding far more tears of joy than of sorrow. She had finally found herself, and in so doing, she had found her passion, her passion for learning—learning in the hope of understanding, understanding as much as she possibly could.

Mid-October, Rose's anthropology professor passed around a brochure about a two-month field study to Kenya the coming spring. Rose's mind began to swirl. She had always wanted to go to Africa. Why? She did not know. She just had. Yes, the idea seemed outlandishly unrealistic, but Rose just couldn't leave it alone. She would have the money once their house sold. Between Randy and her mom, she knew the kids would be well taken care of. Prior to applying for the field study, students had to be accepted into the sponsoring university. Just for fun, Rose applied. Rose decided to let fate decide.

For the third time, everyone—absolutely everyone, except her kids—were aghast. Rose was no longer the person everyone thought she was. She was different. She was now herself and damn proud of it.

Rose and Randy's house finally sold in late October, but the possession date was not till the kid's Christmas break. Rose needed time to find a new home for them all, and she thought the move would best be done during the school break.

Rose thought it silly to rent, given she would have enough to buy a small place outright. As such, in earnest, Rose went house hunting. Around and around and around she went. There was an empty church Rose was exceedingly enamoured with, but with the fix up needed to turn it into a home, it was over the top. After weeks of looking, Rose's best option seemed to be the house right next door to her granny's old house, which was now inhabited, re-inherited by her youngest brother, Jerry. Yes, she was a little trepidatious about living so close to her mom, and it did require a little work prior to their moving in, but all in all, Rose thought it was the best choice.

One frosty winter morning, while making her way to school from their old homestead, a gigantic raven with frost still crisp on its wings, flew down and in front of Rose's minivan. It was startling but breathtakingly beautiful in its near motionless grace, wild and free, so cold it was damn near frozen, but still it soared like there was no tomorrow. As the sky brightened once again, with the raven gone, tears welled up Rose's eyes as she imagined herself as that raven, free as a bird.

Yes ... ravens are birds of prey and carrion, but indigenous cultures consider them tricksters, the deliverers of great wisdom. What has my life been if not a trick, a trick trans-formed into truth.

And so, from then on Rose embraced the raven—corvids—as her spirit or totem animal. Many a night, thereafter, Rose dreamt through the eyes of a raven soaring over mountains and down ravines. One morning, she even awoke feeling like she understood the bone structure of a raven's wing, much like a human arm but folding under instead of up.

Mid-November, Rose learned she had been accepted into both the sponsoring university and the field study program. Rose was going to Kenya.

Oh my God ... oh my God ... I'm going to Kenya!

I felt alive and I felt courageous, for once. Having made so many decisions in the face of grave disapproval, I was becoming "The Little Engine That Could" [12] and it was exhilarating. It was no wonder, however, that my mom responded to my leaving Randy, going back to school, and going to Kenya as she did. She had, after all, been witness to my lifetime of emotional dysregulation and erratically self-destructive behaviour, and as far as she knew, my marriage had been just the ticket, exactly what I had needed to calm myself down and get on with life. Little did she know, but then ... little had she ever wanted to know.

I think back now on how everyone—absolutely everyone—was shocked that I was leaving Randy. No one had any idea how unhappy I was. Although I depended upon our little crowd, had I been using them as decoys for the truth of my miserable life? I now honestly believe that George really was the first real friend I had ever allowed myself to have. George knew me. He knew the real me and he was the only one, at that time, who did.

And so, the second part of my journey began, and it began with an intensity of spirit I had only known once before. I had found a new purpose, a new reason for being. I needed to find out who I was.

Would the real Rose please stand up?

THE BECKONING OF A
NEW BEGINNING

35

SO MUCH TO DO
So Little Time

Rose was so excited; she was on fire. The movers and the moving truck arrived at the hobby-farm on the morning of December 17, 1993. Once their stuff was packed up and the moving truck was en route, Rose, the kids, and the dogs, followed behind in the minivan. She picked up the cats when she went back to clean the next day.

During the next couple of weeks, Rose practiced walking the kids to and from their new school. They would be going to the same elementary school she had gone to many, many moons earlier.

Christmas came and went, so did New Year's Eve.

On January 3, Rose registered the kids at their new school. January 7, the kids, and the dogs moved to their dad's. The plan was that while Rose was away, the kids would come home every couple of days to make sure the cats, which had largely always been outside cats, had enough food and water.

On the morning of January 8, Rose was off to the coast, duffle bag packed, to begin a week's worth of preliminary classes prior to catching the first leg of her high adventure on

January 14, first flying to London, then to Cairo, and finally, to Nairobi, Kenya, to begin a two-month tenting safari through four distinct microclimates.

Was Rose exhausted? Not even a bit. She had never felt so happy, so alive. She was going to Kenya!

Although Rose, with uncommitted carefree abandon, attended a business course at Okanagan College in Kelowna, that college was miniscule in comparison to the university where her pre-Kenyan classes were being held. To say Rose was disorientated would be the grandest of understatements. The day classes were to start, Rose wandered around for three hours prior to finding the right classroom, and by then, the class she'd hoped to attend was—l o n g—over.

Never mind ... at least I will know where it is for tomorrow. Rose chuckled to herself.

After finding student services and getting a map of the campus, outside of missing that one class, Rose's week of classes went without a hitch.

There was another woman, Joan, a bit older than Rose, who had just got divorced herself, and she was also headed to Kenya. The two of them became immediate friends.

And they were off ... Rose and Joan sat together, and stayed in the same rooms together, from Vancouver to London, then London to Cairo, Egypt.

n the past, I quit a great many things I shouldn't have, like going to class, jobs, completing courses, but instead, continued doing a great many things I shouldn't have. No need for details here. Finally, however, on my new path, a path I had freely chosen, a path inspired by my inner most self, I could instinctively intuit when to hold'em and when to fold'em. In listening to my own sense of direction, I started to get the hang of life—the hang of how to be happy while living and learning.

36

LIVING THE DREAM
A Liminal State

*N**O! I can't. It is way too narrow, steep, and dark. I am claustrophobic.*

Rose, you are here now, and this is probably the only chance you will ever have to see what it is like down there—inside the great pyramid—so quit being such a chicken-shit and get going.

After watching Rose's trepidation—hesitation—at the entrance to the narrow, black, downward hole that was leading students into the underworld, a fellow student offered to hold Rose's hand so as to shore-up the courage she was obviously attempting to muster.

Rose had managed to stem the flow of tears that had erupted when she first gazed at the wonders of Giza—at the pyramids and the Great Sphinx—but tears appeared and flowed as Rose descended a shaft leading under the largest pyramid, a shaft from which, Rose worried, she might never emerge. Rose was so scared.

What if there's an earthquake? Or ... the tunnel collapses, and I am—we are all—trapped ... in there?

The city of Cairo was hot, dirty, and the narrow streets were very busy with people—mostly older men—and cars. The smell of unidentifiable foods cooking filled Rose's nose. While wandering through town one afternoon, Rose decided she wanted to try smoking a hookah.

"Oh no ... it will be way too strong for you, lady."

After asking a few different hookah shopkeepers, Rose found a taker. To the surprise of the many men milling about, Rose managed to get herself ushered into the backroom of a shisha shop, where she tried smoking a hookah pipe.

It's not strong at all ... it's like smoking a cigarette. Only smoother.

Wandering through the Egyptian museum, Rose sobbed uncontrollably. Her companions were baffled.

"Why are you crying?"

"I don't know ... it's like I can feel it in my body. It just all feels so ... so intense."

The group's last night in Cairo was spent having dinner on a boat cruise.

How ironic is this ... I am finally cruising down de-Nile.

'Twas while in Cairo, that Kate—the only other smoker—was assigned to Rose and Joan as a third person sharing their rooms and tents. Kate was Rose and Joan's junior by quite a few years, but all three, in being smokers, became quick confidants.

And then, next stop ... Nairobi, Kenya where they boarded a bus to their first Kenyan location—a lakeside resort called Lake Naivasha. Lake Naivasha was beautiful, so lush with tropical vegetation, a pool that desperately needing cleaning, and a giant multi-coloured caged bird. Rose couldn't remember what kind of a bird it was, but in seeing it caged, she felt sorry for it.

The group put up camp on a field down from the dining hall, lounge, and a row of rental rooms, which housed the bathrooms they all used. Members of their group were the only patrons at the time. The place was all theirs and it was great. The dining hall was fancy, and the food was fab.

Rose headed off into the wild blue yonder, ravenous to live, but once she arrived, she was riddled and ruined by the emotional repercussions of her spontaneous quest for adventure. It started in Cairo during down times, but by the time Rose and her cohabitants pitched their tent at their first Kenyan location, distractions were no longer enough to deter or defy Rose's desolation.

The nurse travelling with the group suggested Rose's wretched melancholia was due to her malaria medication, but Rose knew it wasn't. She had finally come to realize what she had done, done to her children, exactly what she swore she would never do. She had abandoned them. She had left them with a man who could barely look after himself, never mind their three dependent little darlings. She was indeed, her biological mother's daughter.

Part of Rose wanted to pick up and fly back home to them as soon as she could, but another part did not. She felt horrible about leaving her children, but she also knew she needed to find out who she was when she was not living in accordance with someone else's expectations. She needed to find out who she was when she was not her mom's daughter, Randy's wife, or her children's mother. Did she even exist without the socially scripted roles she performed?

The pain Rose released while exploring her thoughts and emotions in total isolation, out of reach, and thousands of miles away from everything she had ever known, was unfathomable, at times, almost unbearable. As wave after wave of punishing pain crashed up against Rose's life, she searched, searched inside her heart and soul with every fibre of her being.

Do I love my kids, my family? Do they love me? Do they miss me? Do they even remember me? Are they okay? Should I have left them? What if they hate me now? What have I done to my life?

All dams had been breached and the waters were flowing. From the time Rose was very young, whenever she cried, her eyes would swell up and stay that way for hours. If Rose happened to cry herself to sleep her eyes would be swollen shut by the next morning. It was standard, that is just what happened, but as Rose began to allow her lifetime of pain to drain, the tributaries that fed the coalescing of tears behind her eyes also began to drain. The pressure was dropping. Rose's eyes would still get puffy, sure, but they stopped swelling shut.

But tears were not the only thing that drained. Rose began to sweat. Never before, in her life, could she remember sweating. Rose often wondered why she did not perspire as others did, regardless of heat or energy output, but … there it was. Only in this equatorial hotbox did Rose's body begin to release its collection of physical and emotional toxins. And 'twas not just Rose's pores that relaxed enough to relinquish what was no longer needed. Having prepared for near constant constipation, Rose packed laxatives up the wazoo. A once or twice a week girl at best, when away from home—composure cramped—nothing would be allowed out for weeks. Rose would get sooooo uncomfortable ... but this time ... in giving herself permission to let it *all* out, Rose's constitutional floodgates opened, and the spillways spilled.

Yes, Kenya is typically hot, but this field study occurred right before the rainy season began, so it was *scorching* hot and soddenly humid. As such, everything finally in good working order, Rose was always so freaking hot and sweaty and so freaking dirty because of it; she could barely stand it.

In one location, all had been given strict instructions to zip up their tent at night due to the poisonous scorpions that did their travelling at night. Far too hot to be worried about a few bugs, Rose took her sleeping mat outside and slept under the stars.

If I get bit, then ... I guess I get bit.

Rose was not worried. In the morning, while checking under her mat, Rose saw that three of her little orange—crab-looking—translucent friends, had settled themselves into the sand under her mat.

See ... they did not bite me.

Through it all, Rose could not help but appreciate the uncomplicated nature of how she—they all—were living. They ate; they slept; they learned; they laughed, and they cried tears of both joy and sadness.

Rose had never before seen the diverse colours of dirt that she saw travelling through Kenya. It was all the way from sandy white, through orange to almost red, and then into light brown, dark brown, and almost black. Nor had Rose ever seen people—children—as happy—laughing and smiling—as those she saw in the villages they drove through. Everyone would come out to wave and cheer as they greeted their cavalcade of safari buses en route to their next location.

After making the long, dusty trek into a nearby village—a mile or two away—one morning, Rose was disappointedly surprised to learn that there wasn't a phone to be found anywhere, as that meant that she would not be able to wish her mom a happy birthday. All the village consisted of was a few ram-shackle huts with people selling whatever they sold: water, cigarettes, beer, brightly coloured saris, and sandals made out of old tires. With no phone, radio, or newspapers of any kind, there was no way to find out what was happening back home or anywhere in the world.

I hope Mom's okay ... I hope EVERYTHING is okay.

Curled up in the seat of their safari bus, staring out at the Maasai Mara Plain while listening on a borrowed Walkman to U2—Rose's most favourite band—Rose was consumed by the wonder of it all. So many different animals grazing and wandering peacefully, side by side, till someone's hunger set all to foot. It was all so magnificent in its simplicity.

Without a preconceived role to hide behind, Rose soon recognized that she was not only going to have to start over materially, but she was also going to have to start over emotionally. She was fine while alone, inside herself, wandering around looking at this and looking at that, in a paradise vastly different but strangely similar to her granny's garden. And she was fine in the company of her two tentmates, but she had absolutely no idea how to act or interact while on public display.

Having turned thirty-nine during her sojourn, Rose was no longer a kid, but she was not an adult either. She knew that. She could feel it. Despite being of similar age to her professors, Rose's arrested development had her feeling like she was fifteen years old again—so anxious and self-conscious. Rose felt like a kid, a kid in the presence of all but one man.

For whatever reason, Rose found one of her professors strangely familiar in physical as well as spiritual embodiment. He reminded her of the dark-bearded and mustachioed man she'd seen in her gran's mirror above her bed, so long ago. Now, here he was again, but this time Rose was not afraid, quite the opposite. Rose was captured by him. She was as captured by him as she had been with the eyes of a young boy she'd seen, sitting on his towel at a hot springs she and her family had visited when she was eleven or twelve years old.

Whenever Rose and her hot springs-lad's eyes met, 'twas as if they fell knowingly into each other. So much so that Rose cried when she was told it was time to leave the presence of this young boy, she did not know, had never met or seen before. All the way home, in the back of the family camper, Rose had cried to her recorded copy of Three Dogs Night's, "One is the Loneliest Number." Such was Rose's experience with her professor's eyes. She willingly fell into them and felt he did the same with her.

One night, Rose had a dream wherein the two of them, she, and her psychic consort, were huddled together, each taking comfort from the other in the corner of a very cold, damp, dark cave lit only by glowing crystal stalactites hanging from the ceiling. In another dream, Rose nervously walked up to this man's door and knocked on it. Upon opening his door, Rose saw herself sitting on the bed inside of his room. With this, Rose knew this man to be a masculine reflection of herself, and so, from then on, she felt as if they could lay pictures of their emotions into each other's mind. Rose longed to know what it meant, what she was supposed to do. He was married and his wife and child had accompanied him on their trip so …

Rose was beside herself with angst. She knew how she felt, and she was sure she knew how he felt. The rest would either be, or it would not. Rose knew only time would tell because … it always did.

While pitching their tent one night after a long gruelling day of dry, dusty, dirty travel, Rose stepped ankle-deep into a fresh pile of elephant shit.

In one location, Rose raised her hands to greet her friends—the corvids—and as she did, they began to circle around her hands, round, and round, above her head. In feeling like she knew them, and they knew her, Rose was awash in tears.

Rose saw termites the size of birds and brick-red termite hills that were four feet high.

She held a firefly in the palm of her hand. Rose had always heard of fireflies; she'd seen pictures of them, but ... to one night be holding one in her hand ... it was magic.

Early one morning Rose was awakened by hippos stampeding toward their watering hole, the place their camp got their wash water.

Rose saw the most gigantic crocodile across a massive gorge that in the rainy season, contained a very deep, swiftly running river. It was at that location that Rose stood and consciously decided to breath in what her eyes saw, and her soul felt. She knew from past experience that cameras were of absolutely no use when it came to capturing the spiritual effect a location can have on one's personhood. On her travels, Rose bore witness to the existence of every African animal she could think of. While in Kenya, Rose saw and experienced millions of the most wonderful things.

During a train ride toward the seaside city of Mombasa, Rose saw herself in a mirror for the first time in almost two months. There was a mirror above the sink across from the hole you had to balance yourself over to go to the bathroom. Rose was shocked. She looked so different. She was tanned dark, dark-bronze, and her hair, her hair now, was white, and in cornrows.

Rose had her hair cornrowed in a little hut on a beach by a woman who said: "I have never done this for a woman with white hair before."

Rose's hair had begun to turn grey when she was eighteen years old. At twenty-six, she started dying it, attempting to hide her age. Once her marriage was over, however, Rose decided—promised herself—she would never fake another thing, including her hair colour. To Rose's mind, her grey hair was a testament to how far her times and tribulations had taken her. This pride was only compounded after her two months in the blazing sun had turned what was previously grey hair, into hair as white as snow.

It was at a lovely beach-lined resort on the eastern coast of Kenya, on the Indian Ocean that the happy travellers spent their final few days. It was a hot, sunny paradise in the heat of day and a balmy starlit wonderland at night. Sitting on the beach, with the sound of waves lapping gently in her ears, Rose looked up and into the sky. What she saw was magnificent—stars, hundreds of millions of stars.

She had never—ever—seen so many stars in the sky and they all looked so close … "Why do they look so close?"

'Twas Rose's professor who answered her query. "It's the moisture in the air that makes the stars look so close, the moisture acts as a magnifying glass."

With her heart so full of joy … it was all Rose could do not to burst into tears, release some of the magnified emotion she was carrying.

Toward the end of her trip, Rose believed she had probably cried enough so as to never have to cry again for the rest of her life, but she was wrong. When the day finally came to pack up and go home, Rose began to cry and could not stop crying. Her dream was coming to an end, and she knew she was going to have to wake-up. Yes, she would miss her tentmates, but Rose knew they would remain in touch. Given the bond they had forged during the previous two month, they would remain soul sisters forever, of that Rose was sure but ... the invisible tie that had so unintentionally formed between her and her male counterpart ... that tie, Rose knew, would probably be severed forever.

Yes, she had worked up the courage at times to utter a few phrases here and there. They had even shared a few laughs, but in knowing that soon he would be lost to her forever, she was in agony. She cried and cried. She cried all the way home, remembering again, how much she loved the song, "One is the Loneliest Number."

Rose arrived home on March 20,1994, three days before her eldest's twelfth birthday. She arrived home to a disastrous mess in the house, but a delightful home-cooked meal lovingly prepared by her mom, her precious little girls, and her son. Rose was overcome with emotion in seeing, smelling, and feeling her children's embrace once again. The dream was over. She was home, back to her life, a life in flux. The remainder of the evening was spent with stories and gifts from her travels.

Rose did her best thinking while lying in bed, be it prior to an afternoon nap or before falling asleep at night. During these meditations Rose would think about her life, try to pull the many threads of her life together. Most pressing on Rose's mind since arriving back home, was the quandary she experienced regarding the appearance and abrupt disappearance of her dark-bearded, mustachioed, reflection.

He was there in front of me, I could feel myself in him, but now he is gone. Is he gone forever? Why ... why had I met him, and why ... why am I so heartbroken? I hardly knew him.

Yes, I went to Kenya, and it was fantastic; it was life changing. I saw and did things previously unimaginable, but the whole while I was on an emotional roller coaster.

During an anthropology class, *liminal states* were discussed. To be in a liminal state is to be between structural realities, on the threshold of a new way of being, a new way of understanding and of living. I knew that I was in such a state. I was no longer who I used to be, but I had no idea who I was or who I would become.

My only regret ... leaving was horrifically hard on my children. Not only had their granddad died—a man whom my children loved dearly—their father and I had separated, we moved, they had to change schools, and then I left for two and a half months. In having been so self-absorbed, I robbed my children—all of them—of the emotional support they so desperately needed, so desperately deserved from their mother. I abandoned them in their hours of greatest need.

At the same time though, I cannot help but appreciate the fact that if I had not made some serious changes in my life, there was a good chance my children would have grown up without a mother at all. There is no way I would have survived my previous status quo.

So often I said to George, "... I feel like I am dying, am going to die."

I find it quite remarkable that as a pimply adolescent who hated her appearance, I drew heavy beards and moustaches on any—and all—pictures of myself in order to ruin them. Then, as a very troubled young woman, I saw a distressingly demonic reflection of a dark-bearded, moustachioed man whom I felt I should have known—knew me—in a mirror above my bed. All of this prior to meeting a married man of the same likeness whom I no longer feared, but to whom I felt helplessly—hopelessly—drawn. What does it all mean?

Although I never saw or heard the name of this man spoken ever again, I have thought about him, often, though the years and I do not think I will ever lose my affinity for the depth of feeling—self-understanding—I felt in this man's eyes. He had helped me recognize myself in the mirror of my soul. Was that the point? Could my near magnetic attraction have been a call to find in myself what I saw—felt—in this particular other, to find the deep reservoir of pain, love, loss, and meaning in myself that I felt through him?

37

A PATH LESS TRAVELLED
A Plebeian's Pilgrimage

Rose was home, but coming home was a whole lot harder for Rose than being away had been. Determined to never shapeshift into what was expected again, both family and friends were as uncomfortable around Rose as she was around them. Yes, she and her children had some relearning to do, but that was easy compared to taking up space—being—in the presence of those with whom she had previously associated. In so feeling, Rose focused on her children and the re-modelling of their little home.

One day, on the way home from the grocery store, Rose's oldest said, "Look Mommy, you can see our house from here, but look … it is way over there … all by itself."

"Yes …" Rose could see it. She could feel it.

Something positive that had happened while Rose was away, was that Randy had found himself a girlfriend. It was Rose's hope that this would help her, and her ex-husband move forward on better terms, but it was not to be. Adding another adult or parenting figure to the mix came with challenges. Previously, the kids jockeyed between their mom and dad's house, as they chose, but it quickly became necessary to rein that in. It was difficult but everyone got through it.

Come September, Rose was again a full-time student at the local community college, and she was loving it, having the time of her life again, studying herself and the world through her books. While immersed in studies, Rose was fine, but while not immersed, Rose was alone ... lonely. Although her former tentmates came to visit often and they had a grand old time recounting their grand old times, Rose would have given anything to find a like mind or two with whom to socialize or commune, but such minds, it seemed, existed only in books.

What Rose believed she needed was to transfer to a university. She needed to re-locate, go to a place where she could—would—find like minds. And so, in knowing of no other way, Rose decided to raise anchor on business finally finished and move ... move forward.

Although she could have spent another full year at her community college, Rose applied to the University of Victoria as well as to Simon Fraser University for the coming fall semester. Yes, Rose had tried moving away a few times in the past, but ... no dice. It was always: *home again, home again, jiggety-jig.*

This time, however, Rose believed she was ready to leave, ready to press on. She was ready for greener pastures.

Once Rose learned she had been accepted into both universities, she made her choice. It was to be Simon Fraser University, because that would bring her close to her former tentmates and to her Chris. They all lived in the Vancouver area. Once the decision was made, Rose broke the news to interested parties.

"The kids and I will be moving to Vancouver this summer so I can begin attending Simon Fraser University in the fall."

Coming as no surprise to her, both Randy and her mom were aghast, yet again.

Rose and Randy sorted things out through Family Court Counselling and Rose remained calm while facing down her Mom's semi-silent hostile indignation.

Although never raising her voice while she and her mom were face to face, Rose did have a dream wherein she screamed, "YES, I AM MOVING TO VANCOUVER WHETHER YOU LIKE IT OR NOT!"

That was December of 1994. Shortly thereafter, Rose's mom's cancer returned with a vengeance, and she was gone by March. Coincidence … ? Rose thought not.

Rose knew she was going to be the executor of her mom's estate. Her mom had asked everyone to sign, in agreement, the Last Will and Testament she had prepared when she was first diagnosed with cancer. What Rose didn't know, however, was that the will she would be reading aloud to her siblings and their spouses on the night of her mom's passing, was not the same as the one she had signed a few years earlier. It was different and contained a codicil drafted since Rose had informed her that she and the kids would be moving.

Except for forgiveness on a loan, Rose was largely disin-herited. She was heartbroken. Heartbroken, angry and in a state of disbelief.

Although advised to seek legal advice by the notary Rose had consulted regarding her mother's affairs, Rose was unwavering. "No! If that's the way Mom wanted it, fine! That is the way it will be … I guess."

Rose surmised her mom had construed her latest betrayal as a step too far. Despite trying to convince herself otherwise, Rose couldn't help but believe that her finally breaking free was catalyst for her mom's final resignation.

As George had said, "Honesty does have consequences."

Because her mom had never been religious, was adamantly against any sort of God or higher power, Rose decided it best that she, not a minister, the minister of the church to which her mom belonged, perform the eulogy. Because her mom, with the exception of her church club ladies—whom Rose's mom didn't seem to like much—had no friends, it was in front of the few people who gathered in her parents' yard, that Rose performed a brief service which she ended with Psalm 23. Rose chose this Psalm to read because she remembered reading it aloud in church one day, and it felt appropriate to do so.

Although Rose wished things could have been different between her and her mom, she was grateful to her mom for having lived long enough to allow her to finally stand firm against her. Caving to the expectations of significant others was a pattern Rose had come to realize she had been playing out since childhood: first with her mom, and then with Randy. The pattern had been broken but the residue had still not burnt off.

After Rose's mom had passed, Rose had a very disconcerting dream. In this dream, Rose calmly raised a handgun and shot, point blank, both her mom, and her husband Randy, squarely in the chest while she, without emotion, stood back and watched them bleed.

"Oh my God, George … am I a psychopath?"

"No Rose … you are just very, very, angry. Your dream is perfectly understandable. You need to see your anger—feel your anger—before you can let it go."

Needless to say, George continued to be Rose's sounding board right up to the end, the end of one life and the beginning of the next.

"Do you think I am ready—finally ready—to move forward, start anew, George?"

"Do you feel ready Rose?"

"Yes … I feel strong and I am excited to find out what is at the end of my yellow brick road."[13]

"Well then … you are ready."

As Rose stood up to leave her first real friend's office for the very last time, George offered Rose a hug, a hug that conveyed everything she needed to set her on her way. It conveyed acceptance, approval, affection, and an altruistic anticipation of what the future might hold for her.

Rose and her children left the town of Rose's upbringing, the town where Rose spent the majority of her first forty years in July 1995, four months after the passing of her mom.

With her little house refusing to sell, Rose decided to rent it out. In so far as she needed to get moving and she wasn't sure whether she'd be back or not … she thought the extra income might be useful since she was moving to Vancouver with a seven-year-old, a twelve-year-old and a thirteen-year-old, intending to live on nothing but child support and a student loan.

The first home of the newly placed little family, was on the top floor of a house rented by the owners who lived downstairs. It had three bedrooms and was comfortable enough. It was close to the university, and it was close enough to both an elementary and a high school. Rose's kids would need both. Her two youngest were still in elementary school but her eldest was headed to high school that year.

Wide-eyed and innocent, like a child on Christmas morning, Rose unwrapped disciplinarily diverse classes and cherry-picked her pursuits in accordance with her experiential musings: psychology, philosophy, religious studies/mysticism, literature, sociology, environmental studies, and the humanities. With her studies, Rose fed both her soul and the understanding of her story. Rose finally found her centre. She knew who she was, and so it was, therefore, with no regard whatsoever toward a future career or responsibilities that Rose savoured her *now*. It was just so much better than the her back *then* had ever been.

Shortly before completing her Bachelor of Arts degree in Psychology and the Humanities, Rose went on a hunt for a master's program in Analytical Psychology because it was within the works and thoughts of this branch—most especially Carl

Jung—Rose found heart, her life, and the vision[14] that had over-turned her understanding of things. Unfortunately, Rose could find nothing locally. She would have to move to the States, Eastern Canada, or Europe, and she could not, would not, do that. It had been so hard, so ridiculously hard to settle herself and her kids where they were with no money, no social or emotional support. One do-over had been hard enough. Rose had neither the strength nor the resolve for another but ... she knew she wasn't done.

Although Rose did not find the community of like minds she believed she would find at university, she was having far too much fun exploring all there was to learn and understand to even imagine rejoining the world just yet. She was not ready. Be it luck, fate, or the power of her will to continue, one of Rose's professors suggested she apply for admission to the Master of Arts degree in Liberal Studies through Simon Fraser University. It was a program for mature students firmly placed in their chosen career. Well, Rose was NOT firmly placed in any sort of career, but she was definitely a mature student and there was nothing else she wanted to do, so, why not? Low and behold, she got in.

Once again Rose was in her element. While buried in the subject matter, Rose felt right at home, but amidst her cohort of fellow graduate students, not so much. She felt like a plebe-ian on a pilgrimage with aristocrats. She felt grossly out of place.

What am I doing here? I don't belong here. I am not a professional anything. I am just me, and barely that.

As unaccomplished as she was, Rose had not yet gained enough practice being herself—her true self—in the world to feel like she belonged in a group of adults, never mind a group of upper-middle-class professionals secure in their social standing. With her lack of cultural acumen and social graces, Rose knew she stuck out like a sore thumb.

Every semester, Rose would take on a co-op or temporary job within one of the university departments: psychology, biology, ecology, etc. Rose was able to meet a variety of professors that way and the extra bit of money did help. One semester, with nothing more interesting available, Rose took on the job of caring for a flock of caged sandpipers that were being studied for whatever reason. She lived close so it was no problem zooming up to the university every day to feed and water the birds. Every couple of days she would have to shovel the pen out and hose it down. It was a wet, dirty job but after the way she had treated the family chickens … it was a penance Rose felt happy to pay. She believed she both needed and deserved it.

In hindsight, Rose realized it probably wasn't something she should have shared with her fellow graduate students. It turned out to be one of those tales you tell only to have everyone look away anxious to start up a new conversation. For Rose, the incident had been one among many cautionary tales. Many were Rose's verbal and attitudinal faux pas, but Rose persevered. Her need for approval had been nipped in the bud. All Rose cared about was learning.

Rose's latest intellectual pursuit had her on the hunt for a unifying metaphysical premise, a foundational principle upon which all else could be logically extrapolated. Yes, Rose realized that reality was far too expansive, abstract, and abstruse to study writ large. It had to be broken down into discreet disciplines to be studied, but if reality was ever to be understood as a whole, *Humpty Dumpty's*[15] many pieces would have to be put back together again.

Rose knew she was a piece, but a spec in the dynamic singular whole of existence. She had experienced herself as such during her vision, so she felt sure she would recognize herself, the means, mechanism, and meaning of it all when she came across it. As such, Rose's mission in life expanded. She no longer sought an understanding of her singular *self* so much as she began seeking a fundamental understanding of that to which she was a part—the grand singular *Self*. Everything had to fit together, there could be no incongruence or theoretical dissonance.

Rose searched, and she searched, reading everything she was attracted to, and then ... as if by magic ... she found what she needed in Bishop Berkely, an Irish philosopher's work on immaterialism.[16] Not only did Rose find in Berkely's work the cross-discipline congruence necessary for a first principle, the foundational premise upon which all else—reality itself—could be extrapolated, but quantum physics[17] was presenting an ever-accumulating collection of conundrums solvable only via an immaterial perspective on the nature of reality. It was not a new concept, philosophers and mystics had been espousing similar notions for centuries so ... Rose was so excited—ecstatic—that she decided to present her theory to her cohorts.

To all but her professor, Rose's presentation fell flat.

"Are there any questions ..." Not a word but ...

Never mind ...

With her prof's approval in hand, Rose decided that some sort of a treatise on the nature of reality would be the topic of her graduate thesis. She worked day and night, day, and night for months. Once submissions were being accepted, with her paper all but written, and a supervisor already on board, Rose put forward her proposal. It was turned down. A committee of Rose's peers refused her proposal.

Really?

For whatever reason, 'twas not to be. Of course, Rose was disappointed. She was gutted. External validation would not be forthcoming. There would only be her own sense of personal accomplishment. That would have to be enough.

Heartbroken, Rose managed, with the help of a capstone course, to graduate in June 2001. At forty-six years of age—a year later than she'd planned—Rose completed her Master of Arts degree in Liberal Studies. She could not have been prouder as she walked across the stage, in her graduation garb, in recognition of her accomplishment. Upon completion of her master's, Rose had both her B.A. and her M.L.S. degrees professionally framed and hung on her living room wall.

Yes, Rose would have loved to go on to do a PhD, endeavour to gain the credentials necessary to have her own research, thoughts, and papers funded, but she was exhausted, extremely exhausted, broke, and broken by her disappointment. She did leave open the possibility of maybe someday returning to finish what she had started, but for the time being, Rose felt she needed to focus on getting a job—making money instead of spending it for a change.

With her second degree under her belt and a new life beckoning her forward, Rose wanted her life to be filled with belongings that were hers, things that she had chosen, but damn near everything she owned was from a past that no longer represented her. The only thing Rose had any sort of attachment to was her gran's long, comfy couch, the one she had spent so many nights sleeping on, but it had been twice re-upholstered, and the springs were shot. Besides, Rose did not need that couch to remember her gran. Her gran had taken-up permanent residence in Rose's heart. As such, Rose called an auction house and asked them to give her an estimate on what her house full of belongings was worth.

"Perfect … when can you come and pick it all up?" Once everything was gone, Rose and her kids painted the house before they headed to Ikea to begin again. Ikea was probably not the best place for quality furnishings, but it was the best Rose could do at the time. By the time she and her little family were finished, their little home looked great! Piece by piece, cheap was eventually replaced by quality, but in the interim, Rose was completely at home in her home.

Was I crazy moving myself and my three little ones to Vancouver, a place very different from my small town, intending to live on nothing but child support and a student loan? No ... I do not think I was crazy. I was just extremely naive, extremely immature. I knew in advance it was going to be hard. I just hadn't anticipated the pitch of the learning curve I would be placing myself on.

Was my breaking free the cause of my mom's final resignation? Unsolicited, a card reader once told me that I need not feel responsible for my mom's death because typically, people whose firm grip finally slips, do not take their defeat well. Maybe it was that but then maybe ... just maybe ... in having finally broken free, in my finally having become conscious, Mom knew her job with—for—me was done and she was ready to go home. That is what I now believe.

With time, I have grown ever-more grateful to my mom, for many things. Not only did she teach me a great many practical skills, but she also made me strong, strong enough to survive— eventually thrive—despite having to learn things, every bloody thing, the hardest way possible.

When Mom passed, there were only two things in the topdrawer of her bedside table, and they were both letters. One was the letter I wrote, an apology, after Leonard and I had missed my curfew. The other, was the letter she had written me back. Upon rereading those letters, it was with a heavy heart, I realized that those two letters, together, represented a mother/daughter relationship wherein both parties were heartfeltly stumbling around in the dark trying to find each other. Unfortunately, we never did, not in this lifetime ... but, maybe in the next? I hope so.

There were times—many times—I would get to one of my appointments with George in tears, so in need of a place to unload my pain. Seemingly unfazed as he listened, George would coolly, calmly, and collectedly hand me the box of Kleenex he kept on the floor to the right of his chair.

And there were times—a few times—I asked George, "Can you please ... prescribe me something that will help alleviate the intensity of my suffering? Please George."

But ... his answer would always be the same. "Well, yes ... I can Rose but ...I believe you are strong enough to get through this without."

"Really?"

"Yes, I do!"

With that, each time, I would decide to keep going ... forge ahead with faith in the person I trusted most in the world; I thank my lucky stars I did. How could I have sorted myself out if I my suffering had been subdued, or worse yet, anesthetized. Would my suffering have become more convoluted, even more complex? Would I have been able to set myself free? I wonder ...

'Twas within the cold embers of my anger that I finally found the value in the passive mechanisms of control Mom and Randy had exerted upon me. Without those pressures, from which I was being called to free myself, would I ever have recognized what had me so imprisoned within my own life? As such, how can I be anything but grateful to the both of them?

Without the life I have lived, I would not be who I currently am, and I am ever so grateful for where and who I now am ... not perfect by any stretch of the imagination—perish the thought—but I am now truly myself, learning as I must.

After reading Mom's totally unexpected will aloud to my siblings, I was crushed. I could not understand how Mom could possibly have done to me what she did, even though I was moving away. In hindsight, however, from a different angle, it may not have been the worst thing that could have happened to me. Not only would I have deluded myself into believing I was flush at last, but I also got a much-needed taste of my own medicine. As they say, what goes around comes around.

In return for my thoughtlessness, I received the same. I received what I would not come to understand for a very long while. I made my life and the lives of my children SO much harder than they needed to be.

In having finally become cognizant of what had disabled me, I felt like I had slain my dragon and I could—almost should— proceed with *my* life single-mindedly, single-handedly, to achieve my bliss. I took no one into consideration but myself, not my kids, not my ex-husband, and not my family or family friends.

A year in, my youngest daughter moved back to her dad's because she missed her friends too much. I had ripped her away before she was ready. I was heartbroken. My oldest daughter followed the next year. I was heartbroken again. She eventually returned but my son was lost and alone without any sort of male presence in his life. And what of my ex-husband ... was it fair to take his children so far away so soon after he lost the wife, he *thought* he had? And ... regardless of my relationship with my siblings, my kids loved their aunts and uncles, their cousins. They needed them. They needed the other adults—family friends—they had in their life. They needed someone other than just me ... so easily I had walked away from everyone who had been in my — our — life. As such, after I moved, my children became as isolated as I had always felt, but in never having felt that way before, they were lost. Whether it was right or fair, that is what I did and so ... that is what I have had to openly own.

With my actions came consequences, consequences unknown to me until after I had taken the actions. Many lessons have come as a result of my self-absorption, but as with all my actions, there have always been consequences. If only I had begun learning from them a little sooner.

And what of the failure of my thesis to win graduating — publishing — approval? As mentioned, I felt like I had slain my dragon, and so, as reward, my life would be charmed. I would henceforth live happily ever after. That may well have been a possibility if I did not again — still — suffer delusions of grandeur. In finally finding and following my own path, I was sure I would become someone of considerable import. I had worked hard. I had found what I had been seeking so ... did I not finally deserve formal approval or recognition?

Whether I did, or did not, my ego needed a bit of a trim and I got that, in spades, for years. Does school ever prepare a person for the real world? It certainly did not prepare me. In having been on a path less travelled for so long, I had no idea, I had absolutely no idea.

All this withstanding ... in having lassoed a future through Randy, I was no longer on a frantic search. Instead, I had to keep myself ridiculously busy — distracted — from the erroneous errors of my ways. In having finally lifted myself out of my shadow, however, I was neither frantic nor needed to drive myself to distraction. Sure, I had stuff to work out, tons of stuff to work out, but I was finally, thanks to George, able to hold — embrace — my centre as I muddled forward.

38

THE RUBBER HITS THE ROAD
Bruised Into Becoming

As proud as Rose was of herself, neither of her degrees amounted to a hill of beans when it came to substantive qualifications for a specific job. Yes, she had lots of knowledge, interdisciplinary ideas, and theories, but she had no practical or previous experience in anything relevant … so where would she even start? She couldn't go back to bookkeeping. By that time, things had changed so much she would have to retrain in something she was never interested in the first place.

And so, it began with entry-level jobs in the community service sector. Unfortunately, these jobs paid less than half of what her old bookkeeping jobs paid, so it was a blessing Rose had not yet sold her little house back home. By selling it she could at least pay off her ginormous student loan, a loan so high she could not even afford her monthly payments.

Rose entered the workforce hoping to work her way up the ladder into a senior position of some sort. She was forever applying for advancement but was forever being passed over by people half her age. Agency after agency, it was the same thing. Rose could not figure it out and it frustrated the hell out of her.

Why ... why is this happening?

Six years in, Rose began to wonder if maybe she was supposed to be doing that PhD she'd dreamt of. There was still that program in the states, so she took a road trip down to a two-day orientation seminar. The campus, complete with student housing, laid on the site of an old mission—Jesuit mission as Rose recalled—in Southern California. She would have to attend in person for a week every semester ... she could do that. It would be perfect, but it was SO expensive; her son still lived at home and to what end? Where would a PhD in depth psychology get her? Jungian psychology was not in vogue. She was not a practicing psychotherapist and she had just turned fifty.

Rose ... you are no longer looking for a place to start your life. You are looking for a place to end it. It was a fantastical fantasy, but Rose was able to wake herself up. She got on with it.

By some miracle, some years later, Rose got a job within education working with struggling, troubled and/or disenfranchised youth. She was good at her job. Her boss accepted her for who she was so Rose was quite content for a few years. Several times she thought about using her position as a launch-pad from which to do a PhD. Unfortunately, she was never able to come up with a research question she felt capable of committing to. Rose could not see the value of statistical analysis when it came to problems of living because she had long since come to believe that life—any life—followed an ancestrally driven agenda influenced by the dynamic interplay between a myriad of internal and external factors so … she was hooped as far as a PhD was concerned. Rose could barely find anyone to have a meaningful conversation on the topic, never mind discuss a possible dissertation.

'Twas during this time that Rose received a call from the brother Rose always knew she had, informing her that their mother was in the intensive care unit. She'd had a stroke, a severe stroke. She was conscious but could only speak with her eyes. In having things to say, before it was too late, Rose dashed back to her mother's bedside.

"I know, Mom … I know you love me … you have always loved me. Don't be worried. I forgive you. I understand."

It was not but a month after her bedside soliloquy that Rose, and her two biological sisters were headed back for their mother's funeral. Rose was sad but … she and her mom had found each other. There was peace and love between them.

It was at work that Rose learned how to engage—befriend people—based on practical matters, the more mundane aspects of reality's complexities, but she was still alone. Yes, Rose was still alone but no longer lonely. Many people thought she must be lonely because she was alone, but no.

She'd tried dating, from which she learned a few new—very hard—lessons but nothing ever panned out, and it was just as well. In having found herself so fully, committing so deeply to the fortuitous functioning of the truths she had found and continued to carry, Rose was fine. She felt no holes in her life, so she directed all her energy and all her passion toward the ever-expanding nature of her thoughts through writing.

Coupling the joy of her old journaling days with the joy she experienced at school, delineating her thoughts, Rose would lose time and herself while sitting at her desk just doing what she did, incorporating all into exposés on social issues or what she'd come to understand about her life and the world it was unfolding within. Writing was Rose's release. Playing with thoughts and words was Rose's fun.

After Rose's youngest child—her son—left the nest, Rose moved. She was so done with the strata of the condo she had been living in for the past thirteen years, and having just turned fifty-eight, Rose figured the sooner she moved, the better. Although Rose had envisioned herself growing old in a vibrant urban setting, finances demanded she move further out instead of further in. To Rose's mind, it was pointless to move from one condo into another, so she found herself a little house in the country.

Rose moved on April 26, 2013, and although her little house needed some fixing up, with a garage, backyard, and fireplace, it had everything she wanted. It was within walking distance to all the stores and services she could possibly ever need and … she loved the quiet of having nature all around her. In many ways Rose's new community reminded her of Trail, the little city she grew up in. The only drawback was that the move had increased Rose's commute time to and from work to an hour. With this, Rose was not happy.

Well, low and behold, if shit doesn't happen. On June 11, 2013, on the way home from work—less than two months after she'd moved—Rose was broad-sided on the driver's side. The little white VW bug she'd named Daisy—the car of her dreams— was totaled. Rose and her six-month-old puppy were fine, save soft tissue damage, but the shock to her system was noteworthy. Rose had loved that little car. She had wanted a VW bug since high school. Leonard drove a VW bug.

Off work for the next few months, Rose shuffled around her little house, worked in her little yard, took her dog out on long walks, and wrote to her heart's content. She had a marvellous time at home just doing what she did.

For whatever reason, shortly after Rose returned to work, the location of her office was changed. She was moved from a small area in an alternate school to a cubicle at head office. At first, Rose felt puffed in having her position moved to head office, but the novelty soon wore off. Instead of being with kids struggling, as she had, to fit into the world, Rose was now with adults whose roles and responsibilities were strictly defined and whose beliefs, mostly, conflicted with her own. Rose gave it a go and she really did try but … it was not a good move for Rose. She felt like she was wasting her time, wasting her expertise, and wasting her life.

Egad! I should have become an electrician or a plumber. At least then I would feel like I was useful … accomplishing something.

Rose tried to find a new job but … interview after interview … no luck. Having never looked too far into the future or planned for any sort of retirement, after the purchase of her house, Rose was tapped out. Her coffers were dry. She had not reached the stature she had hoped for, and she no longer felt fulfilled in her job but … she could not just leave a job she was ever so grateful to have.

You see, Rose was making good money and she would have a municipal pension to augment her government pension if she stayed where she was. Rose knew she would have to work till at least sixty-five, seventy-three if she wanted a full pension, given she had gone to school for so long. She was only fifty-eight. Resigned to the fact that her life would have its way with her, Rose got on with it. She would do what she had to do until something changed.

Four years later, Rose noticed a lump on the top of her right thigh. The doctor said, not to worry, it was just a cyst and asked Rose if she wanted to have it out.

"Might just as well."

Because Rose had already planned a trip away to visit her youngest daughter and her family, she booked an appointment to have her lump removed for the following month. By the time Rose got home, her lump was twice the size. It had turned a really odd red and blue colour, and she could feel the little devil in there. 'Twas like her lump had a life of its own hidden in there.

Well, the lump on Rose's right thigh was not a cyst, it was Merkel cell carcinoma.[18] Something had changed.

Rose's oncologist told her that the survival rate for Merkel cell carcinoma was not good. Even with treatment, surgery to remove the lump and surrounding tissue as well as adjacent lymph nodes and a course of radiation, there was only a twenty percent chance she would be alive in five years.

Well … that's great!

Contrary, to her earlier self, Rose was in no particular rush to die. She had learned how to live. She had learned how to enjoy her life, be happy.

"I would suggest you get your affairs in order and then get doing whatever it is you want to do, Rose, because this type of cancer ..."

Sure, it was a bit scary but a strange peace permeated Rose. She felt she'd lived an amazing life so ... if there was more to come, it would be gravy, like the gravy she used to bring home to pour on Clifford's food as a treat. Yes, she would do her best to get well but ultimately ... que sera, sera.

It took a long time for Rose to recover from her treatment. First there was the surgery. Yikes! Rose had to issue a "viewer discretion" warning to those who wanted a peek. Then came intravenous antibiotics at the hospital for an hour, twice a day for a month, to deal with a post-operative infection. This was then followed up by radiation treatments, five days a week for five weeks running. Lastly, there was her recovery from the burns caused by the radiation treatments.

'Twas only during her final appointment with her oncologist that Rose was told, "There is a small chance you will develop bone cancer from the radiation treatments you received."

Again: *Well ... that's great!*

No, it was not a fun time, but Rose got through it with a little—a lot—of help from family and friends. Despite some exceptionally annoying nerve pain that slowly lost its charge over the next few years, Rose was back doing what she did by Christmas.

Luckily, Rose had short and then long-term disability insurance through her work, and she was approved for a government disability pension once her however many weeks were up, so that was good. It would be tight, but she could and would make do financially. Rose thought about going back to work. She had hoped to pay off or at least pay down her mortgage before she retired, but every time Rose even thought about going back to her job, she cringed. She could not make herself do it, especially if she was going to be dead in five years.

No, there was nothing in particular Rose was itching or aching to do before she croaked. She believed she had accomplished all she had come into this life to do; she escaped her prison, and she knew who she was and what she believed or knew to be true. She had a good relationship with her children, and she wanted for nothing, save to perhaps have thicker hair and to quit smoking. Yes, Rose was happy enough working in her little yard or on her little house, taking herself and her dog out into the beautiful countryside she had chosen to live her life out in. She loved to cook herself good meals from scratch. Her hands always felt good in the warm sudsy dishwater she poured to clean up after herself. There was nothing Rose enjoyed more than taking a long, hot bubble bath, slipping on a fresh pair of pjs and then sliding into a bed that sported crisp clean sheets. Rose loved to gaze lovingly around at the many memories attached to the belongings that lived in her home with her. Yes, Rose was happy, ever so happy, happier than she ever thought she would be. Because it was her cancer that had allowed Rose to Zen out, live expecting nothing and being grateful for everything, Rose considered her cancer to be one of the best gifts she had ever received. Was it though …?

Life went on with Rose living the life she had come to enjoy. One day flowed into the next until sometime in August 2018, when Rose received the surprise of her lifetime, and she'd had few. Her biological father's brother—an uncle—had passed away and he had included Rose—his long-lost niece—in his will.

"What? Are you kidding me? Really?" As far as Rose was concerned it was a miracle.

It was not an outrageous sum of money, but it allowed Rose to pay off her mortgage, have her gutters replaced and still have a very nice cushion in the bank. Thanks to an uncle she barely knew, had met maybe once or twice, Rose, if she was sensible—for once—would be able to live comfortably for the rest of her life. Her gratitude was unbounded. So were her children's. They had worried, but they need not worry any longer. It was a miracle, a damn miracle. Rose believed her entire life had been a miracle in the making.

Rose kept thinking about a saying she once heard.

Everything will work out in the end,
and if it hasn't worked out yet, it is not the end.

Rose believed that despite her start in life, everything—absolutely everything—had worked out in the end.

W hat an amazingly lucky stroke of luck—or precognitive anticipatory solution—not to have been able to sell my little house when first I tried. What would I have done with my ginormous student loan without the money from the sale of my little house?

I simply could not understand why I couldn't get anywhere, leap ladders in the fields in which I had worked but ... after the life I had lived, the experiences I'd had and the realizations I had come to, I was stuck between a rock and a hard place. I had promised myself that I would never again pretend to be someone I was not, nor would I ever again pretend to agree when I did not. I had thrown my former motto, *you gotta do what you gotta do if you wanna get what you wanna get*, into the bin and it was only under supervisory duress that I could bring myself to do things I found even a tich daft or detrimental. With this, I probably came off as arrogant, far too big for my britches, and indeed, I probably was. I didn't mean to be, but then, I'd been a lot of things I had not meant to be. The rubber was hitting the road.

Two months after moving to a small house in a place that reminded me of my hometown, I was in a car accident, not a deadly one—of course—but one that necessitated that I be at home, months enough, to have me realize that life without worry or want, strife or striving could be wonderful all by itself.

Soon after I returned to work, no longer amidst the young people I'd felt comfortably myself with, I found myself at head office amongst the movers and shakers, amongst those who I, myself, had always aspired to become. In attempting to fill shoes

I had so long coveted, I grew to feel like an imposter. Feeling like a fraud, once again, the air inflating my over-inflated ego began to dissipate, began hissing as it escaped, as air from a punctured tire or balloon might. With the hot air went all previous aspirations and ambitions toward societally esteemed success. I began to wish for nothing more than to be—just be me—happy in having lived and learned from the life I had led. I was ready to call it a *life*, but I had not prepared my bank account sufficiently. 'Twas not but for my fear of elderly poverty then that I continued to get up and go to work, each and every morning. I had, once again, become afraid.

Four years later, I was diagnosed with a surprise cancer, and the thought of likely only having a few short years left to live, quieted my fears around *having enough*. I had flown by the seat of my pants for most of my life and things had turned out ... so ... again, it was time. It was time to re-establish my faith in the fortuitous functioning of the truths I carried, for whatever time remained for me.

And so, I commenced living my best life only to receive a gift beyond any gift I could possibly have imagined. I was left an inheritance that would allow me to continue to enjoy my best life without financial worry. Was it a coincidental miracle whose timing could not have been better? Or ... I wonder ... could my surprise inheritance have been some sort of cosmic—karmic—reward for having finally understood just exactly who and what I was, no better and no worse than anyone else, just one among billions in a world in search of itself. I can never know for sure but ... I no longer believe in coincidences.

Did I always somehow know I would—could—one day be one of those little old ladies who lived alone, contentedly, in a little house with a garden and a pet or two? I must have because ... assuming, clams are indeed happy, I was always as a happy as a clam in my little houses: the spooky old guest house in the back of my creepy landlord's yard; the little house I bought and fixed up before fate had its way with me; and the little house my children and I lived in prior to my self-seeking strivings. Perhaps I just needed to get to a place where I realized that I was enough, that my enough was more than enough.

EPILOGUE
Home Again, Home Again, Jiggety-Jig

D espite the odds, it has been seven years since I left the larger world, since my cancer diagnosis, and I have never felt better than I do right now. I am in total remission and fully intend to stay that way.

I have a good relationship with my three adult children. I am now a granny to four beautiful grandchildren, and my children's father, Randy, and I have achieved amity. Sadly, since leaving my hometown, my adoptive siblings and I are no longer close. I am just so much different than the sister they used to have. We no longer connect on anything but history, and our hurtful history has grown impenetrable by years—decades —of neglect. With my birth mother gone, my biological siblings and I, with the exception of the brother I always knew I had, have largely lost touch. 'Tis only my biological bro and I who play catch-up by phone every couple of months. I do, however, have an eclectic group of friends with whom I share the ups and downs of life, and I have friendly relations with all of my neighbours. In ceasing to concern myself with a sense of community, it seems, I have found one, a great one. Funny how that works.

In so far as my life is so much different now than it was back then, I have a tough time believing all those fears, all those tears, and all those insincere, callously cavalier years, were actually mine. It all feels so unreal, so distant to me now. With this, I can't help but wonder if my earlier life was a nightmare or some sort of dream I conjured. Could it have been a role in a movie that I had been cast for? If so, surely, I deserved an Academy Award for some of my more perfunctory performances. Perhaps all any of us are doing in this life is following a pre-written script, a pre-determined curriculum of lessons to be passed prior to pressing on. Perhaps Shakespeare was onto something with his line, "All the world's a stage."[19] Whatever my life, true crime, a dream, or *Divine Comedy*,[20] the story has found its conclusion. The curtain has come down, my makeup and costume have come off—stashed away somewhere with my dolls and accordion—and all exploration ceased ... having arrived where I started, knowing the place for the very first time.[21]

I finally, once again, feel as I did during my moments of childhood wonder. Free from all that came before, the essence of daisies fills my heart. I am happy and glad to be alive. I know I belong because if I didn't, I wouldn't be here. On more than one occasion I could have perished by my own hand or the hand of someone—or something—else. By listening to the directions of the little voice I have come to trust, and living in accordance with the rules and rhythms of life; I am wholly fulfilled as I continue to gain ever-greater understandings of the treacherous topography I am here to traverse.

Now the winter of my life, as I do every year when the warmth of spring arrives, I sit—ciggies and a glass of wine in hand—under the sun or stars night after day, night after day, doing what I have done best for the last thirty plus years. I think about stuff. Although it is said that most people cannot see the forest for the trees, from my current vantage point, I have trouble seeing the trees for the forest, so interconnected is the time, space, and fillings of our world, our reality.

To the limits of our scientific expertise, everything that exists, is comprised of nothing but inertia or energy, particles of perhaps intention comprised of mass and spin, but nothing solid, no grit. And given that energy can never be created nor destroyed, only transmuted, or transformed from one state into another, all the energy that ever was, is all the energy that ever will be.[22] With this, everything is forever in balance. In order to maintain this balance, every effect has its cause(s). For every action—thought, feeling, behaviour—there is an equal reciprocal reaction that pops up somewhere, close, or far. This, in combination with the fact that every minute is connected to the next, suggests that everything that happens is a result of what has come before.[23] Such is the dictum underlying the law of karma. And so it is, to my mind, the universe unfolds as it should. It unfolds as determined by what has come before.

Might our world as a whole be on the same journey that I was on? Could the frantically distracted fear, fury, and flux we are currently experiencing be the forebearer of a future seeking itself, a future grounded in a greater understanding of the unified whole of which we are all a part? Only when each of us are able to see how we have contributed to our own—and the larger—drama can we, each and every one of us, stop, drop, and roll so as to summon the courage to join hands like the raindrops and help the marvel of our realm find its way—a better way for us all. As the ancient hermetic principle suggests, "as above, so below; as within, so without."[24]

It is with this hope in mind that I watch as the past and the present usher in our joint future. My companion in this, however, will not be fear because in having been given the eyes to see that "above every layer of perceived chaos there lies order" ... and so on, and so on—until "God" (or the prime mover)[25] is revealed in the order—purpose and design—of the Universe,[26] I know—just know—in the fullness of time, all will be well.

ACKNOWLEDGEMENTS

I would like to thank everyone, absolutely everyone who has ever been in my life—family, friends, foes, as well as teachers, traitors, and transient ties, because all in hindsight have helped direct the journey into understanding that this book is intended to portray.

However, I would like to extend special thanks to my three children, Amanda, Maegan, and Zach, who were, and continue to be, both my inspiration and the anchors that keep me tethered to this life; George Reilly (M.A. Dip. Clin. Psych.), my psychotherapist of almost ten years without whom I cannot even imagine what my life would have been like; Donald Grayston and Stephen Duguid, SFU professors who were invaluable mentors in seeing me on my way, and last but not least, my publishing team at TSPA, Megan Williams (Founder & Owner), Ira Vergani (Chief Operating Officer), Alisen Santa Ana (Editor), and Ashley Russell (Designer), without whom I would never have been able to get this book off the ground.

A giant thank you to all.

ABOUT THE AUTHOR

Brenda Laface, believing she should have been kicked out of high school as a teen, returned to pursue more education as a middle-aged, single mother of three. At university, she received a Bachelor of Arts degree in Psychology and the Humanities. During her undergraduate work, Brenda had an essay published in *The Trumpeter: Journal of Ecosophy*, and another success was in a year when she received a Mahatma Gandhi Humanitarian Award. Not yet ready for the *real world*, Brenda then went on to complete a Master of Arts degree in Liberal Studies. After working in the community and educational service sectors for a number of years, Brenda retired to a little house in Maple Ridge, B.C., where she was *finally* able to complete an autobiographical account of her life from a lost, alone, and terribly confused little girl to someone whose gratitude for the journey she has been on is unbounded. Although her adventures may read like a Greek tragedy, she feels like they were more of a *Hero's Journey* in Women's Studies.

NOTES

1. *The Selfish Gene* was a theory proposed by ethologist Richard Dawkins in his 1976 book of the same name. This theory suggests that individual genes, in a *survival of the fittest battle*, are forever seeking to have themselves replicate into the future.

2. Epigenetics is the study of how gene expression can change within a single lifetime without the necessity of changes in the DNA. A significant study in this field was co-conducted in 2008 through Columbia University and Leiden University on descendants of the Dutch famine (paper published in PNAS).

3. The earliest known use of the term *saving grace* is from the writings of Robert Barnes, a religious reformer of the early sixteenth century. It means: the sudden intervention of God's grace, or forgiveness, for something terrible one has done.

4. One's *reason for being*, refers to one's reason for being alive or one's purpose in life explored by many philosophers (e.g., Sartre, Camus, Kierkegaard).

5. This memory is described in an article that author (B. Laface) wrote entitled, "The Truth of Gaia: Knowings and Proofs," published in *The Trumpeter: Journal of Ecosophy*, Vol. 14, No. 3, WN 56, (1997).

6. The tradition of fortune telling by use of one's day of birth is much older, but this particular rhyme was first recorded in A.E. Bray's *Traditions, Legends, Superstitions, and Sketches of Devonshire* (Vol. II, pp. 287-288) in 1838.

7. This poem, "There Was a Little Girl" was written by the nineteenth century poet, Henry Wadsworth Longfellow.

8. Coined by the sixteenth century mystic and poet, St. John of the Cross, this phrase refers to a passive but exceptionally painful purification of the soul.

9. Biblical quote taken from *Luke 23:34*.

10. Written in the latter half of the fourteenth century by an anonymous Christian mystic, *The Cloud of Unknowing* is a spiritual guide on contemplative prayer. It suggests surrendering one's mind and ego to the realm of the *unknowing*, at which point one may begin to glimpse the nature of God.

11. According to the ancient Greek philosopher Aristotle, there are four fundamental types of answers (i.e., material cause, formal cause, efficient cause, final cause) to "why?" questions, which describe the purpose of a thing's existence (e.g., the final cause of a shovel is to dig).

12. "The Little Engine That Could" refers to an American folktale that was later published in 1930 by Platt & Monk.

13. The idea that the road leading to *the way home* is through accepting the truth, a theme in the 1939 film entitled, *The Wizard of Oz*.

14. Carl Jung termed such visions as indicative of a *transcendent function*, which involves a dialectical process by which an individual is able to integrate both conscious and unconscious aspects of the psyche. To quote Jung: "The way of the transcendent function is an individual destiny."

15. The main character in a late eighteenth century English nursery rhyme, "Humpty Dumpty," an anthropomorphic egg: "Humpty Dumpty sat on a wall, Humpty Dumpty had a great fall; all the king's horses and all the king's men, couldn't put Humpty together again."

16. Bishop Berkeley was an idealist who believed that material things exist only as mental perceptions, exist only in the mind of God (a creator or whatever you believe the *prime mover* to be).

17. Three such conundrums being: 1. the Heisenberg principle of uncertainty—the act of observing something has an effect on what is being observed (i.e., Schrödinger's Cat, thought experiment); 2. the total lack of evidence that sub-atomic particles contain anything other than mass and spin, no actual grit of any kind has ever been found; and 3. quantum entanglement—the fact that particles separated by both time and space can mimic each other's behaviour instantaneously, as if somehow communicating.

18. Merkel Cell Carcinoma is a neuroendocrine carcinoma that attacks tactile nerve cells or receptors (the cells responsible for one's sense of touch). This type of cancer is of increased risk for patients with lymphoma, or with a predisposition toward lymphoma, the type of cancer Rose's biological father succumbed to.

19. Line taken from Shakespeare's play, *As You Like It*, first published in the early seventeenth century.

20. *Divine Comedy* is an Italian narrative poem written by Dante Alighieri between 1308-1321 about the author's journey toward God.

21. Paraphrased ideas from T.S. Eliot's poem, "Little Gidding," originally published in 1942.

22. The first law of Rudolf Clausius's thermodynamics is the law of conservation of energy, as herein mentioned.

23. This idea is the basis of chaos theory (attributed primarily to Edward Norton Lorenz).

24. Referencing a hermetic principle that infers a connection between the macrocosm and the microcosm: the higher realms (above) with the lower realms (below).

25. *Prime mover* by definition is the initiating source of a *thing*.

26. Paraphrased quote by Baruch Spinoza, a seventeenth century philosopher.